LOOKING

FOR

HAMLET

Marvin W. Hunt

palgrave
macmillan

LOOKING FOR HAMLET
Copyright © Marvin W. Hunt, 2007.

All rights reserved. No part of this book may be used or reproduced in any manner whatsoever without written permission except in the case of brief quotations embodied in critical articles or reviews.

First published in 2007 by
PALGRAVE MACMILLAN™
175 Fifth Avenue, New York, N.Y. 10010 and
Houndmills, Basingstoke, Hampshire, England RG21 6XS
Companies and representatives throughout the world.

PALGRAVE MACMILLAN is the global academic imprint of the Palgrave Macmillan division of St. Martin's Press, LLC and of Palgrave Macmillan Ltd. Macmillan® is a registered trademark in the United States, United Kingdom and other countries. Palgrave is a registered trademark in the European Union and other countries.

ISBN-13: 978-1-4039-7036-7
ISBN-10: 1-4039-7036-X

Library of Congress Cataloging-in-Publication Data is available from the Library of Congress.

A catalogue record for this book is available from the British Library.

Design by Newgen Imaging Systems (P) Ltd., Chennai, India.

First edition: December 2007

10 9 8 7 6 5 4 3 2 1

Printed in the United States of America.

CONTENTS

LIST OF ILLUSTRATIONS

The Man in Black: Gallery One

(appears between pages 92 and 93)

The Man in Black: Gallery Two

(appears between pages 164 and 165)

This book is for my parents, Dana and Hazel; my wife,
Robin; and our children, John and Alexandra;
in memory of David Marcus Hunt,
Timothy Reese McLaurin, and Micah Harris.

ACKNOWLEDGEMENTS

I have many people to thank. J. Peder Zane, book review editor at the Raleigh *News and Observer*, insisted such a book as this would be of interest; Mickey Choate, my agent, sold it; my friends Isaac Epps, Mike Massey, David Sanders, David Williamson, Carol Mclaurin, Tom Eamon, Phil and Leslie Bailey, and especially Jim Schiffer helped along the way. The Sarasota Gang—Laury Magnus, Anya Taylor, Tony "The Noose" DiMatteo, Teresa Kennedy, Joe and Joanie Wagner, and Al Shoaf—supplied energy and support. Alan Dessen, Joe Porter (for whom I'm a dead man), and Stephen Greenblatt encouraged me in passing. The editors at Palgrave—Farideh Koohi-Kamali, Chris Chappell, and Rick Delaney—were extraordinarily patient and careful in seeing the book through to publication. I owe a special debt to three people who were engaged with this project from the outset. My good friend Mark Taylor saved me from many errors and contributed as many ideas and observations along the way. I thank Mark and Manhattan College for inviting me to give the 2005 Dante Seminar Lecture, where I presented a version of chapter four. The incomparable Amy Knox Brown, herself a fine writer, edited the first draft of this book with an exacting yet sympathetic eye—actually she has two of them. If there are felicitous moments in *Looking for Hamlet*, Mark and/or Amy probably had a hand in crafting them. I wish also to thank Gene Melton, who oversaw the selection, secured permissions for the illustrations, and compiled the index.

The errors and shortcomings that remain are my own, for which I ask forgiveness, urging you to remember Hamlet's admonition: "Use every man after his desert and who shall scape whipping?"

INTRODUCTION

William Shakespeare's *Hamlet* is an unlikely masterpiece—crowded, ungainly, gratuitous, and impossibly long, more than twice the typical length of a play from the period. Uncut, it runs more than four hours on the stage. At 212 minutes, William Wyler's screen epic *Ben-Hur: A Tale of the Christ* comes in well under the running time of the uncut *Hamlet*. A play so long and so old—written more than four hundred years ago—would seem of improbable interest to us. Furthermore, though it ends in mass violence, for much of *Hamlet* not much happens.

With the exception of the Ghost's appearances in the first act, *Hamlet* is slight on action until the fourth scene of act three, when the Ghost again appears, now for the final time. At this point the pace picks up and the plot steadily moves to a violent crescendo in the great final scene of the play, when Hamlet, Laertes, Claudius, and Gertrude die within the span of a couple of minutes. But until 3.4, *Hamlet* the play is like its protagonist, more talk than action. Earlier, when Polonius—a fatuous though nonetheless dangerous councilor who plays at being a spy, at a dear price—comes upon Hamlet poring over a book, he asks, "What do you read, my lord?" Hamlet's reply might stand as a fitting epithet for much of *Hamlet*: "Words, words, words." Long set speeches are its hallmark. Not only Hamlet's soliloquies, but long monologues by other characters—Claudius, Polonius, the visiting Players—take up an inordinate amount of time.

Even the artistic merits of *Hamlet* have been questioned. None other than T. S. Eliot called it a failure. In *Hamlet*, Eliot argued, Shakespeare's reach exceeded his grasp. Eliot was unable to find what he called "objective correlatives"—events, objects, tangible things that express the inner themes that drive the play. "*Hamlet*," Eliot wrote, "is full of some stuff that the writer could not drag to light, contemplate, or manipulate into art." Eliot believed that in *Hamlet* Shakespeare unleashed drives he could not fully realize, leaving the deepest conflicts and problems to seethe beneath the surface of the play.

And yet, of course, careful readings and imaginative productions of *Hamlet* refute every complaint lodged against it. If *Hamlet* is long on talk and short on action, audiences have delighted in it from the beginning, crowding in to see *Hamlet* from the time of Richard Burbage, who played the first Hamlet in the early seventeenth century, to Kenneth Branagh's film version of *Hamlet* in 1996, and beyond. It is no great risk to say that *Hamlet* is without parallel, the greatest play ever written. None of the works of Sophocles or Aristophanes, Seneca or Plautus, Christopher Marlowe or Ben Jonson, or any playwright to follow compares to Shakespeare's achievement in *Hamlet*.

Hamlet is the most frequently staged not only of Shakespeare's plays but, as far as I can tell, of any play written in any language. From 1879 through 2004 *Hamlet* was produced eighty-two times by the Royal Shakespeare Company and its predecessor, the Shakespeare Memorial Theatre. This is not to mention countless other productions in different venues, beginning a few years after it was written with the first documented performance of the play, aboard a ship anchored off the coast of West Africa. Since then, *Hamlet*/Hamlet has shaped every generation of Western life, from the Enlightenment through Romanticism and the Victorian age; through Edwardian life and the catastrophe of the first World War, through Modernism and World War II, and on through the questioning and fragmentation of Postmodernism. After 400 years *Hamlet* maintains its supreme status in intellectual history. Until recently, when liberal arts colleges and English departments radically altered their curricula to include lesser known (though important) writers and other fields of discourse—rhetoric, scientific writing, and digital communication—virtually every college graduate read (or was supposed to have read) *Hamlet*.

As has been often noted, the play *Hamlet* is inseparable from the character Hamlet, who has 1,506 lines, approximately 39 percent of the total lines of the play. The best minds of four centuries have pursued the character Hamlet in an effort to pin down his meaning, yet their findings have always been provisional and contingent. Hamlet certainly experiences the universal problems of young men—the struggle to create self-identity, to define duty and discover romantic love, to separate oneself from one's parents, to confront internal doubts and misgivings, to prove oneself courageous. But Hamlet embodies much other than tragic youth. He is cowardly, indolent, class conscious, vain, cruel, misogynistic, sophistic, sickly funny. Every age has seen Hamlet, to one degree or another, as a reflection of its own aspirations and neuroses. Yet Hamlet is more than the sum of his parts, or the nature of those reading him. He is, as history shows, something larger, more complex, and more elusive than anyone who confronts him. "Hamlet remains proleptically in tune with the latest present," writes Professor Margreta de Grazia. "At the end of the twentieth century," she adds, "*Hamlet* continued to possess this strange futurity, still gesturing beyond its most recent site of reception. . . ."

This extraordinary appeal is hardly limited to intellectuals, academic specialists, and students. In fact, *Hamlet* is largely responsible for Shakespeare being the most frequently credited screenwriter in Hollywood. With seventy-five film productions by the turn of the twenty-first century, *Hamlet* is second only to *Romeo and Juliet* on the silver screen. Virtually every actor—women as well as men—who has aspired to greatness has played the young man in black.

Hamlet opened one afternoon at the Globe Theatre, perhaps as early as 1599 but probably in 1600, with the thirty-something Richard Burbage, weighing in at 230 pounds, in the lead. Burbage is far from the lithe, tortured young man in black we generally conceive Hamlet to be. Indeed, Gertrude's remark in the duel between Hamlet and Laertes that her son is "fat and scant of breath" could well be a comment on Burbage's weight. Despite the dissonance between the burly, middle-aged Burbage and our image of Hamlet as young, pale, brooding, and sexy, Burbage greatly pleased Shakespeare's audience and, presumably, Shakespeare himself. Indeed, the original *Hamlet* was a smash, and Burbage remained synonymous with the lead part for the rest of his life. Upon his death in 1619, an elegist lamented, among Burbage's many lead roles (which included King Lear and Othello) that there would be "no more young Hamlet."

An especially close relationship seems to have existed between Shakespeare and Burbage, who was four years Shakespeare's junior. An incident recorded in 1602, around the time when *Hamlet* was first produced, tells of a female audience member so smitten by Burbage's performance as Richard III that she asked

Burbage to call at her room under the name of Richard, which was, of course, his name. Shakespeare, the story goes, overheard this exchange and went to the lady's room early. The playwright was "at his game" when Burbage arrived and announced that Richard III had come. Shakespeare sent back a note informing Burbage that William the Conqueror came before Richard III. Even if this story is apocryphal, its suggestion of playful but genuine friendship between Shakespeare and Burbage, the actor who first played Hamlet, may be close to the truth.

If English stages were the main venues for *Hamlet* in the seventeenth century, the play had also traveled far and wide in esoteric venues. A version of *Hamlet*, which survives in a manuscript from 1710, was performed by an English troupe touring Germany during Shakespeare's lifetime. It was staged by the crew of Captain William Keeling aboard the *Red Dragon* off the coast of Sierra Leone in 1607, a mere four years after its print debut. Hamlet, play and character, spread like fire across Europe. Within a few years of its appearance in 1603, there are records of *Hamlet* being performed in Paris and Moscow. Further evidence of *Hamlet*'s early popularity can be seen in the number of times it was printed during the seventeenth century. It appeared seven times (1603, 1604, 1611, 1622?, 1623, 1632, and 1637) in the first half of the century. Six more editions (1664, two in 1676, 1683, 1685, and 1695) were published in the second half, making a total of thirteen publications of *Hamlet* before the eighteenth century. During the Restoration, William Davenant—rumored to have been Shakespeare's natural child—produced an abridged version of *Hamlet*, with Thomas Betterton in the lead role, which was an immediate and enduring hit. Betterton played Hamlet for forty years, well into his seventies.

Since Davenant's time, *Hamlet* has been produced in untold venues great and small. Kenneth Branagh's sumptuous 1996 film version costing millions of dollars was a commercial and critical hit. But the play need not be produced on a grand scale to entertain. I recently saw *Hamlet* staged by the Tiny Ninja Theater in my hometown in which the Melancholic Dane and company were played by fast-food toys.

In case you haven't read it recently, I offer a summary of the play, which, given its prolix nature, isn't easy.

While away at university Hamlet learns of his father's death and returns home to find that his mother has married his dead father's brother. Hamlet doesn't know that for two nights running the ghost of his father has appeared silently to watchmen stationed on the battlements of Elsinore, the castle of his murdered father, now occupied by his uncle, Claudius. On the third night Horatio, Hamlet's best friend from college, makes his appearance. Horatio joins the watch and the ghost appears again. Meanwhile, inside Elsinore, the new king Claudius explains to a general counsel the warlike state of Denmark, and his marriage to Queen Gertrude, and gives permission to Laertes, Hamlet's future rival, to return to Paris, where Laertes is a student. He also attempts to console or placate the grieving Hamlet, addressing the prince as "Our chiefest courtier, cousin, and our son."

Outraged by the stain of what he perceives to be incest—his father's brother marrying his mother—Hamlet retreats into the shadows and contemplates suicide in a soliloquy that quickly transforms itself into a rant against his mother's incestuous conduct and then a harangue against women in general. (Exactly why Hamlet should react to these events with such intense self-loathing is at this point unclear.) Horatio enters the scene, the two friends greet each other, and Horatio tells Hamlet about the ghost's visitations. This conversation sets the stage for Hamlet's meeting with his father's ghost, in which the ghost informs Hamlet privately that Claudius had murdered him while he slept. The ghost charges Hamlet to avenge his death and Hamlet agrees to exact revenge. The busy first act concludes with the ghost leaving the stage, not to appear again for the better part of two acts.

The second act opens with Polonius, the aged counselor to Claudius, warning his daughter Ophelia not to allow herself to be courted by Hamlet, with whom she seems to have a romantic relationship. Next, two more of Hamlet's friends, Rosencrantz and Guildenstern, arrive at Elsinore. They have been recruited—how and from where is not explained—to pry from Hamlet the source of his dark mood. Continuing the conspiratorial theme, Polonius offers to spy on Hamlet. Then, a troupe of traveling actors arrives at Elsinore. Conveniently, Hamlet has met these "tragedians of the city" before, and he enlists them now to stage a version of the murder of his father to be performed before the King and his court, as a means of testing both the veracity of the ghost and the guilt of Claudius. Act Two ends with another of Hamlet's soliloquies, this one commencing with more self-loathing—"O, what a rogue and peasant slave am I!"—and finishing with his resolving to use this play within the play (so, at least, he declares) to "catch the conscience of the King."

The third act begins with a conference among the conspirators—Claudius, Gertrude, Polonius, Rosencrantz, and Guildenstern—but moves quickly to another of Hamlet's soliloquies. This one, beginning "To be, or not to be—that is the question," is perhaps the most famous set speech in all of English literature. On its heels follows a misogynistic assault on Ophelia in which Hamlet rants and rails against her and all her sex as duplicitous whores. The scene abruptly switches to Hamlet's directions to the players followed by a dumb show enacting the poisoning of a king and then the play-within-the-play itself, *The Murder of Gonzago*, which King Claudius interrupts just after the usurping murderer pours poison in the ear of the sleeping king, mirroring the death of King Hamlet. Claudius' calling for the lights unequivocally indicates his guilt.

In the next scene, 3.3, Hamlet comes upon a kneeling Claudius, just after he has confessed guilt, in a gesture that suggests prayer. While Hamlet could easily kill the villainous king at this moment, he does not because, he reasons, killing Claudius at his prayers would send the murdering, usurping, incestuous king to heaven. This is a fateful decision, a point of no return. From here the pace of the play accelerates, and events spin out of control. Hamlet, now extremely mentally and emotionally agitated but with a paradoxical clarity of insight and purpose, visits his mother in her room. In a full-blown rage he charges her with incest and insinuates that perhaps she either knew of or conspired in the murder of her husband, Hamlet's father. All the while Polonius, fatuous and yet sinister at the same time, eavesdrops behind an arras. When he hears the terrified Queen cry, "What wilt thou do? Thou wilt not murder me—Help, ho!" Polonius cries out and Hamlet, mistaking him for the King, stabs the counselor through the curtain, another point of no return. Arriving too late to prevent the killing of this "wretched, rash, intruding fool," which might have averted the catastrophe, the ghost of Hamlet's father appears for the final time. Visible this time to Hamlet only, the Ghost reminds his son that he has still not fulfilled his promise of revenge and commands him to be gentle with his mother, to "leave her to heaven." The Ghost disappears and Hamlet urges his mother, in a tone only slightly less shrill than before the Ghost's intervention, to confess her sins to heaven, begging her "go not to my uncle's bed." The act concludes with Hamlet dragging the body of Polonius offstage.

In the fourth act, the killing of Polonius is revealed. Hamlet is banished to England in the company of Rosencrantz and Guildenstern, who bear a letter from Claudius to the English king commanding the execution of Hamlet. Meanwhile Ophelia, driven mad by the death of her father, appears distracted, singing snatches of old songs about loss and grief. Having learned of his father's murder, Ophelia's brother Laertes has returned to see his sister in her madness. Later a letter to Horatio arrives from Hamlet explaining that he was taken captive by pirates who spared his life in return for favors from Claudius. Still later we will learn that Hamlet had altered the letter to the English king to command the execution of Rosencrantz and Guildenstern. Meanwhile, Claudius enlists Laertes in a plot to kill Hamlet, and the fourth act ends with the Queen's report that Ophelia has drowned herself. The motivation is now in place for Laertes' own revenge against Hamlet, as the two rivals—their fathers murdered and the woman they claim to have loved drowned—become mirror images of each other.

As we shall see, Shakespeare inherited most of *Hamlet*, both plot and characters, from Danish and English sources, but the two scenes of the final act, which are probably wholly Shakespeare's inventions, are the most powerful of the play. The first has Hamlet and Horatio, friends to the end, coming upon a gravedigger shoveling a fresh grave. This is to be Ophelia's final apartment, of course, though Hamlet and Horatio, newly arrived at Elsinore, do not at first know that. Hamlet and the gravedigger have a ghastly but brilliant conversation about human remains, the emblem of the skull, death, stink, horror. This darkly profound scene, the supreme thematic moment in *Hamlet*, sets up the gory final movement in which four remaining principal characters—Hamlet, Laertes, Claudius, and Gertrude—are killed, and the nation of Denmark is left in the hands of the conquering Fortinbras, Prince of Norway.

In *Looking for Hamlet*, I make the argument that Shakespeare's greatest tragedy enacts a radical and unprecedented internalization of reality. I then attempt to show how the resulting sense of a palpable interiority has reflected and shaped the intellectual history of the West, making *Hamlet* the single most important work in constructing who we are, especially in how we understand our psychological, intellectual, and emotional beings. I begin with an exploration of the sources of Shakespeare's play. The typical reader or viewer may assume that *Hamlet* originated with Shakespeare, but this is by no means the case. Its origins go far back into Danish history. The first recorded version of the Hamlet story was provided by a Danish historian, Saxo the Grammarian, writing in the twelfth century. Moreover, important aspects of Hamlet's character—his presumed madness, for example—date even farther back, to Roman character types. In 1570, a heavily moralized version of the Hamlet story by François Belleforest was published in French. In the 1580s, the saga of Hamlet was written as a play—now lost— probably by Thomas Kyd. Kyd's version, the so-called Old or Ur-*Hamlet*, was enormously popular on the London stage at the beginning of Shakespeare's career, but was never printed. This lost version is perhaps the most important missing link in literary history. Clearly, the prehistory of Shakespeare's play, which shaped it in innumerable and irrecoverable ways, is essential to confront at the outset of the search for Hamlet.

In the next chapter of *Looking for Hamlet*, I consider the vexed, bewilderingly complex early printing history of Shakespeare's play. *Hamlet* appeared in three different though related versions, two of which (in 1603 and 1604) were printed during Shakespeare's lifetime; the third appeared in 1623, seven years after his death. In time, these three versions of the play coalesced into a more or less stable version of *Hamlet* that has been published and produced countless times since. It is important to realize that our *Hamlet* is a version of the play never produced in Shakespeare's time. Its composite nature means that the *Hamlet* we read and see today is an artificial construct, something quite different from what was performed by Shakespeare's acting company at the turn of the seventeenth century.

Next, in a consideration of the great fifth act, I attempt to show why *Hamlet* the play is such a pivotal work: the fact that it relocates reality from outside the human mind to within it, taking us from a medieval mindset that held reality to be objective, anterior, and superior to human experience, to a modern, or more precisely, an early modern view that holds reality to be in large part, if not entirely, a function of subjective experience. *Hamlet* with its myriad representations of the human psyche presses a radical new belief—or fear: that what goes on inside our heads is what is ultimately real. "There is nothing either good or bad," Hamlet says in perhaps the most radical statement in the play, "but thinking makes it so." This relocation from objective to subjective realms is expressed in figures of confinement—prisons, chapels, closets, a nutshell, an arras, and, ultimately, the human skull, this finite container of infinite reaches of memory, thought, dream, desire, fear, all that can be felt and said.

The remainder of *Looking for Hamlet* offers a history of reception, exploring how generations of readers and viewers have interpreted *Hamlet* the play and Hamlet the prince. Now, more than four centuries after it first appeared in print, *Hamlet* should seem very old. And in some senses it does. Many aspects of the drama—the sword play, the Ghost, the splendidly ornate language—may seem antiquated today. But from another perspective, *Hamlet* shows no indication of aging. In fact, it achieves the opposite. One of the implicit claims of this book is that *Hamlet* is a sort of miracle child, a creature that defies—or until quite recently, has defied—the universal law that influence fades over time. Though clouds may be gathering on the horizon, clouds that may one day eclipse the play, *Hamlet* is now more central to the Western world—indeed to the entire world—than ever.

Hamlet the character, I argue, is the collective dead son of Western history, the lost child that haunts our culture, perpetually killed and resurrected again in each performance before succeeding generations. The embryonic conception of Hamlet as a dead son appears in eighteenth-century England but is really born in Germany at the beginning of the Romantic period late in that century. The high period of European Romanticism during the early nineteenth century reacted to Hamlet with a powerful collective grief, a grief that amounts to a lament for the child who dies within us as we age. In effect, Hamlet the character functions as a repository of lament and sadness, an emblem of lost youth and potential, of what might have been. Samuel Taylor Coleridge, a great poet who saw himself as a melancholic failure, expressed the unspoken thought of millions of others when he said, "I have a smack of Hamlet in me."

I continue this exploration of the play's reception in the context of a growing recognition of and emphasis on disorders of the mind, notably depression, which Shakespeare and his generation signified by the word melancholy. It is apparent that Hamlet, aside from his playing the fool, really is the Melancholic Dane. He is clinically depressed, we would say, or perhaps, bipolar. As the Western world becomes increasingly concerned with the operations of the mind, Hamlet assumes a more central position in our culture. An explosion of interest in Shakespeare's play accompanied the formalization of the study of psychology in the nineteenth century, and with the continued growth of the study of the human mind, writing about *Hamlet* proliferated through the modern and postmodern periods. And as the play garners more intellectual attention, it enjoys ever greater popularity, with the number of film and stage versions increasing exponentially in the last hundred years. Clearly, academic and popular interests fuel each other.

In the final chapter of *Looking for Hamlet*, I take up the personal search for Hamlet, one that has occupied the lives of untold numbers of people. I offer Hamlet as a sort of missing person, impossible to locate definitively though seemingly close, in a cultural, historical, and personal sense. At the same time that we search for someone or something else, we are also hunting for ourselves, constantly engaged in an internal search for who we are as individuals. The point of *Looking for Hamlet* is this search for something missing, a present absence we pursue as a means of finding and knowing ourselves. But, of course, Hamlet the character is not merely an inert object—a mirror, to call upon a convenient and familiar metaphor, in which we see ourselves reflected. Indeed, to a remarkable degree Hamlet has shaped what we are. Because it registers and defines so much of what it means to be human, *Hamlet*/Hamlet touches the heart and mind in ways, and at depths, that no other play can match. It speaks to us directly across history and represents, at the deepest levels, a shaping fantasy, as Shakespeare's Theseus says in *A Midsummer Night's Dream*, that gives a local habitation and a name to what is dead or dying within us, our lost selves.

The *Hamlet* bibliography, it has been said, is second in size to that of Christ himself. In 1959 Harry Levin calculated that from the publication of Horace Howard Furness' Variorum Edition of *Hamlet* in 1877 to 1937, a new item was added to Hamletiana every twelve days. "One is released," Levin wrote, "by these very circumstances, from the obligation to be definitive or, on the other hand, from the endeavor to be wholly original." It is safe to say that this pace has only increased since Levin published *The Question of Hamlet* in 1959. Given the enormous amount and variety of commentary on the play, any effort at providing a comprehensive history of reception would have to be prodigious indeed. To the extent to which such a history could be achieved, Gary Taylor, in *Reinventing Shakespeare*, has done so, from the Restoration to the late 1980s. My approach has been to construct a narrative of reception—*a* narrative, not *the* narrative—focused on major issues in the play, and the major figures within the Anglo-American and European traditions that have responded to those issues. Even so, I have by no means considered all important commentaries on the character and the play, and some readers will fault me on that account. I attempt to compensate for the short shrift given in the text of *Looking for Hamlet* to stage and film versions of the play through the galleries, which offer a brief history of *Hamlet* in performance.

In keeping with recent practice, rather than crowding this work with footnotes or endnotes, I offer a bibliographic essay at the end of *Looking for Hamlet* in which I catalogue and comment on my sources.

ONE

THE PREHISTORY
OF HAMLET

SAXO GRAMMATICUS

The story presented in *Hamlet* did not originate with Shakespeare. In order to appreciate Shakespeare's achievement, we must therefore bring to light what we can of the material Shakespeare inherited and from which he produced his play. Indeed, as will become clear as we go along, commentators who ignore Shakespeare's source material are sometimes led to make unsupportable claims for the playwright's character and motivation. The story of Hamlet took shape five hundred years before Shakespeare's play, from still far more ancient material. The earliest account of Hamlet was written in Latin by the Danish historian Saxo Grammaticus during the twelfth century. Saxo lays out the general plot and characters that eventually evolve into Shakespeare's *Hamlet*. His story proceeds this way. Horwendil, king of Denmark, is murdered by his brother Feng, who then marries his brother's wife, Queen Gerutha, and becomes king, thus depriving Horwendil's son, Amleth, of the throne. The fact that Horwendil's murder is committed openly, known to all, is significant. It means, of course, that the Amleth legend has no need for a private means of revealing the nature of the murder to the hero. The ghost is a post-Danish addition to the story, appearing perhaps in the 1580s when the legend was rendered as a stage play in a version that was never printed and thus is missing.

After his father is killed, Amleth feigns madness to avoid suspicion and to buy himself time to engineer his revenge against Feng. Amleth becomes, Saxo writes, "utterly listless and unclean, flinging himself on the ground and bespattering his person with foul and filthy dirt. His discolored face and visage smutched with slime denoted foolish and grotesque madness. All he said was of a piece with these follies; all that he did savored of utter lethargy." As part of this strategy, Amleth spends his time carving wooden stakes. When asked why, he replies cryptically that with these he will avenge his father's killers. Amleth's assumption of the guise of a madman clearly prefigures Hamlet's strategy in Shakespeare's play, and so is an aspect of the character that Shakespeare inherited from Saxo, if indirectly, since it is unlikely that Shakespeare had access to Saxo's version.

Meanwhile Feng, suspecting that Amleth is not really mad, devises two stratagems to flush him out: first, he sends "a fair woman" to seduce Amleth; and second, if the seduction doesn't work, he'll send "a counselor" to eavesdrop on Amleth and his mother in her chamber. In Feng's first scheme, Amleth is tipped off by a "foster-brother," and leads the woman to a secluded spot, "a distant and impenetrable fen," where he has sex with her while avoiding detection by Feng's agents.

Feng then moves to his backup plan, planting a spy in his wife's chamber. Whatever may be the immediate source of Shakespeare's 3.4 in which Hamlet kills Polonius and harangues his mother, its distant origin is undoubtedly this episode from the Amleth saga. Coming to his mother's chamber, Amleth discovers the spy hiding in the straw covering the floor and stabs the unnamed counselor. Amleth then cuts the body into pieces, which he boils and throws into a sewer, where the eavesdropper's remains are eaten by swine. While Shakespeare's Hamlet doesn't abuse Polonius' corpse this way, his dragging the body offstage with the words, "I'll lug the guts into the neighbor room" echoes that abuse. Having dispensed with the spy, Amleth returns to his mother, berating her for marrying incestuously. "Most infamous of women!" he cries, "dost thou seek with such lying lamentations to hide thy most heavy guilt? Wantoning like a harlot, thou hast entered a wicked and abominable state of wedlock, embracing with incestuous bosom thy husband's slayer, and wheedling with filthy lures of blandishment him who had slain the father of thy son." She is, he says, little better than a mare, a brute beast. The debt, however indirect, of Shakespeare's 3.4 to this episode in Saxo is underscored when Amleth goes on to tell his mother that in order to escape treachery he has had to pretend madness, that he has had to make himself a fool to rectify a circumstance that his mother was complicit in creating. In this we might hear Hamlet's insistence to Gertrude that "It is not madness / That I have uttered"—that is, that his madness has been a guise. Unmistakably, when Saxo writes that "[w]ith such reproaches, he rent the heart of his mother, and redeemed her to walk in the ways of virtue," we hear Hamlet's much more intense plea that his mother "[l]et [not] the bloat King tempt you again to bed, / Pinch wanton on your cheek, call you his mouse / And let him for a pair of reechy kisses, / Or paddling in your neck with his damned fingers, / Make you to ravel all this matter out, / That I essentially am not in madness / But mad in craft."

The outline of Shakespeare's plot continues to follow Saxo rather closely until the fifth act of *Hamlet*, the Graveyard Scene, which owes nothing to Saxo's version, and the duel with Laertes, who has no parallel in Danish saga. When Feng discovers that Amleth has eluded his traps, he exiles the young prince to England in the company of two retainers who carry a letter to the British king instructing him to have the hero killed. Amleth, however, wins the confidence and trust of the king by issuing a number of prophesies that come true, then altering the letter so that it commands the deaths of the retainers rather than himself. After the British king executes Feng's henchmen, and after a year's absence, Amleth returns to Denmark just as the court, at his mother's behest, is observing Amleth's obsequies. Amleth's entrance astonishes the crowd, who clamor in wonderment how he is still alive. Amleth, while telling of his sojourn in England, plies the courtiers with alcohol. When they are drunk and incapacitated, Amleth pulls down the wall hangings, covering the sleepers, ties them together with the staves he had carved and sets the bundle on fire, immolating the entire court. While the flames rage, Amleth goes to Feng's chamber, confronts him with his crimes, and slays the king with the king's sword.

Thus ends Book Three of Saxo's *History of the Danes*, which covers only the first half of Amleth's life, the half that Shakespeare adopted and adapted. But the legend of Amleth as recorded by Saxo continues far beyond Shakespeare's version. Shakespeare's Hamlet dies while accomplishing his revenge, but his prototype Amleth looks forward to a remarkable career after the killing of Feng. After cleansing the Danish court of a corrupt regime, he is made king of Denmark, returns to England, wins the hand of the Queen of Scotland, and ultimately is betrayed and killed in battle.

FRANÇOIS DE BELLEFOREST

After Saxo but before Shakespeare, the Hamlet story is told again, with much moralizing and small but significant alterations, by François de Belleforest in his *Histories Tragiques* in 1570 and translated into English in 1608, five years after the first edition of Shakespeare's *Hamlet* appeared in print. From Belleforest we gain new details that have a significant bearing on Shakespeare's play. We learn from Belleforest that Fengon, the usurping brother, had "incestuously abused" the Queen while her husband, Horvendile, was still alive. "An unfortunate and wicked woman," Queen Geruth "made divers men think that she had been the causer of the murder." Belleforest asks, "Where shall a man find a more wicked and bold woman" whom "we leave in the extremity of lasciviousness?"

As in Saxo, Belleforest's hero, here named Hamblet, hides behind the counterfeit of madness, but the *Histories Tragiques* takes the characterization a step further by adding that Hamblet "had been at the school of the Roman Prince," Junius Brutus, whose fashion and wisdom he imitated. Belleforest's Hamblet "rents and tears his clothes, wallowing in the dirt and mire, his face all filthy and black." He "runs through the streets like a man distraught." Like Amleth, Hamblet sharpens sticks in front of the fire, muttering, "I prepare piercing darts and sharp arrows to revenge my father's death." Foolish courtiers, Belleforest writes, "esteemed these his words as nothing; but men of quick spirits, and such as had a deeper reach" understood that "under that kind of folly there lay hidden a great and rare subtlety." This cloaking of wisdom in the guise of madness follows Saxo, who associates Hamlet with the Roman Brutus, as well as with the Bible's David, who feigned madness at the court of Achish (1 Samuel 10–15). Thus the concept of the wise fool, which I discuss in another chapter, may be the deepest and most ancient aspect of Hamlet's character, a concept registered in the name Amleth, which etymologically suggests the notion of the fool or idiot. Yet the character Amleth/Hamblet clearly strategically employs, as his ancestor Junius Brutus had, the *appearance* of folly as a supremely wise and effective means of evading his murdering uncle.

As in Saxo's account, Belleforest's evil Fengon sends a woman to seduce Hamblet. And as in Saxo, a boyhood friend who had been "nourished" with the prince warns Hamblet of the trap. Belleforest adds a significant detail about this woman, that "from her infancy [she] loved and favored" Hamblet, "whom she loved more than herself." Belleforest, the rigid moralist, equivocates on the matter of whether Hamblet has sex with her, writing that "[t]he prince deceived the courtiers and the lady's expectation that affirmed and swore that he never once offered to have his pleasure of the woman, although in subtlety he affirmed the contrary."

Like Saxo's Feng, Belleforest's Fengon decides that Hamblet should be closeted with his mother, to whom he might confess his intentions. But in Belleforest's version of the story, the spy—a "counselor"—hides himself behind a wall hanging rather than under the straw as in Saxo. Hamblet enters and begins to crow "like a cock beating his arms against the hangings." Feeling something stir behind the arras, Hamblet cries "a rat, a rat"—and stabs the counselor. Similarly, Shakespeare's Hamlet prefaces his stabbing of Polonius behind the arras with "How now! A rat! Dead for a ducat, dead!" After dragging the corpse from behind the curtain, Belleforest's Hamblet, like Saxo's Amleth, cuts the body to pieces, boils them, and dumps the parts into a privy where they are eaten by hogs.

Having disposed of the counselor, Hamblet then turns his attentions to his mother, berating her in much harsher terms than Saxo's Amleth does. Hamblet calls her "a vile, wanton adulteress" who nightly embraces "the traitorous villainous tyrant that murdered my father." "Is this the part of a queen and daughter to a king?" he asks, "to live like a brute beast (and like a mare that yieldeth her body to the horse that hath beaten her companion away), to follow the pleasure of an abominable king that hath murdered a far more honester and better man than himself in massacring Horvendile, the honor and glory of the Danes?" As we see later in Shakespeare, Belleforest's Hamblet viciously whips his mother with bestial analogies. "O, queen Geruth," he says, "it is the part of a bitch to couple with many." Geruth is less and worse than a beast. Even "lions, tigers, ounces and leopards fight for the safety and defense of their whelps," he says. To the moralizing Belleforest—this tone is not so evident in Saxo—it must be "unbridled desire" that leads the queen to the arms of the tyrant Fengon.

Hamblet tells his mother that he is "constrained to *play* the part of a mad man" (my emphasis). This explicit reference to playing may be quite important: it may stand as the moment when the saga of Hamblet becomes incipiently a drama, when historiography becomes theater, a destiny that will be fulfilled by Shakespeare, who will exuberantly explore the nature of playing and contrast various forms of acting with his own actor-hero's inward reality.

This action rises to an angry crescendo as Hamblet turns his mother's attention to his own unfortunate circumstance: "the face of a madman serveth to cover my gallant countenance; and the gestures of a fool are fit for me, to the end that guiding myself wisely therein, I may preserve my life for the Danes." In a statement that even more closely prefigures Shakespeare's Closet Scene than did the parallel scene in Saxo, Belleforest's Hamblet says, "weep not to see my folly but rather sigh and lament your own offense, tormenting your conscience." His vituperative tirade forces a confession from Geruth: she was wrong to marry Fengon, she says, "the cruel tyrant and murderer of thy father, and my loyal spouse." But she did not, she insists, conspire in or consent to the death of her husband. In her last gesture in this scene, Hamblet's mother swears loyalty to her son in his plan to avenge the death of his father; she soon proves his loyal ally.

Once the killing of the counselor is discovered, Fengon announces that Hamblet is to be exiled to England accompanied by two "faithful ministers." Hamblet instructs his mother not to grieve at his exile but to pretend happiness, and to hang the walls with tapestries fastened with nails, and also to keep the sharpened brands Hamblet has made. After his absence of a year, she is to organize a celebration of his funeral.

Fengon's henchmen, Shakespeare's characters Rosencrantz and Guildenstern, bear a letter to the English king ordering the murder of Hamblet. Supremely wise, the hero obtains the letter and alters it to command the deaths of the henchmen. This accomplished, Hamblet charms the English king with prophesies, discussed below, that come true. For his success Hamblet is rewarded with gold that he melts into staves. The prince returns to Denmark just as the court, according to the instructions Hamblet had left with his mother, is celebrating his funeral. The crowd drinks and carouses while Hamblet in plain sight feigns distraction. Once they pass out, the wall hangings are brought down on the drunken revelers, whom Hamblet stitches up with staves. He sets the human bundle on fire. Hamblet then makes his way to Fengon's tent, where, as in Saxo's account, he cuts down the usurping king with the king's own sword, foreshadowing Hamlet's killing of Claudius.

In Saxo Grammaticus' account of Amleth and in Belleforest's reworking of this material in his story of Hamblet, we can clearly see the lineaments of Shakespeare's plot and his characters. Horwendil/Horvendile is Hamlet's father; Feng/Fengon is

Claudius; Gerutha/Geruth is Gertrude; Amleth/Hamblet is Hamlet; the "fair woman"—unnamed in both accounts—is the prototype of Ophelia, though she is not called a daughter in the Danish saga; the unnamed foster brother who warns the hero about the setup with the woman is a version of Hamlet's friend, Horatio; the "counselor" killed, boiled, and fed to swine is the prototype of Polonius (called Corambis in Belleforest's *Histoires tragiques* and in the first edition of Shakespeare's play); the two retainers who accompany the hero to England are versions of Rosencrantz and Gildenstern (which are names of two of the most noble families in Danish history). Like his prototypes in Saxo and Belleforest, Hamlet is the son of a father whose murderer married his mother and took Hamlet's place as king. As in the earlier accounts, Shakespeare's Hamlet feigns madness as a means of buying time to plot revenge against his father's killer, though it is far from clear in Shakespeare's play the degree to which Hamlet feigns madness or slips into actual insanity. Hamlet's antics, furthermore, appear tame compared to those of his prototype, who is filthy and crows "like a noisy cock."

The scene in Geruth's chamber is clearly reflected in 3.4 of *Hamlet* when Hamlet confronts his mother in her bedchamber, but Shakespeare incorporates a telling difference. Whereas Amleth's assault upon Geruth succeeds in making an ally of her, Hamlet's shrill and violent attack upon his mother fails. The failure is the effect of something present in Shakespeare's play that is missing from the Danish sources: the ghost of Hamlet's father. In 3.4 the ghost appears only to Hamlet, not to his mother. This creates for Gertrude the appearance that Hamlet is hallucinating. The fear that her son is mad leads Gertrude to betray Hamlet in subtle ways, and so set into motion a series of events that will condemn innocent people, herself included, to death.

The Danish hero's return from England, just as a funeral is being staged, provides the context for the opening of Shakespeare's 5.1, when Hamlet and Horatio arrive just as the court prepares for the burial of Ophelia. But Shakespeare uses nothing of the second half of the prince's life in Danish lore, which includes Amleth/Hamblet becoming king of Denmark.

In addition to elements of plot and character, Shakespeare's *Hamlet* incorporates aspects of tone and imagery that have their origins in the early sources. When Amleth/Hamblet charges his mother with having entered an incestuous marriage, for example, he repeatedly employs the imagery of bestiality, which permeates Shakespeare's play from early to late. In 1.2, his first soliloquy, Hamlet laments that "a beast that wants discourse of reason / Would have mourned longer—." After lamenting in bitter disbelief that his mother has married his father's brother, Hamlet picks up the most obvious of Belleforest's themes: "O most wicked speed! To post / With such dexterity to incestuous sheets. . . ." We may also hear an echo of Belleforest's misogynistic rantings in Hamlet's earlier pronouncement: "Frailty, thy name is Woman."

Perhaps even more significant are elements seemingly inspired by the Danish Hamlet's prophesies to the English king. Invited to feast at court, Hamblet—who is noticeably more melancholic than Saxo's Amleth—refuses to eat, claiming that the meat has been dipped in blood, that the beer has been brewed with water tainted with iron, that the meat upon which they dine "stinketh and savoreth of man's flesh, and [is scented] like the savor of dead carrion, being since cast in the vault." Each of these divinations proves true. As it turns out, the bread had been made of wheat cropped from a field where the skeletons of fallen soldiers were found, where "great heaps of wounded skulls might well appear," the ground made more fertile by human blood. Next it is shown that their beer was brewed from river water. Nearby, the King's men dig into the riverbed and find "a great store of swords and rusty armor."

The last of these prophesies is most interesting. It is discovered that the hogs butchered for the feast honoring Hamblet had fed on the body of a "thief that had been hanged for his demerits." The flesh of animals who have fed on men is eaten by men. Just as Hamblet had fed Fengon's counselor, the prototype of Polonius, to hogs, in England Hamblet as guest of the English king refuses to eat. His host and company are dining on pork fatted on human flesh.

Shakespeare's Hamlet seems obsessed with this strangely recursive process wherein creatures that feed on human flesh are in turn eaten by men. In 4.3, responding to Claudius's "Now, Hamlet, where's Polonius?" Hamlet offers up a cryptic reply. "At supper," he says, easily tripping up the narrowly focused, increasingly desperate Claudius. "At supper?" the king asks, "Where?"

> HAMLET: Not where he eats, but where 'a is eaten. A certain convocation of politic
> worms are e'en at him. Your worm is your only emperor for diet. We fat all
> creatures else to fat us, and we fat ourselves for maggots. Your fat king and
> your lean beggar is but variable service—two dishes, but to one table—that's
> the end.
> KING: Alas, alas!

HAMLET: A man may fish with the worm that hath eat of a king, and eat of the
fish that hath fed of that worm.

KING: What dost thou mean by this?

HAMLET: Nothing but to show you how a king may go a progress through the
guts of a beggar.

Hamlet offers another variation on the uses of putrefied flesh in 5.1 while contemplating the skull of the jester Yorick, marveling at "what base uses we may return, Horatio":

> Why may
> not imagination trace the noble dust of Alexander till 'a
> find it stopping a bunghole?
>
> HORATIO: 'Twere to consider too curiously, to consider so.
>
> HAMLET: No, faith, not a jot, but to follow him thither with modesty enough, and
> likelihood to lead it: Alexander died, Alexander was buried, Alexander
> returneth to dust, the dust is earth, of earth we make loam, and why of that
> loam whereto he was converted might they not stop a beer-barrel?
> Imperious Caesar, dead and turned to clay,
> Might stop a hole to keep the wind away.

A bunghole is the hole through which a cask or barrel is filled and emptied, but it perhaps echoed for Shakespeare's audience the anus, through which waste is passed.

The smell of death, as Stephen Greenblatt has noted, permeated daily life in Shakespeare's time, especially, ironically, in churches and church yards, where the dead were buried. The smell of death permeates the two scenes of *Hamlet*—4.3 and 5.1—we've been considering. In 4.3. after Claudius asks a second time, "Where is Polonius?" Hamlet replies,

> In heaven. Send thither to see. If your messenger find
> him not there, seek him i' th' other place yourself. But if
> indeed you find him not within this month, *you shall nose*
> *him* as you go up the stairs into the lobby.
>
> (my emphasis)

5.1, a darkly powerful scene, is centered on the most terrifying of sights, the human skull; it is also about the foulest of odors. Holding Yorick's skull, Hamlet asks

Horatio, "Dost thou think Alexander looked 'o this fashion i' th' earth?" "E'en so," Horatio replies. "And smelt so? Pah!" Hamlet exclaims, throwing down the death's head.

If much of the content and tone of Danish myth find their way into Shakespeare's play, it cannot be determined exactly how that occurred. We cannot definitively answer the basic question whether Shakespeare even knew these stories of Hamlet as they appear in Saxo and Belleforest. This mystery remains because the path of transmission from the Danish story to Shakespeare is missing a vitally important link, a missing play from the 1580s upon which Shakespeare certainly relied in the writing of his *Hamlet*.

THE UR-*HAMLET*

Elements of Shakespeare's play that do not appear in the Danish sources—the Ghost, Laertes, the visiting players, *The Murder of Gonzago* interlude, Hamlet's great soliloquies, the gravedigger scene—are of particular importance in the search for Hamlet. The counselor Corambis in Belleforest, for example, has no son, so at some later point in the evolution of the story the character of Laertes appeared as a foil to Prince Hamlet. Similarly, much of the material in the second and third acts of Shakespeare's play—the arrival of the players at court and Hamlet's advice on acting, the dumb show and the play within the play—have no precedent in Saxo or Belleforest. There are two possibilities that might explain these additions: one, they are Shakespeare's inventions; two, they are the inventions of some intermediate source between Belleforest and Shakespeare's play. Conjectural evidence suggests that many if not all of these new elements were introduced to the Hamlet story when it took the shape of a drama in the missing Ur-*Hamlet*.

The Ghost is the most significant aspect of Shakespeare's play not found in the Danish histories. This figure, so central to *Hamlet*, probably entered the plot when the Danish material took the shape of a Senecan revenge play, a type of bloody and bombastic drama that was enormously popular in England in the 1580s, named after the first-century Roman tragedian Seneca. Shakespeare's main contribution to this genre is his *Titus Andronicus*, written in the first half of the 1590s. Among Shakespeare's most obscure works, *Titus* over the last decade or so has received increased attention, most notably as a 1999 film by Julie Taymor starring Sir Anthony Hopkins as Titus.

At its core Shakespeare's *Hamlet*, like *Titus Andronicus*, is a revenge play. The king has been murdered and his brother has taken his wife and queen. Son Hamlet has been robbed of both father and mother. He suspects treachery but doesn't have the proof until the ghost of his father appears to tell him what has happened. Hereafter, Hamlet is assigned to revenge; through a tortuous process that costs many lives, including his own, he finally gets even. This is the same basic plot line as the most iconic of the surviving revenge tragedies, Thomas Kyd's *The Spanish Tragedy*. In fact *The Spanish Tragedy* and Shakespeare's *Hamlet* share too many elements great and small—a secret murder, a ghost, demands for revenge, feigned madness, the genuine madness of a female character, the hero's delay and self-reproach, etc.—for the relationship between the two to be coincidental. Rather, these similarities point to a third source, the missing Ur-*Hamlet*, whose author was probably Kyd himself.

It is not out of the question that Shakespeare knew Belleforest's work—the *Histoires Tragiques*, enormously popular in France, was reprinted six times by the beginning of the seventeenth century and translated into English five years after Shakespeare's *Hamlet* appeared in print. Shakespeare's immediate source for *Hamlet*, however, was more probably the lost Ur-*Hamlet* of the 1580s, which was never printed and so had no chance of surviving the centuries. This lost play is without a doubt the most important missing document in Shakespeare studies. Discovering the Ur-*Hamlet* would provide answers to vital questions about Shakespeare's play—what it owed to its predecessors, how it took shape in Shakespeare's incomparable imagination, whether and how Hamlet the character evolved through the process of revision, how the play was staged and performed. The Ur-*Hamlet* is perhaps the most painful absence in literature, an empty space that can be filled only with speculation. It is an untraceable umbra, an invisible halo around the play, as palpable and yet unknowable as a shadow.

Still, we can surmise some of what the Ur-*Hamlet* must have contained. We know from evidence, which I will discuss later, that it featured a ghostly father who commanded his son to avenge his murder. This must mean that, as in the Danish sources, the Claudius figure was the villain of the old play, the murderer of Hamlet's father. It's probable also that in the old play Hamlet, as in the Danish and French sources, feigned madness as a cover for his revenge. Since no trace of the Laertes character exists in the Danish sources, it is reasonable to suppose that Laertes—and perhaps Horatio—premiered in the old play, though we cannot be sure. Nor can we be certain that the players appeared there, or that Hamlet staged there a play-within-the-play as a means of testing the king's guilt. We can surmise, however, that Polonius had an expanded role in the Ur-*Hamlet* under the name of Corambis, which he is called in Belleforest and in the first printed version of Shakespeare's play.

What is absolutely certain is that in the decade before Shakespeare wrote his *Hamlet*, the old *Hamlet* play had achieved iconic status. In 1589, Thomas Nashe, writing "To the Gentlemen Students" of Oxford and Cambridge, in a preface attached to Robert Greene's prose romance *Menaphon*, mocks hack translators and leaden scribblers who are passing themselves off as dramatists: "Yet English Seneca read by candle light yields many good sentences, as 'blood is a beggar,' and so forth: and if you entreat him fair in the frosty morning, he will afford you whole *Hamlets*. I should say handfuls of tragical speeches." Apparently, the old *Hamlet* contained an abundance of violent and maudlin speeches, the kinds of declamations that Shakespeare's Hamlet censures in his advice to the players on acting. While we can't know exactly what Nashe means by "handfuls of tragical speeches," Shakespeare's play contains, as far as I can tell, nothing that can really be called a set speech of a Senecan nature, which may suggest one manner in which Shakespeare, when he has Hamlet urge a naturalistic performance style, is signaling an important alteration of the material he inherited.

Nearly a decade after Nashe referred to scriveners as English Senecas, Frances Meres in his *Palladis Tamia*, or *Wits Treasury*, singles out Shakespeare as England's own Seneca and also its Plautus. In addition to mentioning Shakespeare's "sugared sonnets [circulated] among private friends," Meres offers a nearly complete list of Shakespeare's plays written in or before 1598. The fact that his list does not include *Hamlet* suggests that Shakespeare had not yet written, or at least not produced, it by 1598. It would follow, then, that Nashe's reference to *Hamlet* and the "English Seneca" in 1589, does not point to Shakespeare as the author of the old play. Additional evidence of an apparently non-Shakespearean play about Hamlet is offered by Philip Henslowe, the manager of the Lord Admiral's Men, who listed a play by that name staged at Newinton Butts, a playhouse across the Thames in Southwark that may have been owned by Chamberlain's Men, the company (after 1603 The King's Men) with which Shakespeare would be associated for the rest of his career. But this occurs in 1594, the year Shakespeare joined that company, rather too early, as I argue below, to have been his work.

Two years later, in 1596, Thomas Lodge, in his *Wit's Misery, and The World's Madness*, includes a curious remark about "the Visard of the ghost which cried so miserably at the Theatre like an oyster wife, Hamlet revenge." Tradition has it that Shakespeare himself played the role of the ghost in *Hamlet*. It is tempting to imagine Will's face behind "the Visard of the ghost" crying something like what he would later render as, "If thou didst ever thy dear father love . . . Revenge his foul and most unnatural murder." Lodge's remark is even more tantalizingly biographical if by "Theatre" he is referring to the Theatre, London's first public playhouse, opened in 1576, and the primary venue for Lord Chamberlain's men. If Shakespeare did not create the character of Hamlet's father's ghost, he may have played that part in a production of the old *Hamlet*.

Evidence of what the Ur-*Hamlet* contained is provided by a German play from the seventeenth century, *Der Bestrafte Brudermord oder Prinz Hamlet aus Dannemark*, translated as *Fratricide Punished*. The text comes from a manuscript dated October 27, 1710, but the play was performed by an English company touring Germany decades earlier, before 1626 in fact, and then again between 1660 and 1690. The opening is patently un-Shakespearean, a prologue in which Night and the Furies call for revenge against the new king and his wife, which has no parallel in Shakespeare's play. Otherwise this truncated, touring version of *Hamlet* has all the main elements of Shakespeare's version, opening with a tense exchange between two soldiers, followed immediately by the appearance of the Ghost, the entrance of Horatio and then of Hamlet, who is informed of the visitation of the ghost of his father. A meeting of the Ghost and Hamlet paralleling 1.5 follows, after which Hamlet reunites with his friends, which is followed by a meeting of the King, Queen, Hamlet, and Corambus that parallels Shakespeare's 1.2. The second act of *Fratricide Punished* opens the same way as 3.1 of *Hamlet*, with the King, Queen, and Corambus discussing Hamlet's unusual behavior, after which Ophelia enters and reports his cruel antics, followed by his angry confrontation with Ophelia, mirroring the second phase of Shakespeare's 3.1. Next, Hamlet confides to Horatio that he's pretending madness, followed by the arrival of the players and the plan to stage the play-within-the-play. The second act concludes with the dumb show and what in *Hamlet* is *The Murder of Gonzago*. Act three opens with the scene (3.3 of *Hamlet*) in which Hamlet chooses not to kill Claudius while he is praying. This is shortly followed by the closet scene in which Hamlet stabs Corambus behind the arras. The scene continues, as in Shakespeare's play, with the Ghost appearing to Hamlet but not to his mother the Queen. Jens and Phantasmo, clowns who have no counterparts in *Hamlet*, discuss "the queer goings on at court," which is followed by the entry of Ophelia, mad. Next, the King determines to send Hamlet to England, followed by another scene of Ophelia distracted. Act four opens with Hamlet tricking the Two Ruffians (cf. Rosencrantz and Guildenstern), who accompany him to England, into shooting each other to death, a compelling bit of stage business that Shakespeare—who once directed a man to be chased off stage by a bear—didn't write into his several versions of *Hamlet*.

This episode is followed by the arrival of Leonhardus (Laertes) in Denmark to avenge the death of his father, Corambus. The King and Leonhardus plot to kill Hamlet, with the King suggesting, as he does in the first edition of Shakespeare's *Hamlet*, that the tip of the rapier be poisoned. The fourth act concludes with Ophelia entering distracted once again, this time carrying flowers. Near the beginning of the final act of *Fratricide Punished* Hamlet and Horatio are reunited. In the next scene, the Queen announces Ophelia's suicide, and the final sword play commences, with Hamlet getting the first hit. Leonhardus then wounds Hamlet with the poisoned sword; weapons are dropped and inadvertently exchanged, after which Hamlet wounds Leonhardus, who confesses the plot of the poisoned sword. In the meantime, the Queen drinks from a chalice of poisoned wine, and Hamlet stabs the King, after which both Leonhardus and Hamlet die, but not before Hamlet kills Phantazmo.

Clearly, *Fratricide Punished* is very close to Shakespeare's play. It must have been based on some version of his *Hamlet*, or the Ur-*Hamlet* that Shakespeare inherited and breathed new life into around the turn of the seventeenth century. At the same time, differences between this work and Shakespeare's play are also telling. Fortinbras, into whose hands Denmark is commended in Shakespeare's play, doesn't appear at the end of the German version. There is no equivalent to the Gravedigger Scene, nor is there a gravedigger scene in any of the sources and influences of Shakespeare's play.

Judging from the absence of such a scene in earlier works, we can fairly deduce that 5.1 is the most original scene in Shakespeare's play. Still, as I explained above, there are elements of tone and imagery in 5.1 of Shakespeare's *Hamlet*—the smell of death, the tasting of it, the handling of it—unaccounted for in the acknowledged sources of the play, that seem to point to Shakespeare's awareness of Saxo or Belleforest or both.

DATING *HAMLET*

A significant minority of commentators, among them Peter Alexander and Harold Bloom, believe that Shakespeare himself wrote the Ur-*Hamlet*. This is unlikely. Shakespeare probably didn't arrive in London until the late 1580s, by which time the old *Hamlet* was already a staple of the London stage. As I mentioned above, this old play seems to have been heavy on declamatory speeches, a feature Shakespeare's play notably lacks. It seems much more probable that Shakespeare reworked the old Hamlet play sometime between 1599 and 1602. Some scholars—James Shapiro, for example—place it in 1599, the year the Globe Theatre opened and Shakespeare wrote three other masterpieces, *Henry V, As You Like It,* and *Julius Caesar. Julius Caesar* seems to have been fresh in Shakespeare's memory when he wrote *Hamlet,* since Caesar is mentioned twice in that play, in the first and third acts.

As for the latest possible date, Shakespeare's play was written before July 26, 1602, when it was entered in the Stationers' Register, a comprehensive registry begun in 1557 of nearly all works printed, or intended to be printed, for sale in England. The *Hamlet* entry is by James Roberts, who had entered four other plays by Shakespeare, though he printed only two: "Entered for his copy under the hands of Master Pasfeild and Master waterson warden A book called The Revenge of HAMLETT Prince [of] Denmarke as it was latelie acted by the Lord Chamberleyne his servantes." The first edition of *Hamlet* was printed the following year, 1603.

In all likelihood Shakespeare's *Hamlet* was first performed sometime after 1598, when it was not included in Shakespeare's plays listed by Meres in *Palladis Tamia,* and before the execution of the Earl of Essex in February 1601. The evidence for this comes from a passage written by the pedant Gabriel Harvey on a blank half page of his volume of Chaucer's *Works,* which he purchased and signed in 1598: "The younger sort takes much delight in Shakespeare's *Venus, & Adonis*

[1593]: but his [*The Rape of*] *Lucrece* [1594], & his tragedy of *Hamlet, Prince of Denmark* have it in them, to please the wiser sort."

Harvey's gossipy remarks, which speak of Essex in the present tense, suggest a date for *Hamlet* later than September 1599 but before February 1601, when the Earl of Essex's errant career came crashing down in humiliating cascade of defeat, disgrace, treason, and execution. His demise had been set in motion nearly two years earlier when the young firebrand, on behalf of the Queen, led an expeditionary force of 17,000 men into the green hills and bogs of Ireland, to put down an insurgency led by the valiant, wily, and ruthless Hugh O'Neill, Second Earl of Tyrone. Instead of confronting Tyrone directly at Ulster, Essex wasted his troops' energies and supplies in a series of inconclusive encounters over southern Ireland. This terrible strategic and tactical mistake doomed the expedition to failure. Facing a hopeless situation, Essex cut his losses and signed a treaty with Tyrone that provided Elizabeth with less than even a Pyrrhic victory: Tyrone had succeeded in humiliating the great English Queen.

Essex retreated to England in September 1599 and settled into his London residence, stung, seething, and stewing in embarrassment, paranoia, and anger. Over the coming months Essex solidified a coterie of powerful and disaffected noblemen—among them Shakespeare's patron Henry Wriothesley, the Third Earl of Southampton—to oppose the Queen. The conspirators committed themselves to a plainly treasonous course of action, amounting to an attempt to overthrow Elizabeth. When the uprising failed, Essex was confined to the tower, stripped of his lucrative subsidies, tried and convicted of treason, and sentenced to die. On February 25, 1601, the Earl and his co-conspirators were beheaded in the Tower of London.

In the run-up to the failed coup, Shakespeare had his most dangerous brush with *realpolitik*. Someone, presumably Southampton, enlisted the Lord Chamberlain's Men to stage one of Shakespeare's old plays, *Richard II*, in which the legitimate monarch Richard is publicly deposed and replaced by the worthy usurper Bullingbrook. Needless to say, this did not set well with the Queen, who complained angrily to her Keeper of the Records for the Tower, William Lambarde, "I am Richard II. Know ye not that?" Lambarde reassured Her Majesty by noting that though Elizabeth had raised Essex to great office, he had a "wicked imagination." Elizabeth's reply to her advisor is telling. Perhaps registering the fear produced by the gathering gloom of age, she multiplied the influence of this performance, propagating it, and playing it in both open and closed venues. "He that will forget God, will also forget his benefactor," she says. "This tragedy was played 40tie times in open streets and *houses*" (my emphasis).

Many scholars have seen an allusion to the Essex rebellion of 1601 in Rosencrantz's suggestion in 2.2 of *Hamlet* that the players newly arrived at Elsinore have been banned from acting in the city. Rosencrantz remarks that "their inhibition comes by the means of the late innovation." Since "inhibition" carries a sense of legal prohibition, Rosencrantz's comment might reasonably allude to a punishment imposed upon Chamberlain's Men for its role in the events leading to Essex's execution in February 1601. Still, it must be said that no evidence survives to indicate that Shakespeare's acting company was punished for its role in the Essex uprising.

Evidence for dating *Hamlet* later in 1601, perhaps even 1602, is also provided by the subsequent exchange between Rosencrantz and Hamlet concerning the rivalry between child and adult acting companies, the "War of the Theatres." This "war" amounted to a contest between competing acting troupes, one made up entirely of boys and the other composed of men playing adult male roles and boys playing the female roles. The chief evidence of this "war" is a series of attacks and counterattacks conducted via satiric caricatures between playwrights Thomas Dekker and John Marston on the side of the adult acting companies, and Ben Jonson, who at the time—1600–1601—was writing plays for child acting companies. "The War of the Theatres" reached its peak when Dekker (with Marston) in *Satiromastix* and Jonson in *The Poetaster* lampooned each other in retaliatory plays. The fact that both *Satiromastix* and *The Poetaster* were entered in the Stationers' Register in late 1601 may suggest that *Hamlet* was written at about the same time, perhaps even later, in 1602. In July of that year, when *Hamlet* was entered in the Register, the intent to publish the play noted that the play to be printed "was latelie Acted by the Lord Chamberleyne his servants," "latelie" meaning recently.

Shakespeare's sources are of obvious importance in the search for Hamlet. In order to grasp the character and play in anything like totality, we must know what material Shakespeare was reworking, what he had before him at his desk when he wrote. And yet, that is impossible to fathom. Informed by all available evidence, our powers to reconstruct this particular moment, the weeks or months that it took Shakespeare to write *Hamlet*, can never be entirely successful. Untold mysteries, the bulk of which we may not yet even recognize, would be revealed with the discovery of the Ur-*Hamlet*. This painful absence, and the unbridgeable gulf it creates, will likely prevent us from ever discovering precisely how and when Shakespeare wrote *Hamlet*.

The exact date of *Hamlet*—where in the 1599–1602 window it was written—is interesting, of course, if impossible to determine. More important than the precise date of its composition is the recognition that *Hamlet* was created near the end of Queen Elizabeth's reign. It's a late Elizabethan rather than a Jacobean play. If its final moment, with Fortinbras on the verge of assuming the crown of Denmark, presages the ascension in 1603 of the Scot James to the English throne, the play itself is a register of the collective experience of an English nation facing the imminent passing of the aged Queen Elizabeth. At the conclusion of his discourse on the reeking death's head of Yorick the Jester in 5.1, Hamlet commands an indefinite "you" to get "to my lady's chamber and tell her, let her paint an inch thick, to this favor she must come; make her laugh at that." This reference to inch-thick makeup covering a skull seems to allude to aging Elizabeth, who was fifty-seven in 1600, missing many of her teeth, the remaining stained yellow, and given to wearing gowns that exposed her body to her navel. Her face ravaged by smallpox and the cumulative effects of time, Elizabeth wore makeup half an inch thick. The once youthful and sexually alluring Virgin Queen was now herself a living *memento mori*, a painted skull—at once an image of imminent death and an emblem of the death of an age that in her forty-four-year reign she had singularly defined.

TWO

THE THREE
HAMLETS

*T*he textual history of *Hamlet* is impossibly complicated but nonetheless
critically important. Three different editions of the play appeared over a
twenty-year span, from 1603 to 1623. The first two versions appeared in
virtual tandem—in 1603 (Q1) and 1604/5 (Q2)—but are radically different from
each other. These were published as play books, relatively inexpensive documents
printed in the quarto format (hence the Q designation) made up of sheets of paper
folded twice to make four leaves and eight pages. About the size of modern paper-
back books, quartos were printed, gathered, and sold, generally unbound. Only
two copies of Q1, discovered in 1823, survive; seven copies of Q2 exist, of which
three are dated 1604, the others 1605. In addition to these quartos, a third version
of *Hamlet* appeared in the first collected edition of Shakespeare's plays, which
printed thirty-six of them in the large folio format, seven years after his death. The
First Folio of 1623 (F1) is made up of sheets of paper folded once to make two
leaves and four pages. Often sumptuously illustrated and bound in leather, folios
were expensive books. Their costly materials testify to importance, registering a
belief that folio works—whatever they were—were preserved in an enduring
format. This first collected edition is evidence of the recognition of Shakespeare's
importance in his own century.

Indeed, in his dedicatory poem in the First Folio, Ben Jonson, who loved
Shakespeare, he said, "on this side of idolatry," enthroned Shakespeare atop the

pantheon of dramatists. Jonson inaugurates Bardolatry, the cultlike worship of Shakespeare as the supreme cultural and literary icon of the English-speaking world, a stature that has only grown with time. Jonson praises Shakespeare as transhistorical, "not of an age, but for all time!" "Triumph, my Britain," he writes, "thou has one to show / To whom all scenes of Europe homage owe." It is clear even to the casual observer that Jonson was right. Shakespeare is for all time. The only possible complaint Jonson can muster is that Shakespeare had "small Latin, and less Greek." But this is a quibble, true only when Shakespeare's knowledge of classical languages is compared to that of Jonson, who was the preeminent classicist of his age, and it may not, in fact, be a complaint at all. Jonson's "Though thou hadst small Latin, and less Greek / From whence to honor thee, I would not seek / For names, but call forth thundering Aeschylus, / Euripides and Sophocles to us" might be understood to mean "even if you had only small Latin and less Greek, I would still rank you with Aeschylus, Euripides and Sophocles."

In 1616, the year Shakespeare died, Jonson had become the first English playwright to oversee the publication of his own collected plays. This was unprecedented among English dramatists, because playwrights like Shakespeare and Jonson wrote as members of acting syndicates and had little reason, it appears, to see their work in print. In flush times, acting companies wanted to keep these plays away from the public because the company itself might want to stage them at a later date. Moreover, because there was nothing like modern copyright law in existence, the printer rather than the author profited from the publication of a play, particularly in the printing of stolen or pirated versions of plays.

Indeed, the pirating of plays was not uncommon, especially as far as Shakespeare is concerned. Like the quarto editions of *Titus Andronicus* (1594), *Richard III* (1597), and *Romeo and Juliet* (1597), the 1603 *Hamlet* may have been an unauthorized publication. The evidence suggests to many scholars that it was a memorial reconstruction of a staged version of Shakespeare's play, put together by an actor who played two minor roles. Not surprisingly, he remembered his own lines very well; less perfectly the words of others on stage with him; and rather poorly the lines of principal characters in the play, especially Hamlet himself, who delivered the most famous speeches of the play alone on stage. In keeping with the theory of Q1 as a bootlegged version of *Hamlet*, this edition is a drastically shorter version of the play, about half the length of later versions.

Only a year later, perhaps to supercede this version of the play, the Second Quarto of *Hamlet* appeared. At 3,902 lines, Q2 is nearly twice the length of Q1. Its title page announces that this version is "newly imprinted and enlarged to almost as much again as it was, according to the true and perfect copy." This claim boasts authority, suggesting that Shakespeare himself authorized and perhaps even oversaw the publication of this edition. Since the eighteenth century Q2 has most often served as the "copy text" of *Hamlet*, the version on which editors base their own editions.

Since, until quite recently, editions of *Hamlet* were composites of these three distinct versions of the play—1603, 1604, and 1623—we must necessarily closely consider these three early printed versions individually and examine the relationships among them.

THE FIRST QUARTO

Traditionally, Q1 has been categorized as one of the "bad quartos" in Shakespeare's canon, the term "bad" designating a play book that records a corrupted version of a play. This long-established view holds that Q1 was reconstructed from memory by the actor who played Marcellus—an officer early in the play—and the very brief roles of Lucianus and Voltemand (Voltemar in Q1) in the play within the play of 2.2. Of course different actors might have played these roles, which would mean that three actors are responsible for Q1, but it is just as likely that all three roles were played by the same actor, a premise supported by the possibility that Q1 is based upon a touring version of *Hamlet*, in which the same actor would play multiple roles where possible, to keep the number of required players at a minimum. In any case, the attribution of Q1 to this actor or actors rests upon the overwhelming agreement—as much as 93 percent—between these roles in Q1 and later, more authoritative versions of *Hamlet* discussed below.

The primary significance of the title page (see figure 2.1) rests on the fact that until 1603 Shakespeare's acting company had been under the patronage of Henry Carey, Lord Hundson, the Queen's Chamberlain. But with the death of Elizabeth in the spring of 1603 and the ascension of James I, Lord Chamberlain's Men came under royal patronage as The King's Men. The fact that the title page of Q1 reflects the royal imprimatur—"his highness servants"—suggests that the printer was

THE

Tragicall Hiftorie of

HAMLET

Prince of Denmarke

By William Shake-fpeare.

As it hath beene diuerfe times acted by his Highneffe fer-
uants in the Cittie of London : as alfo in the two V-
niuerfities of Cambridge and Oxford, and elfe-where

At London printed for N.L. and Iohn Trundell.
1603.

Figure. 2.1   THE / Tragicall History of / HAMLET / Prince of Denmarke / By
William Shake-speare. / As it hath beene diverse times acted by His Highness ser- / vants
in the Cittie of London : as also in the two U / niversities of Cambridge and Oxford, and
elsewhere / At London printed for N.L. and John Trundell / 1603. By permission of the
Huntington Library.

capitalizing on the new royal status of Shakespeare's acting company. This distinction, perhaps more so than the intrinsic merit of Q1 as a text of *Hamlet*, may account for its publication. But there is more to the story. Though lost, the actual text from which the play was imperfectly reconstructed appears to be derived from a provincial touring version of *Hamlet*, radically abridged—a production, perhaps, by Shakespeare's own acting company, The King's Men. Since the title page announces that this version was performed not only in London but also in Oxford, Cambridge, "and elsewhere," it's likely that whoever was responsible for this version of *Hamlet* wanted to cash in on the popularity of a stage version that enjoyed some currency as a touring play.

The brevity of Q1—at 2,224 lines, about half the length of later versions—is another reason to believe that this version is based upon a touring production of the play. It stands to reason that a touring *Hamlet* would be pared down more or less to the essentials of the drama, streamlined so that it could be performed by a minimal touring cast. Circumstantial evidence further supports this theory. At various times in Shakespeare's professional life—the late 1580s through 1613—the plague swept through London, killing thousands and creating massive disruptions of civic life. The best minds of the age had not discovered even the efficacy of basic sanitation, much less the etiology of the plague, which was spread through fleas carried by rats on ships arriving from distant ports. The pestilence would overwhelm London with terrifying alacrity. In 1601–1602, there is no record of the plague in London, yet it came with a vengeance in 1603, the year Q1 was published, breaking out in April after the Queen's death in March and raging throughout the remainder of the year. Of the 38,244 deaths in London and its suburbs in 1603, the plague accounted for more than 30,000. The week of September 1, 1603, was a particularly terrible one, in which the city recorded 2,495 plague deaths.

During plague times, theaters, like other public places that brought lots of people together, were shut down. Such was the case in 1593 and 1594 when Shakespeare the dramatist was idled by the plague. He used this forced hiatus to write two great nondramatic poems, *Venus and Adonis* and *The Rape of Lucrece*. In the 1603 outbreak, virtually all public events were cancelled. The year-round fair at Smithfield was closed, school terms were deferred or transferred out of town. Anybody healthy enough to travel fled the vicious contagion enveloping London. Like the schools and fairs, the theaters were closed. Following the general exodus, Shakespeare's acting company may have attempted to outrun the plague by going on tour, where they performed the shortened version of *Hamlet* that is the inspiration for the memorial reconstruction of Q1. This might explain the apparent portability of the version of *Hamlet* rendered as Q1.

Q1 is marked by inversions, omissions, and garbled lines, all attributable to the imperfect operation of memory. The most obvious cases are Hamlet's famous soliloquies delivered by the lead character often alone on stage, and hence not as well heard or recalled by another actor compiling the text later. A comparison of Hamlet's famous "To be or not to be" in Q1 and Q2 is instructive. I have italicized phrases that are common, either the same or recognizably similar, in both versions. In the more authoritative Q2, Hamlet's soliloquy—with spelling modernized—is as follows.

> *To be, or not to be*—that is the question;
> Whether 'tis nobler in the mind to suffer
> The slings and arrows of outrageous fortune,
> Or to take arms against a sea of troubles,
> And by opposing end them; *To die; to sleep*—
> No more, and by a sleep to say we end
> The heartache and the thousand natural shocks
> That flesh is heir to; 'tis a consummation
> Devoutly to be wished—*to die, to sleep*—
> *To sleep, perchance to dream*—ay, there's the rub,
> For in *that sleep of death* what dreams may come,
> When we have shuffled off this mortal coil,
> Must give us pause: there's the respect
> That makes *calamity* of so long life.
> For *who would bear* the whips and *scorns* of time,
> *Th' oppressor's wrong, the proud man's contumely,*
> The pangs of despised love, the law's delay,
> The insolence of office and the spurns
> That patient merit of th' unworthy takes,
> When he himself *might his quietus make*
> *With a bare bodkin. Who would fardels bear*
> *To grunt and sweat under a weary life*
> *But that the dread of something after death,*
> (*The undiscovered country from whose bourn*
> No traveler returns) *puzzles the will*
> *And makes us rather bear those ills we have*

Than fly to others we know not of.
Thus *conscience does make* cowards—
And thus the native hue of resolution
Is sicklied o'er with the pale cast of thought,
And enterprises of pitch and moment
With this regard their currents turn awry
And lose the name of action.

Now consider the same speech, with spelling modernized, as it appears (much earlier in the play) in Q1.

To be, or not to be—ay, there's the point
To Die, to sleep—is that all? Ay, all:
No, *to sleep, to dream*—ah marry, there it goes,
For *in that dream of death,* when we're awaked
And *borne* before an everlasting judge,
From whence no passenger ever returned—
The undiscovered country, at whose sight
The happy smile and the accursed damned—
But for this, the joyful hope of this,
Who'd bear the *scorns* and flattery of the world,
Scorned by the right rich, the rich cursed of the poor,
The widow being *oppressed,* the orphan *wronged,*
The taste of hunger or a tyrant's reign,
And thousand more *calamities* besides,
To grunt and sweat under this weary life,
When that *he may his full quietus make*
With a bare bodkin? Who would this *endure,*
But for a hope *of something after death,*
Which *puzzles the* brain and doth confound the sense,
Which *makes us rather bear those evils we have*
Than fly to others that we know not of?
Ay, that. O, *this conscience makes cowards of us all.*

According to the theory of memorial reconstruction, the actor (or actors) responsible for this speech in Q1 remembered its general structure and many of its most memorable words and phrases. He recalled the initial formulation, "To be or not to be" but dropped "Whether 'tis nobler . . ." altogether, picking up "To die, to sleep" (which appears twice in Q2) and adding the meaningless filler, "ah marry, there it goes." Q2's "that sleep of death" becomes "that dream of death" in Q1. He remembered the phrase "undiscovered country" but couldn't recollect its context, substituting "borne" (meaning "carried to") for "bourn" (meaning a boundary) from which "no traveler returns." In this position Q1 offers "an everlasting judge," a phrase that has no parallel in Q2. Q2's "the dread of something after death" becomes "the hope of something after death" in Q1.

Likewise, important words in Q2 appear scattered and altered in Q1. "Scorns" is used in two variants, "scorns" and "Scorned," "oppressor's" becomes "oppressed." "[H]e may his full quietus make / With a bare bodkin" imperfectly renders "he himself might his quietus make / With a bare bodkin." The actor remembered "which makes us rather bear those ills we have / Than fly to others we know not of" almost exactly, substituting "evils" for "ills," which he might have misheard rather than misremembered, and adding "that" to the second line to destroy its meter. The memorable "Thus conscience does make cowards of us all" closes Hamlet's soliloquy in Q1 as "O, this conscience makes cowards of us all."

Not everyone subscribes to the traditional view of Q1 as a memorial reconstruction. In recent years, a competing argument—which might be called the ensemble theory—has been used to challenge the Marcellus/Lucianus/Voltemar formulation as the "recorder" for the first edition of *Hamlet*. According to the ensemble theory, the entire cast of a production might have recited to a scribe their lines as they had been performed or as they remembered performing them. The ensemble theory in no way negates the memorial basis of Q1, of which the evidence is compelling. But by positing that the text is closer to a reconstruction by the troupe, the cast of a performing version of *Hamlet*, rather than by incidental actors in it, the theory carries with it implicitly greater authority. It carries the suggestion of group approval, and if the group we are talking about is The King's Men, the premier acting company in the nation whose principal author was William Shakespeare— Shakespeare's name appears on the title page of Q1—then we have quite a more formidable artifact on our hands in Q1, even if its flaws make it unsuitable to serve as the foundation of a modern version of the play.

The overall pace and efficiency of Q1 reflect a more or less complete staged version of *Hamlet*, a theatrical adaptation perhaps supervised by Shakespeare himself. Recently, it has been argued that Q1 *Hamlet* reflects "a conscious reworking designed to shorten and speed up the play in preparation for the stage." This would by nature be a textual fixing of an ephemeral event to some extent dependant on the memory of players, and the care they took to recount their lines exactly. In assessing Q1, we have to consider unfathomable contingencies—how tired or drunk or rushed or careful the actors were to present their roles accurately—and how much these same factors affected the accuracy of the scribe who took down their words.

But dramatic efficiency is essential to the theory of Q1 as a version of a staged *Hamlet*. Consider, for example, Q1's version of 1.5, when the Ghost addressing Hamlet explains the circumstances of his murder. Near the beginning of this account in Q1, Hamlet Sr. inserts the urgent qualifier, "Brief let me be." Accordingly, the story he tells of being murdered by his brother who then marries his widow, his "seeming-virtuous queen," and usurps the throne, is pared down. His first lines framing the scene, "'Tis given out, that sleeping in my orchard / A serpent stung me" through to the Ghost's departing remark "Hamlet adieu, adieu, adieu. Remember me," covers only forty-five lines in Q1. This is brief enough. In the longer Q2, however, the exchange between dead father and soon to be dead son is sixty or so lines long. Accommodating the expansion of this scene, Q2 drops the ghost's "Brief let me be" twenty-four lines later in the speech, after a contextual indicator, "But soft, me thinks I scent the morning air."

In Q1 this exchange is nicely framed by "briefe let me be" and "Hamlet, adieu, adieu, adieu. Remember me." It recounts the story of murder and remarriage with considerable narrative efficiency, conveying the essential evidence of regicide and incest, stumbling only in the repetition of "Brief let me be" seventeen lines into the account. We learn that "A Serpent stung me. So the whole ear of Denmark / Is with a forged process of my death rankly abused"; and that "He that did sting thy father's heart / Now wears the crown." Hamlet's reply to his father is close to that of Q2: "O my prophetic soul! my uncle, my uncle!" The essentials of the speech are intact. Lewdness courts in the shape of heaven, and moving from a celestial bed, lust will prey on garbage; the usurper, we learn, entered the orchard and poured the poison in the ear of the sleeping king; the action of the poison was swift, thickening the blood, and leaving "all my smooth body, barked, and tettered over":

> Thus was I sleeping by a brother's hand
> Of crown, of queen, of life, of dignity
> At once deprived, no reckoning made of,
> But sent unto my grave,
> With all my accounts and sins upon my head.
> O horrible, most horrible!

Q1 simplifies, from three lines of Q2 to a single line, the ghost's following injunction: "If thou hast nature in thee, bear it not," before the ghost turns his attention to Hamlet's mother, commanding his son to "leave her to heaven" and five lines later departing with "Hamlet, adieu, adieu, adieu. Remember me." The important point is that Q1 has the virtue, common to performance-based texts, of speeding up the action.

The efficiency essential to the ensemble theory of Q1 *Hamlet* is most apparent in the only episode—scene 14, paralleling 4.6, 4.7, and 5.2 of Q2—found in Q1 and not in either of the two later editions. This surprisingly intimate meeting between Horatio and Gertrude—the only such encounter in the play—is almost always omitted from modern texts of *Hamlet*. It is the most substantial excision from modern *Hamlet*s, whose editors generally favor inclusion rather than exclusion, further bloating the already gigantic text of the play.

But it clearly functioned importantly in the play as represented in Q1. Horatio informs the Queen (Gertred in Q1) that Hamlet is back in Denmark and that a letter from him has arrived recounting how, en route to England, he had discovered the king's plot to have the two friends (Rossencraft and Gilderstone in Q1) engineer his murder. The Queen remarks, "Then I perceive there's treason in *his* looks / That seem'd to sugar o're *his* villanie / For murderous minds are always jealous" (my emphasis). If we take the possessive pronouns "his" to refer to the King, and not Hamlet, then Gertred is again siding with her son, consistent with her characterization in Q1 as innocent of complicity in her husband's killing. At 11.85–6, the Closet Scene, she exclaims to Hamlet, "I swear by heaven / I never knew of this most horrid murder." The tantalizing exception to this claim of innocence is 9.112 of Q1, when the player queen remarks that "None weds the second but *she* kills the first," where Q2 and F1 read, "None wed the second but *who* killed the first." No modern edition that I know of accepts the Q1 reading here.

Horatio then tells Gertred that Hamlet intends to come to court, adding cryptically: "Observe the king, and you shall quickly find, / Hamlet being here, things fell not to his mind." Here, the context indicates that "his" must refer to Claudius. Horatio also confides that Hamlet has engineered the deaths of Rossencraft and Gilderstone—"so [that] all was done without discovery"—and the scene ends with Gertred thanking Horatio "With thousand mother's blessings to my son." This scene not only reinforces an important aspect of Gertrude's character—her desire to protect her son (though not with absolute certainty)—it does so with remarkable efficiency. Indeed, dramatic efficiency is the point. Like the earlier scene, this one packages information in such a way as to convey in the shortest time information—Hamlet's return, the altering of the letter, the dispatching of the false friends—that is scattered over several scenes in the later texts. This compression is consistent with the needs of a shortened touring version of the play.

Whatever the genesis of Q1, it is the closest version of *Hamlet* that we have to the play as it was actually performed in Shakespeare's age. Twice the length of what could be played in "this two hours traffic of the stage" (the typical length of a play, according to the chorus of *Romeo and Juliet*), Q2 and F1 are far too long to have been performed as published. In Shakespeare's age, as in any age, plays must run at a clip or risk losing the audience. Performed without pause or intermission, Shakespeare's tragedies are brilliantly fast, and they get faster after *Hamlet*. *Macbeth*, for instance, at 2,084 lines, is especially frenetic. The play lacks a back-story to explain the missing Macbeth child or children, that baby or babies of whom Lady Macbeth remarks "I have given suck and know / How tender tis to love the babe that milks me." The Scottish Play exists only in the present and future dimensions: Lady Macbeth feels "now / The future in the instant," and her husband wishes that "here, / But here, upon this bank and shoal of time, / We'd jump the life to come." The play moves forward at a breathtaking pace, slowing to an agonizing crawl only in Macbeth's "Tomorrow and tomorrow and tomorrow" speech. Much longer than *Macbeth*, *Othello* nevertheless runs at a breakneck pace, covering only two or three nights (and the time between acts one and two) in a taut dramatic narrative leading to a swift and violent catastrophe.

Q1 *Hamlet* may be only a brief chronicle, flawed in ways that make it unfit to serve as the basis for modern editions of *Hamlet*. Yet because it was in all likelihood actually performed by Shakespeare's own acting company, it is of unique importance. Without this quarto play book, of which only two copies have survived, we would not have any good idea how *Hamlet* was staged in Shakespeare's time.

Still, to return to the claim I briefly alluded to in the last chapter—the possibility that Q1 is a version of Ur-*Hamlet*—I don't find in Q1 anything like set speeches of a Senecan nature, no booming talk, no "handfuls of tragical speeches" that Nashe witnessed in the 1580s *Hamlet*. In fact, nowhere in Shakespeare do we find junk speeches of the kind Nashe's comment suggests. Even in his early plays— *Titus Andronicus*, for example—Shakespeare is too careful an artist for this kind of hackneyed work. Even in primitive Q1, the Ghost is something extraordinary, as many scholars have noted, unlike any other before it. While ghosts were typically bogeymen meant to terrify the hero and his audience, the Q1 Ghost is a rounded character, rendered with a psychological and emotional complexity not found in typical ghosts of the Senecan tradition. On these grounds alone, I am tempted to divorce Shakespeare from the Ur-*Hamlet*.

I want to draw attention, finally, to one particular resonance of Q1 *Hamlet*. It duplicates the problem Hamlet himself faces: the onerous burden of remembering something that's inevitably being forgotten. The maligned Q1 reconstructs from memory—either a single memory or a concert of memories—a prince who is enjoined with the task of remembering. In time, as we know, Hamlet seems to lose the powerful poignancy and immediacy of his dead father's vivid demand to revenge his murder. In 3.4 the Ghost appears to him in his mother's chamber in order, he tells his son, to "to whet thy almost blunted purpose." A play about fading memory is, in other words, a product of fading memory, a memorial reconstruction of a memorial reconstruction, a *Hamlet* for Hamlet.

THE SECOND QUARTO

The Q1 *Hamlet* is the platform of later incarnations of the character, one stripped of (or has not yet acquired) the intellectual, psychological and emotional complexity of later versions. Notably, Hamlet in Q1 is not a man who significantly delays his pursuit of revenge. He is not nearly the tortured figure, paralyzed by thought and introspection, that we know him to be. Hamlet of Q1 is primal and primitive, the first and least sophisticated version of Shakespeare's most complex character. He is an outward projection of what in later versions will become Shakespeare's most inwardly directed character. Q1 Hamlet is rather flat, a character fit for an audience that was watching and listening (and expecting action) rather than reading. He registers little of the profound thought, brilliant language, and psychological complexity of the Hamlet we know today.

The fully realized *Hamlet*, the basis for modern editions of the play, appears a year after the First Quarto, in 1604 (some copies are dated 1605) as the Second or Good Quarto, at 4,056 lines the longest of the three versions of the play. The term "good quarto" effectively distinguishes Q2 from Q1, the "bad quarto," but is otherwise misleading, for it was not very carefully printed. Still, there is every reason to think that Q2 is close to what Shakespeare had written as *Hamlet*. Indeed, "written" is the operative word, for rather than being a performance text, Q2 is a literary text, a version for the page rather than the stage. With a running time of more than four hours, Q2 is twice the length of a typical theatrical production in Shakespeare's day. Accordingly, just as Q1 is an outwardly focused work, a projection onto the stage, Q2 is inwardly focused, developing the character of Hamlet from within, creating the illusion of roundness, a fully human status that only literature, as opposed to stage productions, can create.

For these reasons, Q2 *Hamlet* is the foundation for most modern editions of the play. Its title indicates a desire to supercede the earlier, corrupt text (see figure 2.2).

The claim to authority on the title page of Q2 may tell us something about Shakespeare himself at the height of his career. In 1604 William Shakespeare was already the most successful playwright in English history. Though he would never collect his works, as his friend Jonson did his, it is inconceivable that he was unaware of his own importance. After all, he was more than a decade into a career of unparalleled artistic development, writing not only plays but enormously successful nondramatic poems and sonnets.

Shakespeare the playwright had first drawn public notice in 1592, quite early in his career, while he was finishing the sequence of three *Henry VI* plays. This first, and most infamous reference to Shakespeare came from a dissolute pamphleteer and playwright, Robert Greene (1558–92). Six years Shakespeare's senior, Greene was one of the so-called University Wits, men such as Thomas Lodge and George Peele, who had been educated at Cambridge or Oxford and turned to

THE
Tragicall Historie of
HAMLET,
Prince of Denmarke.

By William Shakespeare.

[handwritten annotation: who with some errors not to be abowed in that age, had vndoubtedly a larger soule of poesie then for any of our nation, was the first who to shun ye paine of continuall ryming ...]

Newly imprinted and enlarged to almoſt as much
againe as it was, according to the true and perfeſt
Coppie.

[handwritten annotation: ... more properly Prose ... into which the English ...]

AT LONDON,
Printed by I. R. for N. L. and are to be ſold at his
ſhoppe vnder Saint Dunſtons Church in
Fleetſtreet. 1604.

Figure 2.2 THE / Tragicall History of / HAMLET / Prince of Denmarke / by William Shakespeare. / Newly imprinted and enlarged to almost as much / againe as it was, according to the true and perfect / Coppie / AT LONDON, / Printed by I. R. for N.l. and are to be sold At his / shoppe under Saint Dunstons Church in / Fleetstreet. 1604. By permission of the Folger Shakespeare Library.

writing (mainly plays) rather than taking up more respectable careers. The Cambridge-educated Greene achieved considerable success as a writer, publishing thirty-six titles in all. But he was afflicted with a wretched character, and a weakness for drink. A liar, backstabber, and double-dealer, he shamelessly squandered his wife's inheritance and lived thereafter by a sequence of schemes and cons. By the time Shakespeare began writing plays around 1590, Greene must have presented a sorry sight indeed—a hugely obese, reeking derelict who drank away what little money he was able to eke out from those who still pitied him. He died, it was reported, after a surfeit of pickled herring and Rhenish wine.

In 1592, the last year of his life, while living in extreme poverty with a poor shoemaker, he wrote an apology for his life titled *A Groats-Worth of Witte, Brought with a Million of Repentance*. Under a thin Italianate veneer, Greene surveys his unfortunate course from a man of substance and education to utter ruin. The pamphlet ends with a curious "Address" to his fellow University Wits, warning them against spending their time writing plays. Attacking actors, Greene writes, "Yes trust them not, for there is an upstart Crow, beautified with our feathers, that with his *Tygers hart wrapt in a Players hyde*, supposes he is as well able to bombast out a blanke verse as the best of you: and being an absolute *Johannes factotum*, is in his owne conceit the onely Shakes-scene in a countrey" (emphasis in original). "Shakes-scene" puns on Shakespeare's name, of course, and the line "Tygers hart wrapt in a Players hyde" is a slightly altered line from Shakespeare's *3 Henry IV*, "O tiger's heart wrapped in a woman's hide!" Greene accuses Shakespeare of being a poser ("an upstart Crow"), implies that he is a thief of other men's wit ("beautified with our feathers"), a hack ("bombast"), a pedant ("*Johannes factotum*"), and self-important ("in his owne conceit"). Park Honan, one of Shakespeare's finest biographers, calls Greene's remarks "a virtual rape of Shakespeare." He notes that the envious, dying Greene must have been attending to Shakespeare's plays with a very careful ear since none of the Henry plays was in print in 1592, when Greene parodied the line from *3 Henry VI*. It's a safe bet that other playwrights were also paying equally close attention to this budding master, who, in his early work, was, along with the doomed Kit Marlowe, virtually inventing the history play.

Too proud to take Greene's insult lying down, Shakespeare appears to have threatened some kind of action against Greene's publisher, Henry Chettle, perhaps calling upon friends to pressure Chettle (who some think was actually the author of *A Groats-Worth of Witte*) for a retraction. The effort was successful. In

December 1592 Chettle issued a profuse apology for Greene's attack, claiming he had met the wronged man and discovered "his demeanor no less civil than he [is] excellent in the quality he professes. Besides," he continues, "divers of worship have reported his uprightness in dealing, which argues honesty, and his facetious grace in writing, that approves his art." Shakespeare must have felt vindicated by this apology, but he wasn't finished with Greene—he would lift the plot of his late Romance, *The Winter's Tale*, from Greene's *Pandosto*.

In 1592, in the nascent world of print culture, Shakespeare was a budding superstar. The next year his enormously popular nondramatic poem *Venus and Adonis* would be published, and the following year his second nondramatic work, *The Rape of Lucrece*, even more acclaimed and respected than *Venus and Adonis*, would appear. Shakespeare's awareness of his own importance as a writer was surely deepened six years later with the publication of *Palladis Tamia* or *Wit's Treasury* (1598) by Frances Meres, a Cambridge- and Oxford-educated rector and clergyman. A thoroughly unoriginal and even turgid work, *Palladis Tamia* includes a survey of living English writers in which he considers Shakespeare's place among them. Precisely because Meres is undiscriminating and unoriginal, his remarks on Shakespeare are all the more important. He's a sort of pollster, articulating what others are thinking, presenting the consensus opinion of his time. Meres praises both *Venus and Adonis* and *The Rape of Lucrece*, as well as Shakespeare's "sugred Sonnets" then circulating among friends. He then turns his attention to Shakespeare as playwright, offering praise in terms all the more extraordinary when we consider that Shakespeare had yet to reach full maturity as a dramatist; he had not yet written *As You Like It, Henry V, Julius Caesar, Hamlet, Macbeth*, or *The Tempest*. "As Plautus and Seneca are accounted the best for Comedy and Tragedy among the Latins," Meres proclaims, "so Shakespeare among the English is the most excellent in both kinds for the stage." He then lists, perhaps incompletely, Shakespeare's plays: among comedies, *Two Gentlemen of Verona, The Comedy of Errors, Loves Labors Lost, Loves Labors Won* (possibly a lost play), *A Midsummer Night's Dream*, and *The Merchant of Venice*; and among tragedies, *Richard II, Richard III, Henry IV, King John, Titus Andronicus*, and *Romeo and Juliet*.

Shakespeare surely read Meres's extraordinary praise of himself. This thirty-four-year-old poet/playwright of common birth from rural England, though lacking a university education, was now enormously successful and becoming a very wealthy man. And it must have spoken deeply to him, the claim that he was

Plautus and Seneca in one. Plautus, Seneca, and Shakespeare. It sounds almost divine, one step down from the Holy Trinity. But Meres does not simply present us with Shakespeare as an equal to Plautus and Seneca. Instead, Shakespeare embodies the two Roman dramatists, exclusive masters of comedy and tragedy, in one artist.

Indeed, 1598 was a great year for Shakespeare. His 1594 *The Rape of Lucrece* appeared in quarto that year. In addition, six of his plays appeared in quarto, five of which included Shakespeare's name on the title page. Though play books were common, it was unusual for the names of dramatists, who existed in the same nearly anonymous realm as modern screenwriters, to appear on them. But Shakespeare's career belies that trend. Beginning in 1600, in fact, his name regularly appears on title pages of his plays, and by 1608, the so-called Pied Bull quarto of *King Lear* carries Shakespeare's name, "M. William Shak-speare" followed by "His" above and before the title of the play. Shakespeare's name is more prominent than the title.

By the time of the publication of Q2 *Hamlet* in 1604 or 1605, William Shakespeare was celebrated, singularly successful, a literary giant in an impressive literary culture. The title of the Q2 *Hamlet*, in short, announces with authority the work of a triumphant writer. Q2 is the real McCoy, newly corrected and twice the length of Q1, made from a perfect copy of the play—a tantalizing suggestion that this version is close to Shakespeare's own hand.

It is in Q2 that attention shifts from the plot of *Hamlet* to the character of Hamlet himself. Here, Hamlet emerges as the compelling figure the world has admired and puzzled over for four centuries, a young man of incomparable intelligence, unblinkered honesty, wit, and unparalleled eloquence; a young man in black by turns charming and nasty, engaged and aloof, direct and subtle, acutely sensitive yet capable of naked viciousness; the student at Wittenberg University who comes home to find his father dead and his mother married to his father's brother; who learns the truth privately from his father's ghost; who kills an innocent man whose young daughter he drives to madness and suicide; who assails his own mother; who engineers the execution of two false friends, who becomes a scourging minister bent on cleansing his world of sin and transgression; who holds one true friend dear, discourses with a skull, and thinks too much; who, though overweight and out of shape (according to his mother) and in his thirties, out-duels his younger opponent and dies by the treachery of a murderer king who has fouled his mother; whose last word is "silence" and whose lifeless body, accorded the rites of a soldier, is carried up to a scaffold. While Q1 had included most of the elements of the plot of *Hamlet*, the subjective aspects of the Prince—his inner life—emerge only in Q2.

The most celebrated aspect of Hamlet's character is his inwardness, the powerful sense we have that Hamlet's magnificent words are the record of a mind, a psyche, and a heart at work, the interior of a person or self grappling with overwhelming burdens brought on by his father's murder and his mother's remarriage. If we are looking for Hamlet, we should attend first to this emotional, psychological, and intellectual life of the character. Objective phenomena, visible appearances, shapes and forms, have only a secondary claim to reality in *Hamlet*; what is inside Hamlet, what is unseen, is actual. This inwardness, the implications of which I explore in a later chapter, is the great advance Q2 makes over Q1.

In 1.2 of Q2, for example, Hamlet's first encounter with the king and queen at court, Hamlet opposes external appearance with internal reality, an opposition greatly attenuated in the much shorter version of this speech in Q1. To his mother's question of why his father's death "seems" so singular, Hamlet replies:

> 'Seems' madam—nay it is, I know not 'seems.'
> 'Tis not alone my inky cloak [good] mother
> Nor customary suits of solemn black,
> Nor windy suspiration of forced breath,
> No, nor the fruitful river in the eye,
> Nor the dejected havior of the visage
> Together with all forms, moods, shapes of grief,
> That can denote me truly. These indeed 'seem,'
> For they are actions that a man might play,
> But I have that within which passes show,
> These but the trappings and the suits of woe.

The trappings and suits of woe, the gestures and vestments of grief—Hamlet's black cloak, his sighs, his tears, his ruined face, together with all other forms, moods, and shapes of grief—are visible registers of something invisible within himself, some interior reality that cannot be faked or played, something that passes show. There is a self that experiences a reality both deeper and more elusive than what is or can be manifested.

This interiority is most convincingly expressed in Hamlet's famous soliloquies—Q2 is the only version that contains all four—the first of which comes in 1.2 shortly after Hamlet's reply to his mother just discussed. The stage clears of all but Hamlet.

> O that this too too [sullied] flesh would melt,
> Thaw and resolve itself into a dew,
> Or that the Everlasting had not fixed
> His cannon 'gainst self-slaughter. O God, God,
> How weary, stale, flat and unprofitable
> Seem to me all the uses of this world!
> Fie on't, ah, fie, 'tis an unweeded garden
> That grows to seed, things rank and gross in nature
> Possess it merely. That it should come thus:
> But two months dead—nay not so much, not two—
> So excellent a king, that was to this
> Hyperion to a satyr, so loving to my mother,
> That he might not beteem the winds of heaven
> Visit her face too roughly. Heaven and earth,
> Must I remember? Why, she should hang on him
> As if increase of appetite had grown
> By what it fed on. And yet within a month
> (Let me not think on't—Frailty, thy name is Woman),
> A little month, or e're those shoes were old,
> With which she followed my poor father's body
> Like Niobe, all tears. Why she—
> O God, a beast that wants discourse of reason
> Would have mourned longer—married with my uncle,
> My father's brother (but no more like my father,
> Than I to Hercules). Within a month,
> Ere yet the salt of most unrighteous tears
> Had left the flushing in her galled eyes,
> She married. O most wicked speed! To post
> With such dexterity to incestuous sheets,
> It is not, nor it cannot come to good;
> But break, my heart, for I must hold my tongue.

Here the operations of the mind and heart correspond in a logic that achieves the palpable effect of interiority. Hamlet opens with a threat to kill himself, a claim that presupposes a real self that can be destroyed. It may be a hollow threat, a trick, a gesture, but it comes from someone we already believe to be authentic. A universal weariness and *ennui*—the feeling that the world is stale, flat, and unprofitable—follows from the threatened suicide. The entire world is contracted to a garden, unweeded, inhabited by "things rank and gross in nature." Suddenly Hamlet's thought shifts to his father's death— "But two months dead: Nay not so much, not two," then to his father's Hyperion-like excellencies and his gentle and courteous treatment of his Queen, whose face he shielded from the wind. She, in turn, would hang upon her royal husband "as if increase of appetite had grown / By what it fed on."

"Fed on" leads to a repugnant thought of his mother's sexuality, which is sickening to Hamlet. He generalizes his disgust to all women: "Frailty, thy name is Woman." To Hamlet women are incapable of the strength necessary to remain loyal, in this case to her king and husband. Though in Q1 Gertred insists that she is innocent of her husband's murder, and though we can assume that this characterization is not substantially altered in later incarnations of the play, including Q2, she surely knows that by marrying Claudius she has destroyed her son's chance to become king of Denmark. Emerging from this speech is a deeply engrained misogyny, a hatred of women that, as we shall see in later chapters, has troubled many commentators, despite the fact that for centuries women have played Hamlet on stage and, in the twentieth century, on screen, and that the Melancholic Prince has undergone a marked feminization over time, transforming from the rotund, thirty-something Burbage, "fat and scant of breath," to the handsome, trimly athletic and often epicene Hamlet of our time.

As his 1.2 soliloquy draws to a close, Hamlet returns to the question of how long his father has been dead, shrinking the time in half. It's been "A little month" since the funeral, which was hastily followed by his mother's remarriage. The thought surprises and outrages him. He explodes emotionally, his mind turning to beasts, as Amleth's had in the parallel scene in the Danish legend. An animal without the ability to reason would have grieved longer than Gertrude. Further contracting time, Hamlet claims it was less than a month before she remarried, posting "With such dexterity to incestuous sheets." But he must stop thinking on it. This extraordinary speech of thirty lines ends with a need to throttle speech itself, the medium though which inwardness, the matter of the heart, is conveyed—"break, my heart, for I must hold my tongue."

Hamlet has given varying timelines in the same speech. But it doesn't really matter, I think, that later Ophelia insists, in response to Hamlet's "my father died within [these] two hours," that it was "twice two months." What matters is the unstable inner reality of Hamlet, deeply tied to memory, leaping from suicide to unweeded gardens to a timeline of grief to educated analogies, to the increase of appetite on what it craves, to heaven and truncated time, then to incest, and finally to pronouncement that none of this can ever be good.

A similarly turbulent and unstable internal life is evident in the second soliloquy, at the end of the second act, a speech that, along with the similarly toned fourth soliloquy, was radically abridged in productions prior to, and after, the Romantic revolution that championed Hamlet as a young man plagued by thought. This speech directs its considerable venom not against women or murderers so much as against Hamlet himself, attacking that person who inhabits customary suits of solemn black as "a dull and muddy-mettled rascal," a sleepy "John-a-dreames, unpregnant of my cause." "Am I a coward?" he asks. No, nobody plucks his beard or tweaks his nose in insult, yet he continues to define himself as pigeon-livered, without gall. Only an ass, he says, would fail to act when his father had been murdered and his mother prostituted. Hamlet is a man "Prompted to my revenge by heaven and hell" who instead of getting on with it, unpacks his heart "with words" like a whore.

In this soliloquy, memory, thought, and language—which lack the necessary property of action—paradoxically inspire a plan of action. This notion comes immediately to Hamlet in the idea of the play-within-the play, depicting what only he, the Ghost, and Claudius know—the details of his father's murder, the weapon (poison), and the means (poured into the ear while sleeping). This entertainment will test both the Ghost's veracity and Claudius's guilt, Hamlet concludes approvingly. "The play's the thing / Wherein I'll catch the conscience of the King."

Hamlet's third soliloquy, near the beginning of the third act, is the most famous speech in English literature. This soliloquy is surprisingly impersonal, or rather depersonalized. Even the threat, explicit in the first soliloquy, to destroy the self is here only abstract. Couched in absolute terms, "To be or not to be," it is stripped of context. Beginning with the ultimate alternatives—being and nonbeing—Hamlet casts the discussion in ethical rather than personal terms, asking whether it is nobler to endure the "sea of troubles" that is life, or by opposing, end them. To die, he reasons, is to experience a kind of sleep, implying a peace and respite that is "a consummation / Devoutly to be wished." But if death is a kind of sleep devoutly to be wished for, why then don't we fly to this sleep? But this commonplace analogy between sleep and death produces a startling turn. Hamlet is obliged to consider what dreams may come in the sleep of death. The thought of these dreams, the mind's ability to cast itself into the region of death and contemplate what must be experienced there—this is what gives us pause and brings the mind to terror and unwillingness to destroy the self, no matter how tawdry, oppressive, or painful life may be. Hamlet's list of insults and injuries to which flesh is heir—the oppressor's wrong, the proud man's contumely, etc.—ends with "the dread of something after death, / (The undiscovered country, from whose bourn / No traveler returns) puzzles the will." The dread of what this undiscovered country may hold paralyzes us, making us tolerate the indignities of this life rather than rush to other horrors of which we know nothing.

Hamlet's fears and imaginings anticipate those of the condemned Claudio from *Measure for Measure*, composed probably in 1604, the year that Q2 *Hamlet* appeared. Like Hamlet, Claudio, facing what seems his imminent death, projects his thought into the realm of death. Speaking to his sister, who has the ability to release him from this sentence, Claudio contrasts here and there, now and then, crossing the existential boundary from which no traveler returns:

> Ah, but to die, and go we know not where
> To lie in cold obstruction and to rot,
> The sensible warm motion to become
> A kneaded clod, and the delighted spirit
> To bathe in fiery floods, or to reside
> In thrilling region of thick-ribbed ice;
> To be imprisoned in the viewless winds
> And blown with restless violence round about
> The pendent world; or to be worse than worst
> Of those that lawless and uncertain thought
> Imagine howling— 'tis too horrible!

The weariest and most loathed worldly life
That age, ache, penury, and imprisonment
Can lay on nature is a paradise
To what we fear of death.

Hamlet, in contrast to the genuinely terrified Claudio of *Measure for Measure*, commands a unique authority in his exploration of the realm of death exactly because he has been there. He has walked with his ghostly father into the undiscovered country and returned from it. At the end of 1.4 he exits the stage with the Ghost, presumably crossing into the realm of the dead. When he crosses back to the realm of the living, he has acquired a new intimacy with the dead, which father and son together exploit in the following Cellarage Scene (1.5) at the expense of Horatio and Marcellus.

Despite his inaction, Hamlet is being transformed over the course of the play. In 3.4, notably, after the killing of Polonius and the final appearance of his father's ghost, he becomes something more than an accidental killer. Now a scourging minister, he accuses his mother in the Closet Scene of 3.4 of incestuous corruption, berating her blackest sins in the language of disease:

Lay not that flattering unction to your soul
That not your trespass but my madness speaks.
It will but skin and film the ulcerous place
Whiles rank corruption mining all within
Infects unseen.

He becomes the voice of righteous indignation, something of a puritan and something of a hypocrite; he's committed murder but demands that his mother refuse sex and confess her sins to heaven: "Repent what's past, avoid what is to come," he says. "Forgive me this my virtue," he asks his mother,

For in the fatness of these pursy times
Virtue itself of Vice must pardon beg.
Yea, curb and woo for leave to do him good.

Hamlet sets himself up as his mother's confessor, a kind of fundamentalist preacher, hating her sex. He's an amalgam of Malvolio and Angelo, the ascetic prudes undone by desire and ambition in *Twelfth Night* and *Measure for Measure*. There is especially much in Hamlet of Angelo, the absolute moralist who loathes the thought of sex, or thinks he does. Hamlet again accuses Gertrude of wallowing in the foul corruption of an incestuous bed, calling upon her to repent and confess her sins to heaven, ironically setting his own "virtue" against her vice before parting. Bidding her goodnight, he begs her, "go not to my uncle's bed /—Assume a virtue, if you have it not." He continues:

> Let not the bloat King tempt you again to bed,
> Pinch wanton on your cheek, call you his mouse
> And let him for a pair of reechy kisses,
> Or paddling in your neck with his damned fingers,
> Make you to ravel all this matter out
> That I essentially am not in madness
> But mad in craft.

As the scene concludes, Hamlet turns to the dead body of Polonius, ending with a perfect couplet. "This counselor," he says, "Is now most still, most secret, and most grave, / Who was in life a foolish prating knave." Now the wheels that will doom Hamlet and the others have been set in motion.

This ability to place the self on the other side of life is a principal concern of Hamlet's final great soliloquy near the end of the fourth act, a speech unique to Q2 that has often been cut from production because it adds little to the action but also because it underscores Hamlet's imprisonment within the confines of thought, a cowardly retreat from action that detracts from his role as righteous Avenger. Preparing to leave for England, Hamlet is informed that the young Norwegian Prince Fortinbras is crossing Denmark to attack Poland. One of Fortinbras' captains points out the uselessness of this campaign. "We go to gain a little patch of ground," he tells Hamlet, "That hath in it no profit but the name." Huge expenditures of blood and treasure will be paid for no good reason. When the captain leaves,

Hamlet is alone to contemplate his circumstance, which now appears to him more urgent than ever. He has killed Polonius, been banished to England, and still Claudius lives, possessed of his crown, his ambitions, and his queen. "How all occasions do inform against me," Hamlet exclaims,

> And spur my dull revenge. What is a man
> If his chief good and market of his time
> Be but to sleep and feed? A beast—no more
> Sure he that made us with such large discourse,
> Looking before and after, gave us not
> The capability and godlike reason
> To fust in us unused. Now whether it be
> Bestial oblivion or some craven scruple
> Of thinking too precisely on th' event
> (A thought which quartered hath but one part wisdom
> And ever three parts coward) I do not know
> Why yet I live to say this thing's to do,
> Sith I have cause and will and strength and means
> To do't. Examples gross as earth exhort me—
> Witness this army of such mass and charge,
> Led by a delicate and tender prince
> Whose spirit with divine ambition puffed
> Makes mouths at the invisible event
> Exposing what is mortal and unsure
> To all that fortune, death and danger dare,
> Even for an eggshell. Rightly to be great,
> Is not to stir without great argument
> But greatly to find quarrel in a straw
> When honour's at the stake. How stand I then
> That have a father killed, a mother stained,
> Excitements of my reason and my blood,
> And let all sleep; while to my shame I see
> The imminent death of twenty thousand men
> That for a fantasy and trick of fame
> Go to their graves like beds, fight for a plot
> Whereon the numbers cannot try the cause,
> Which is not tomb enough and continent
> To hide the slain? O, from this time forth,
> My thoughts be bloody or be nothing worth.

The initial suggestion that the intensity of his memory of his father is fading—that the motive for revenge has been dulled—is followed by a contrast of human beings with lower orders of creation. What distinguishes man above other creatures is his "large discourse," that is, the power of human mind and language to remember and anticipate, to reinhabit the past and project beyond the present into the future—"looking before and after."

And this God-like reason, Hamlet understands, must not be wasted. He then considers two possibilities why he has yet to accomplish his revenge. One is "bestial oblivion," the possibility that he has become deracinated, stripped of the very reason with which God imbued man; the other, contradictorily, is the habit "of thinking too precisely on th' event," which may, in fact, be merely a cover for cowardice. This might explain "why yet I live to say this thing's to do." In contrast to Hamlet's paralysis, "examples gross as earth" exhort him to action. Finding a convenient other person to compare himself unflatteringly to, Hamlet notes that even the "delicate and tender" Fortinbras can lead his Norwegian army into battle. Ambitious Fortinbras "Makes mouths at the invisible event"—that is, dismisses the unseen, unrealized future—"Exposing what is mortal, and unsure, / To all that fortune, death and danger dare." And Fortinbras will undertake this perilous mission, "Even for an eggshell." Compared to Fortinbras, who marshals an entire army toward oblivion, how much sorrier is the inaction of Hamlet, whose father has been murdered and his mother "stained." Reason and passion spur him to revenge and yet he is "all sleep." To his shame, he imagines the "imminent death of twenty thousand men / that for a fantasy and trick of fame / Go to their graves like beds," fighting for a plot of land which is not worth the killing of so many, nor can supply the ground to bury them. He resolves that if so many will die for so little, then he must kill and perhaps die for a much greater cause, the loss of father and mother: "O, from this time forth, / My thoughts be bloody or be nothing worth." The catastrophe of 5.2 is already taking shape on the horizon, a growing inevitability that will come to slaughter in the final scene.

If Q1 presents us with an outwardly focused man of action, the avenger of his father's murder and usurpation, Q2 refocuses Hamlet as a figure of immense psychological complexity. In the evolution from Q1 to Q2, he becomes a man working, as it were, from within, motivated as much by the dictates of his own inner reality as by his father's external, objective call for revenge. As we enter the fifth act, Hamlet is a man fulfilling his own rather than someone else's destiny. What he has done to others and what they have done to him pointed him in this direction, for sure, but what he has thought and felt and said to himself—these are more important than any external exigency in directing him to his violent end.

It is for the next version of the play to enrich and deepen Hamlet's complex interiority and supply to the world the full realization of literature's most important character, one whose unprecedented skepticism casts a shadow over the centuries to come, both reflecting the doubts and anxieties of future generations while determining the shape of things to come.

THE FIRST FOLIO HAMLET

The *Hamlet* that appeared in the first collected edition of Shakespeare's plays in 1623, seven years after the playwright's death, is the last significant version of the play. This collected edition, known as the First Folio, presents thirty-six of the thirty-seven plays (*Pericles* is missing) attributed to Shakespeare in the large, expensive format reserved for important books. The First Folio divides Shakespeare's canon into comedies, histories, and tragedies, and was edited by two members of Shakespeare's acting company, John Heminges and Henry Condell, to whom Shakespeare had left in his will money "to buy them rings." It has long been a commonplace assumption that Shakespeare cared little or nothing about preserving and bequeathing his plays to the future. The fact that eighteen plays were printed in his lifetime has been explained as acts of piracy (as in the Q1 *Hamlet*), correction (as in Q2 *Hamlet*), or quick profit (as in *The Merry Wives of Windsor*). But the gifts to Heminges and Condell may indicate otherwise. Not only does his will, which included a gift to Richard Burbage, indicate that Shakespeare kept in touch with his old friends even after his retirement to Stratford, the money willed to Heminges and Condell suggests his desire to preserve his dramatic works, implying a promise from these two men, who as shareholders in The Kings' Men presumably had access to the most authoritative texts, that they would oversee the publication of his collected works.

THE TRAGEDIE OF

HAMLET, Prince of Denmarke.

Actus Primus. Scœna Prima.

Enter Barnardo and Francisco two Centinels.

Barnardo.

Ho's there?

Fran. Nay answer me: Stand & vnfold your selfe.

Bar. Long liue the King.

Fran. Barnardo?

Bar. He.

Fran. You come most carefully vpon your houre.

Bar. 'Tis now strook twelue, get thee to bed Francisco.

Fran. For this releefe much thankes: 'Tis bitter cold, And I am sicke at heart.

Barn. Haue you had quiet Guard?

Fran. Not a Mouse stirring.

Barn. Well, goodnight. If you do meet Horatio and Marcellus, the Riuals of my Watch, bid them make hast.

Enter Horatio and Marcellus.

Fran. I thinke I heare them. Stand: who's there?

Hor. Friends to this ground.

Mar. And Leige-men to the Dane.

Fran. Giue you good night.

Mar. O farwel honest Soldier, who hath relieu'd you?

Fra. Barnardo ha's my place: giue you goodnight.

Exit Fran.

Mar. Holla Barnardo.

Bar. Say, what is Horatio there?

Hor. A peece of him.

Bar. Welcome Horatio, welcome good Marcellus.

Mar. What, ha's this thing appear'd againe to night.

Bar. I haue seene nothing.

Mar. Horatio saies, 'tis but our Fantasie, And will not let beleefe take hold of him Touching this dreaded sight, twice seene of vs, Therefore I haue intreated him along With vs, to watch the minutes of this Night, That if againe this Apparition come, He may approue our eyes, and speake to it.

Hor. Tush, tush, 'twill not appeare.

Bar. Sit downe a-while, And let vs once againe assaile your eares, That are so fortified against our Story, What we two Nights haue seene.

Hor. Well, sit we downe, And let vs heare Barnardo speake of this.

Barn. Last night of all, When yond same Starre that's Westward from the Pole Had made his course t'illume that part of Heauen

Where now it burnes, Marcellus and my selfe, The Bell then beating one.

Mar. Peace, breake thee of: Looke where it comes againe.

Enter the Ghost.

Barn. In the same figure, like the King that's dead.

Mar. Thou art a Scholler; speake to it Horatio.

Barn. Lookes it not like the King? Marke it Horatio.

Hora. Most like: It harrowes me with fear & wonder

Barn. It would be spoke too.

Mar. Question it Horatio.

Hor. What art thou that vsurp'st this time of night, Together with that Faire and Warlike forme In which the Maiesty of buried Denmarke Did sometimes march: By Heauen I charge thee speake.

Mar. It is offended.

Barn. See, it stalkes away.

Hor. Stay: speake; speake: I Charge thee, speake.

Exit the Ghost.

Mar. 'Tis gone, and will not answer.

Barn. How now Horatio? You tremble & look pale: Is not this something more then Fantasie? What thinke you on't?

Hor. Before my God, I might not this beleeue Without the sensible and true auouch Of mine owne eyes.

Mar. Is it not like the King?

Hor. As thou art to thy selfe, Such was the very Armour he had on, When th'Ambitious Norwey combatted: So frown'd he once, when in an angry parle He smot the sledded Pollax on the Ice. 'Tis strange.

Mar. Thus twice before, and iust at this dead houre, With Martiall stalke, hath he gone by our Watch.

Hor. In what particular thought to work, I know not: But in the grosse and scope of my Opinion, This boades some strange erruption to our State.

Mar. Good now sit downe, & tell me he that knowes Why this same strict and most obseruant Watch, So nightly toyles the subiect of the Land, And why such dayly Cast of Brazon Cannon And Forraigne Mart for Implements of warre: Why such impresse of Ship-wrights, whose sore Taske Do's not diuide the Sunday from the weeke, What might be toward, that this sweaty hast Doth make the Night ioynt-Labourer with the day: Who is't that can informe me?

Hor. That can I,

At

Figure 2.3 *Hamlet* appears seventh among the Tragedies in the First Folio (1623), the first collected edition of his plays. This version divides the play into acts and scenes. By permission of the Folger Shakespeare Library.

If Q2 *Hamlet* is implicitly addressed to readers as opposed to playgoers, the First Folio version is explicitly so. The dedicatory epistle prefacing the book announces the work "to the great Variety of Readers," a theme to which Heminges and Condell return later in the dedication. They exhort us to "Read him, therefore; and again and again: And if then you doe not like him, surely you are in some manifest Danger, not to understand him. And so we leave you to other of his friends [referring to the dedicatory poems by Ben Jonson and Hugh Holland that follow], whom if you need, can be your guides: if you need them not, you can lead your selves, and others. And such Readers we wish him." These remarks underscore the degree to which the F1 text is a work of the page rather than the stage. Even so, this is a truth that needs qualifying.

Traditionally, scholars have concluded that this version is based on Q2, since it has much in common with that version of the play, F1 being only slightly shorter than Q2. The editors of the 2006 Arden *Hamlet* find 220 lines in Q2 and F1 that are identical but caution us that, even in the case of substantive agreements, Q2 and F1 accord only 36 percent of the time. Q2 contains approximately 222 lines that have no equivalent in F1, according to the Arden editors, and F1 contains 88 lines with no counterpart in Q2. In some ways, in fact, Q1 and F1 appear to be more closely related than Q2 and F1 are. Q1 and F1, for example, share some readings that are different in Q2. At other times, more significantly, F1 and Q1 share the same cuts. Hamlet's last soliloquy, containing his meditation on the army of Fortinbras, makes this point tellingly. Both Q1 and F1 preempt the speech at virtually the same line, and pick up the action again at the same place. This would seem to indicate that whoever put together the F1 text had only the Q1 text at hand or, having Q1 and Q2 at hand, consciously decided to excise Hamlet's fourth speech—that is, to intentionally follow Q1 rather than Q2.

Two aspects of *Hamlet* unique to F1, material that doesn't appear in either Q1 or Q2, require special attention. The first issue concerns Hamlet's curious remarks in the second act about the child acting companies, which appears only in F1. In 1600, acting companies made up entirely of child actors were a recent addition to London's already crowded theatrical milieu. Since the first public theater in England, the eponymous Theatre in Shoreditch, was erected in 1576, the rise of theater as a dominant entertainment had been meteoric. By the time of *Hamlet*, a quarter century later, the booming theatrical life of London was highly competitive. In 1599—the year that the Theatre was dismantled and its timbers hauled south through the city across the Thames and reconstructed as the Globe, Shakespeare's principal venue—there were more than ten public theaters operating in London and its suburbs, as well as the private theater of Blackfriars. And this doesn't take into account smaller theatrical venues associated with inns and taverns. Furthermore, the competition for audiences wasn't limited to competing plays and playhouses, since fairs and animal baiting rinks vied for public attention and money.

By 1600 or 1601 child acting companies seem to have been a painful thorn in the side of adult acting companies, competing with them for audiences and revenue. In 2.2 of F1, Rosincrance (Rosencrantz in Q2) announces the arrival of the traveling players. Hamlet asks why they are not playing in the city. Rosincrance replies that "I think their inhibition comes by the means of the late innovation." The mention of an "innovation"—perhaps a reference to the inhibition of plays in London (which may have been a result of Lord Chamberlain's Men's involvement in the Essex uprising of 1601)—occurs in Q2 as well as F1, but F1 alone carries Hamlet and Rosincrance's subsequent comments on the ascendancy of child acting companies that were depriving adult companies of audiences and income, a competition that resulted in the so-called War of the Theatres. Interestingly, while Q2 contains no reference to the child acting companies, Q1's Gilderstone (Guildenstern in Q2) notes that "the principal public audience that came [to the visiting company's London productions] are turned to private plays, and to the humour of children." In F1, when Hamlet asks whether the players are now as highly esteemed as they used to be, or whether they are "grow[n] rusty," Rosincrance replies, "Nay,"

> Their endeavour keeps in the wonted pace. But there is, sir, an aerie of children, little eyases that cry out on the top of the question and are most tyrannically clapped for 't: These are now the fashion, and so berattled the common stages (so they call them) that many wearing rapiers are afraid of goose-quills, and dare scarce come thither.

> HAMLET: What, are they children? Who maintains 'em? How are they escotted? Will they pursue the quality no longer than they can sing? Will they not say afterwards, if they should grow themselves to [become] common players— as it is most like if their means are not better—their writers do them wrong to make them exclaim against their own succession?

"Aery" means nest and "eyases" are unfledged hawks. Mere hatchlings, that is, shouting at the tops of their high-pitched voices on the stages of London, armed with goose-quills rather than swords, are now all the rage. Hamlet seems puzzled, as Shakespeare himself perhaps was. But Hamlet's interest is not so much in the contesting playwrights but in how the boy actors are maintained and supported, how they are "escoted." Don't the children realize that they will grow up to be adult actors and so their poets do them wrong supplying them with plays in which they exclaim against their own succession? That is to say, don't they realize that they are threatening their own futures as adult actors? Rosincrance agrees: "Faith, there has been much to-do on both sides, and the nation holds it no sin, to [incite] them to controversy. There was for a while no money bid for argument unless the poet and the player went to cuffs in the question." "There has been much to do on both sides" suggests the recent nature of the controversy, which reached its peak in 1601, suggesting a date for *Hamlet* closer to 1600 or 1601 rather than 1599. The fact, moreover, that Q1 alludes to popularity of the child acting companies (the public's attention is turned "to the humour of children") and F1 significantly amplifies the subject, while Q2 doesn't mention the War of the Theatres at all, may indicate a closer relationship, at least in 2.2, between Q1 and F1 than between Q2 and F1.

In this context, it is interesting to note that the passage the visiting players relate later in 2.2—the story of Priam's slaughter—concerns the fate of old rather than young people. Hamlet notes the age of the visiting actors. He greets one as an "old friend," noting his face is "valanc'd"—bearded—since the last time they met. He expresses concern that one of the younger member's voice "be not cracked"— too low, that is, to play the role of a woman. In the killing of Priam itself, there is no place for children. Everything about this speech asserts age. Hiding in the Trojan Horse, Pyrrhus, his "sable arms / Black as his purpose," prepares to ambush "Old grandsire Priam." "[R]everend" (aged) Priam, hopelessly outmatched, wields an "antique sword." Old Hecuba, his wife, wearing a blanket for a robe "about her lank and all-o'er teemed loins," runs madly about as Pyrrhus butchers her husband.

The War of the Theatres may have been a mock exercise designed to draw attention to the playwrights involved in the quarrel, but Rosincrance's suggestion of tempers flaring—poets and players going to cuffs in the scripts—is intriguing. Jonson, a veteran of the continental wars, who had killed a man in a duel and escaped prosecution only by the fact that he could claim the benefit of the clergy, claimed that he "beat [John] Marston, and took his pistol from him." Marston, who wrote for adult companies, and Jonson, who wrote for the child companies, were combatants in The War of the Theatres. The tone of Hamlet's exchange with

Rosincrance in F1 suggests that Shakespeare remained largely aloof from the "war" itself, while he maintained a cautious attitude toward the child acting companies, which enjoyed their vogue and then faded quickly out of existence.

The War of the Theatres digression in F1 is important in the search for *Hamlet*. Not only does it open a window on a matter of topical interest, helping to date the play, it presents Hamlet as more of an actor than a university student. Taking Hamlet noticeably out of character, this scene portrays him as intimately involved in a theatrical milieu similar to that of London circa 1601, a habitué of the world of playing, conversant with the goings-on in the theater. Shakespeare, we remember, was not only a poet and playwright but an accomplished actor (he's listed among the actors in Jonson's plays) and a shareholder in his acting company. In Hamlet's conversation with Rosincrance concerning the child acting companies and later in his instructions to the players, we might speculate that Hamlet comes perhaps closest to the character of his creator. Shakespeare, a man of the theater rather than the academy, was bound up by playing—his formal education ended with grammar school, and his life was devoted to the theater.

But the War of the Theatres digression tells us little about Hamlet the character, about his depth, his introspection, his interior being. More significant in that regard is the exchange between Hamlet and Rosincrance and Guildensterne in their initial encounter with these visitors in 2.2, which appears only in F1. After a scholarly greeting interwoven with bawdy entendre—Rosincrance and Guildensterne live about the "waist" of Fortune, "in the middle of her favour," about her "secret parts"—Rosincrance remarks that "the world's grown honest." Hamlet replies that Doomsday must be near, and then asks why Fortune has brought these boyhood friends to Denmark, "to this prison hither":

GUILDENSTERNE: Prison, my Lord?

HAMLET: Denmark's a Prison.

ROSINCRANCE: Then is the world one.

HAMLET: A goodly one, in which there are many confines, wards, and dungeons—Denmark being one o' th' worst.

ROSINCRANCE: We think not so, my Lord.

HAMLET: Why then 'tis none to you; for there is nothing either good or bad, but thinking makes it so. To me it is a prison.

ROSINCRANCE: Why then your ambition makes it one: 'tis too narrow for your mind.

HAMLET: O God, I could be bounded in a nutshell and count my self a king of
infinite space—were it not that I have bad dreams.

This exchange significantly deepens the interiority that Hamlet conveys, the presence of an extraordinary man—intelligent, thoughtful, acutely sensitive, and
princely—confessing a radical skepticism about life.

Hamlet introduces the mental image of confinement, picking up the idea of a
prison from his ghostly father's mention of his own "prison-house" in 1.5. Here in
2.2, the entire world is a prison—"a goodly one," suggesting not a virtuous world
but an impressively large one. Hamlet then subdivides this global prison into confines, wards, and dungeons, of which Denmark is "one o' th' worst." Though his
interlocutors protest—"We think not so, my lord"—Hamlet radically subjec-
tivizes this metaphor. If they do not think Denmark is a prison, "Why then 'tis
none to you." But for Hamlet it is a prison because, he says, "there is nothing either
good or bad but thinking makes it so."

The speech presents us with a sequence of restrictive interior spaces that termi-
nates in the smallest of confining spaces, the nutshell, a tiny place that paradoxically holds the kingdom of infinity of which Hamlet is monarch: "I could be
bounded in *a nutshell*, and count my self a king of *infinite space*" (my emphasis).
This would be, but that he has "bad dreams." Prison is the reality of individual perception, of subjective experience. It is a waking dream, in which the self attempts to
contain all within itself, a subject I treat at length in a later chapter. To Hamlet, if
not to his visiting school fellows, Denmark is a prison.

This radical relativism, perhaps owing something to Shakespeare's reading of
essays by the great French skeptic Michel Montaigne, internalizes reality. This is a
dangerous notion, one that in Shakespeare's time was commonly associated with
the force of evil that opposes God's dominion over the world. In Christopher
Marlowe's *Dr. Faustus*, a play staged around the time that Greene attacked
Shakespeare in *A Groats-Worth of Witte*, Faustus asks Mephistopheles where is
hell. The devil replies, "Hell hath no limits, nor is circumscribed / In one self place.
But where we are is hell / And where hell is there must we ever be." Dislocating hell,

relativizing it, positioning the place of supreme punishment inside the mind—this strikes Faustus, who thinks "hell's a fable," as amusing and liberating: "How? Now in hell? Nay, and this be hell, I'll willingly be damned here. What! Sleeping, eating, walking, and disputing?" To be sure, the final scene of Marlowe's play vividly reasserts the existential reality of hell. In the Elizabethan staging of *Faustus*, he is dragged down through the trap door in the middle of the stage known as "the mouth of hell." His end comes appropriately as he stares into this horror show, renouncing learning and the fruits of the mind. "Ugly hell, gape not," he cries, "come not Lucifer! / I'll burn my books."

It is not incidental to the skepticism of the antic Faustus, in some ways a prototype of Hamlet, that Marlowe was reputed to be an atheist. The son of a Canterbury shoemaker, he had been a brilliant student. He entered Cambridge as a sisar—a boy who showed promise but had no money to pay tuition. In short order, he earned a bachelor's degree and then was virtually done with his masters degree when, in 1587, the record reflects, the University refused to grant Marlowe the degree, crediting rumors that he "was determined to have gone beyond the seas to Rheims and there to remain." The Cambridge authorities feared that Marlowe had converted to Catholicism and intended to join the counter-Reformation. But this seems not to have been the case at all, for in an unprecedented move, the Queen's Privy Council, comprised of her most powerful and intimate advisors, interceded on Marlowe's behalf. The Council noted that Marlowe "had done her majesty good service, and deserved to be rewarded for his faithful dealing," and ordered that "he should be furthered in the degree he was to take this next Commencement because it was not in her majesty's pleasure that anyone employed, as he had been, in matters touching the benefit of his country should be defamed by those that are ignorant in th' affairs he went about."

Despite Marlowe's service to the state, allegations of atheism persisted. In 1593, just before Marlowe's death, his onetime roommate Thomas Kyd, the likely author of the Ur-*Hamlet*, swore, probably under torture, that Marlowe was an atheist. Kyd, attempting to clear himself of the charge that he, too, was an nonbeliever, denied that he "should love or be familiar friend with one so irreligious," and later alleged that Marlowe would "jest at the divine scriptures" and "gibe at prayers." And Kyd wasn't alone in leveling such damning accusations. Arrested under suspicion of treason, another government spy, one Richard

Cholmely, charged that Marlowe "is able to show more sound reasons for atheism than any divine in England is able to give to prove divinity." In May 1593, aged twenty-nine, Marlowe was stabbed to death in a private room of an inn in Deptford by a probable agent of Elizabeth's secret service, thus bringing to an abrupt close the meteoric theatrical career of a dark, mercurial playwright who was Shakespeare's exact contemporary, who was almost certainly a government spy, and seems to have died for it.

Roughly eighty years after Marlowe's death, John Milton's Lucifer, in Book I of *Paradise Lost*, expresses the same radical skepticism. Like Faustus, Milton's Satan dislocates hell, internalizing it, bringing it within the confines of individual psychology. In what is really an extension of Hamlet's "there is nothing either good or bad, but thinking makes it so," Lucifer, tragically, heroically, welcomes his minions to this dark new world, irrevocably damned but unbowed. "Hail horrors," the fallen angel shouts, "hail"

> Infernal world, and thou profoundest Hell
> Receive thy new Possessor: One who brings
> A mind not to be changed by Place or Time.
> The mind is its own place, and in itself
> Can make a Heaven of Hell, a Hell of Heaven

This radical claim—that heaven can be made into hell and hell into heaven by the mere configuration of the mind—is traceable to an obscure medieval cleric, Amaury de Bène (d. 1207). De Bène advocated an early pantheism, the belief that God is immanent everywhere in nature. If God is love, it follows that God must also be hatred, since God is everything. De Bène's more radical belief was that there is no hell or heaven, no resurrection, no damnation, only a diffusion of God into nature, by the process of corruption, rotting, turning to loam. God, being the first principle of the universe, must contain all experiences, even decay and oblivion. Shakespeare's age characterized de Bène, as it did Marlowe, as an atheist. Interestingly, Innocent III condemned Amaurian doctrine "not so much heresy as it is insanity."

After his death, it is reported, de Bène's remains were ordered exhumed and his bones to be scattered on unconsecrated ground. The priest presiding at Ophelia's funeral wishes a similar desecration of her remains in 5.1 of *Hamlet*. "But that great command [of Claudius] o'ersways the order," he complains,

> She should in ground unsanctified been lodged
> Till the last trumpet: for charitable prayers,
> Flints and pebbles should be thrown on her.

He continues in this condemnatory mode

> We should profane the service of the dead
> To sing a requiem and such rest to her
> As to peace-parted souls

until Laertes rebukes him as a "churlish priest": "A ministering angel shall my sister be / When thou liest howling."

At this point, Laertes jumps into the grave with Ophelia's body. The grave is, of course, another emblem of restriction, a place of confinement that holds its contents for eternity. Hamlet steps forth to challenge Laertes but only Q1 contains the stage direction that "*Hamlet leaps / in after Leartes* [sic]." "This is I," he shouts, "Hamlet the Dane." The two struggle for a moment before being separated as Hamlet professes that he loved Ophelia, "as dear as twenty brothers could," according to Q1; Q2 and F1 raise this stake to forty thousand brothers. The three *Hamlet*s record the Prince's boasts that if Laertes will weep, fight, fast, tear himself, drink vinegar, eat a crocodile, Hamlet will do the same. He demands that he and Laertes be buried alive with Ophelia.

5.2 is so well known that I will point out only the significant differences among the three versions leading up to this final banquet and sword fight. The exposition covering Hamlet's time in England and his engineering of the deaths of Rosencrantz and Gildenstern, which has been covered with greater efficiency in the unique scene 14 of Q1, is developed at length in Q2 and F1. Likewise, Hamlet's insistence that "They are not near my conscience" appears only in Q2 and F1. At this point the foppish Osric enters. The verbal sparing between Hamlet and Osric is much reduced in both Q1 and F1, again suggesting more than an accidental or incidental affinity between these two texts published twenty years apart. All three include the report that Claudius, now clearly Machiavellian, covers his tracks by placing his wager on Hamlet in the upcoming sword fight. Only Q2 and F1 have Horatio warning Hamlet that he will likely lose the contest with Laertes, and Hamlet replying that he has been in continual practice during his exile in England and so will win the match. All three texts include the cheerless and poignant mention of Hamlet being sick at heart: "Thou wouldst not think how ill all's here about my heart—but it is no matter" (Q2). When Horatio suggests that Hamlet should back down from the challenge, Q1 abbreviates Hamlet's beautiful "We defy augury" speech to barely three lines: "if danger be now / Why then it is not to come, there's a [predestined] providence / in the fall of a sparrow." Except for incidental differences, Hamlet's famous meditation on the operation of providence in the complex of time is the same in Q2 and F1.

The banquet begins and the combatants prepare to fight. All three texts contain Hamlet's apology to Laertes, attributing the harm he has caused Laertes to Hamlet's madness and proclaiming that he has "shot mine arrow o're the house, / And hurt my brother," though F1 has the telling misreading of "Mother" for "brother." Laertes accepts Hamlet's apology but insists on the satisfaction of a duel. Q1 greatly reduces the subsequent dialogue, excluding such significant details as Claudius' promise to reward Hamlet with a pearl in his cup if Hamlet makes the first or second hit. Q1 lacks Gertrude's curiously disparaging remark to her husband, after Hamlet lands his second hit, that her son is "fat and scant of breath." Gertrude then drinks from the cup of poisoned wine as Hamlet and Laertes engage for a third time. Q1 and F1 contain stage directions indicating that Hamlet and Laertes (unknowingly) exchange rapiers, Q1 indicating more of the action with "*both are wounded / Leartes falls down. The Queen falls down and dies.*" The three *Hamlets* now draw attention to the stricken Queen, who cries (in F1), "the drink, the drink, O my dear *Hamlet*, / The drink, the drink, / I am poison'd." At Hamlet's "Treachery! seek it out," Laertes confesses that treachery is here, with him. Hamlet has not "half an hour of life" left, Laertes says, Q2 misreading "the treacherous instrument is in *my* hand" for "*thy* hand" (my emphasis). Hamlet then turns on Claudius, stabbing him and forcing the dregs of poison wine down his throat. All three texts have Laertes and Hamlet exchanging forgiveness, but Q1 lacks Hamlet's striking but curiously inappropriate "this fell sergeant Death / Is strict in his arrest."

In Q2 and F1, the dying Hamlet asks Horatio to "report me and my causes aright / To the unsatisfied" (Q2). All three versions contain Horatio's threat to fall on his sword like Brutus. Horatio seems almost jealous of this select royal company, each of whom dies in part or whole by poisoning. "I am more an antique Roman than a Dane," Horatio says, recalling the end of *Julius Caesar*, written in 1599, still fresh in Shakespeare's mind. But Hamlet uses the last of his fading strength to wrest the cup from Horatio. "Let go," Hamlet insists, "I'll ha't!" He begs Horatio to live:

> O God, Horatio, what a wounded name
> Things standing thus unknown, shall I leave behind me!
> If thou didst ever hold me in thy heart,
> Absent thee from felicity a while
> And in this harsh world draw thy breath in pain
> To tell my story.

With "he has my dying voice," Hamlet endorses the young Fortinbras—this "delicate and tender prince," he had called him in the fourth act—as the next king of Denmark. In Q1 his last words are "heaven receive my soul"; in Q2 his dying words are "the rest is silence." F1 appends, perhaps, a vestige of the powerful stage presence of Richard Burbage, the first Hamlet—adding "O, O, O, O" after "The rest is silence."

Horatio, newly designated historian, cradles Hamlet as his last breath leaves him. "Now cracks a noble heart," he says.

> Good night, sweet prince
> And flights of angels sing thee to thy death.

Fortinbras, under whose titular command the remaining events fall, wonders at the slaughter. "O proud death, / What feast is toward in thine eternal cell, / That thou so many princes at a shot / So bloodily hast struck?" He tacitly assumes the kingship of Denmark, noting that he has "some rights of memory in this kingdom / Which now to claim my vantage doth invite me." He orders that Hamlet be given the tribute of a soldier, ordering four captains to carry Hamlet up to a scaffold, "For he was likely, had he been put on, / To have proved most royal. And for his passage / The soldiers' music and the rite of war / Speak loudly for him." The play concludes with Fortinbras' ordering a salute: "Go, bid the soldiers shoot."

In the following chapter I return to Hamlet's radical skepticism, considering how matters "good or bad" suggest that the ultimate issues of good and evil are functions of thought. Reality is subjective, contingent, and particular, a matter of individual perspective. The infinite reality of the world can be no more than the infinite reality of the particular mind experiencing the world. This internalization of value, this shifting attention away from heaven, the image of infinity, to the form of our own skulls, the smelly finite emblem of mortality, may be the play's major contribution to the development of modern (and postmodern) thought.

THREE

YORICK'S SKULL: RELOCATING REALITY IN *HAMLET*

*A*s we have seen, in *Hamlet* Shakespeare saves the best for last. Abridged in Q1 but fully realized in Q2 and F1, the fifth act is the greatest of the great play's movements. In the two scenes that constitute it, Hamlet fulfills his destiny as tragic hero, and carries into the last days and hours of his life the affective power of the interiority developed through the earlier acts, especially the soliloquies. The previous four acts are prologue to a finale that brings a man of deep thought and feeling, facing an outrageous and daunting circumstance, to his inevitable death.

The final scene of Hamlet draws its tremendous power from the penultimate 5.1. Without this great preamble, 5.2 would appear hollow, perhaps even farcical. Here, in 5.1, Shakespeare recreates the morbid power of 4.3 of *Romeo and Juliet* (1595) when Juliet, having taken a sedative so powerful as to mimic death, imagines waking up among the dead in the Capulet vault "Where for this many hundred years the bones / Of all my buried ancestors are packed":

> Alack, alack, is it not like[ly] that I,
> So early waking—what with loathsome smells,
> And shrieks like mandrakes torn out of the earth,

That living mortals, hearing them, run mad—
Or, if I wake, shall I not be distraught,
Environed with all these hideous fears,
And madly play with my forefathers' joints,
And pluck the mangled Tybalt from his shroud,
And, in this rage, with some great kinsman's bone
As with a club dash out my desp'rate brains.

The terrible circumstance of both scenes, 4.3 of *Romeo and Juliet* and 5.1 of *Hamlet*, is that the living find themselves among the remains of the dead, forced to confront their own ultimate demise.

Hamlet's fifth act opens with two "clowns," comic actors who were enormously popular in Shakespeare's day, digging a grave. Hamlet, back from England, enters the scene with Horatio as the two friends are passing through a graveyard. This route, not found in Grammaticus or Belleforest, foreshadows Hamlet's own death, of course. Neither Hamlet nor Horatio is aware that the grave being dug is for Ophelia, the most innocent of *Hamlet*'s casualties, who has drowned herself. Because she has committed suicide, the reluctant priest attending her burial will soon remind us that by the standards of the Church she is the most certainly damned.

Hamlet listens as the gravedigger and his simple assistant exercise their maudlin wit through jokes that play on the implacable permanence of death. Who builds stronger than either the mason, the shipwright, or the carpenter, the first clown asks? The gallows-maker, his well-rehearsed assistant replies, because his structures outlive a thousand tenants. A few lines later the gravedigger sends his assistant off to fetch a drink, and he never again takes the stage.

The gravedigger—probably played in Shakespeare's time by the great comic actor Robert Armin, who in 1599 succeeded the legendary Will Kemp as the principal comic actor in Lord Chamberlain's Men—remains, to parry brilliantly with Hamlet. Shortly after Hamlet and Horatio enter the scene, the gravedigger tosses up a skull from the grave. Hamlet notices what it is missing: the tongue, the instrument of speech, the very thing at which Hamlet excels. "That skull had a tongue in it, and could sing once," he says. The gravedigger throws the skull to the ground, Hamlet says, "as if t'were Cain's jawbone, that did the first murder!" linking the skull's missing jaw to his own circumstance via "the primal eldest curse," as Claudius had earlier termed it, the killing of a brother. He continues, speculating that this skull might be the remains of a politician that "would circumvent God," or those of a courtier, "which could say 'Good / morrow, sweet lord, how dost thou, sweet lord?' " or "Lord Such-a-One" himself, "that praised another 'Lord Such-a-One's horse.' " Or it could be "my Lady Worm," who's now "chapless and knocked about the mazard with a sexton's spade." "Chapless" or "chopless" refers to the missing jaw bone. Chops, the gift of the jaw that enables singing, talking, the exercise of reason and madness, all that adds up to life. Only as ghosts can the dead talk without jaws. This is the salient difference between ghosts and the merely dead. Very soon Hamlet will join the jawless, the chopfallen, a fate that he is simultaneously attracted to and repelled by. But for now he is among the living, those who speak. It makes Hamlet's own joints ache to see these bones thrown about the gravesite.

When the Clown tosses up another skull, Hamlet again seizes the opportunity to reanimate this head with language. "Why may not that be the skull of a lawyer?" Hamlet asks. Where are all his arguments, his quibbles, and nice distinctions now? Why, Hamlet asks facetiously, doesn't this skull threaten the gravedigger with a charge of battery, since he's tossing this absent presence about so indifferently? How could this gravedigger be so callous? Hamlet wonders. "Custom hath made it in him a property of easiness," Horatio replies.

Perhaps, Hamlet continues, this skull belonged to a great land developer constantly occupied with bonds and titles and statutes and fines, "procedures for converting an entailed estate to a freehold." F1 follows with Hamlet's punning on fines and recoveries: "Is this the fine of his fines, and the recovery of his recoveries, to have his fine pate full of fine dirt?" Then Hamlet brilliantly advances this ghoulish logic with "the very conveyances of his lands will scarcely [fit] in this box," echoing the theme of internalization, confinement. To Hamlet's question, "and must the inheritor himself have no more [space than this]?" Horatio assents, "Not a jot more, my Lord."

Hamlet wonders whose grave the Clown is working at. His question functions as a straight man's setup of the professional clown. The gravedigger plays upon Hamlet's literalism with his own: "Mine Sir." Not to be outdone, Hamlet says, "I think it be thine, indeed, for thou liest in't." Despite his deferential "sir," the Clown is Hamlet's better: "You lie out on 't, sir, and therefore 'tis not yours. For my part I do not lie in't, yet it is mine." Hamlet quibbles: "Thou dost lie in't, to be in't and say it is thine. 'Tis for the dead, not the quick. Therefore thou liest." But the Clown is prepared for this turn: "'Tis a quick lie, sir, 'twill away again from me to you." The lie will quickly rebound from him to Hamlet. Hamlet is the liar, the true clown. Such an exchange of values, making fools of wise men, gravediggers of princes, is the fundamental skill and purpose of clowns in Shakespeare.

This contest of wits is too much for Hamlet to handle, so he shifts his ground again. "What man dost thou dig it for?" he asks, a straight question to which the Clown answers: "for no man, sir." "What woman then?" he asks. But the Clown won't give up the antic: "For none neither." "Who," then, "is to be buried in't?" "One that was a woman," the gravedigger replies, "but rest her soul, she's dead." Hamlet, whose potent wit had played so skillfully and easily upon the literalism of Claudius and his mother in the first act, assumes here their role, as a victim of the superior wit of the Clown. Hamlet concedes defeat by saying to Horatio: "How absolute the knave is! We must speak by the card [punctiliously] or equivocation will undo us." He then complains to Horatio that the respect for rank and status has eroded over the years, a problem that was familiar in the late Elizabethan age when commoners were, by dress and manner, encroaching on higher orders of society: "the age is grown so picked," Hamlet reckons, "that the toe of the peasant comes so near the heels of our courtier, he galls his kibe" (that is, rubs his chilblain).

In Q2 and F1 Hamlet asks how long the gravedigger has been at his occupation, and we learn that he began the day that young Hamlet, who has been sent to England, was born. Why was Hamlet sent to England? Hamlet (who has not revealed his identity) asks. Because he was mad, the Clown replies. He'll recover his wits there; if not, it won't matter since in England all men are as mad as he, the Clown says. Following this laugh at the audience's expense, the Clown remarks that he has been a sexton, man and boy, for thirty years. Thus we learn that, though still a student, Hamlet is thirty years old. This is a detail missing in Q1, which makes Hamlet considerably younger. Though we are accustomed to thinking of Hamlet as youthful, Q2 and F1 cast him as a man well into his prime, an age well suited to Burbage, who was in his thirties when he first played the role.

The conversation between Hamlet and the gravedigger turns next to the question of how long it takes a body to rot in the grave. Alluding to the ravages of the plague, the gravedigger remarks that if a body "be not rotten before he die (as we have many pocky corpses that will scarce hold the laying in) 'a will last you some eight year—or nine year—a tanner will last you nine years." The plague regularly swept England, carrying off many hundreds of people. It closed the theaters in 1593, forcing Shakespeare to turn his hand to nondramatic poetry. 1603, the year the Queen died and *Hamlet* first appeared in print, was another terrible year, as we have seen. Appearing in April, the plague raged all summer and into the fall, killing more than 30,000 in London and its suburbs. By the time *Hamlet* appeared in print—the exact date isn't known—the London air might have been filled with the choking stench of death.

Hamlet's contemplation of Yorick's chopfallen skull follows. We learn that Yorick has lain in the ground "three and twenty years," and that Hamlet Sr.'s jester had insulted the gravedigger, once pouring a bottle of wine on his head. "A pestilence on him for a mad rogue," he says, recalling the plague. Hamlet takes up the skull, his gorge rising—his stomach sickened—at the sight and smell of the death's-head. As I mentioned earlier, at the conclusion of his meditation on Yorick's skull, Hamlet seems to allude to the aged Queen Elizabeth with "Now get you to my lady's chamber, and tell her, let her paint [her face] an inch thick, to this favor she must come." He then recalls other rulers, Alexander and Caesar, who have followed the same course to an ignoble end, where their flesh is eaten by worms, which will in turn be eaten by the living. This line of thought, amounting to a parody of the Eucharist, strikes Horatio as taking things too far. "'Twere to consider too curiously, to consider so," he says. Hamlet disagrees, "No, faith, not a jot," and traces Alexander the Great's decomposition into loam "to stop a beer-barrel."

> Imperious Caesar, dead and turn'd to clay,
> Might stop a hole to keep the wind away.

The smell of rotting human flesh hovers over the final two acts of the play, as does Hamlet's concern with the grotesquely cannibalistic pattern of dining on creatures that have dined on human flesh. These morbid aspects, as I suggested earlier, Shakespeare probably inherited from the tradition of Amleth/Hamblet, where the hero murders the prototype of Polonius and feeds his body to hogs and later refuses to eat the flesh of hogs that have fed on men.

The discourse on skulls of 5.1 points to the paradoxical containment of the infinite reaches of the human mind within the finite space of the cranium. The skull is the empty vessel that once held endless possibility. The drive to contain the infinite, to convey the palpable sense of interiority, is evident early in *Hamlet*, at the Ghost's first appearance. He appears, Horatio reports, "armed at point, exactly cap-a-pie"— that is, in full armor. A metal jacket cloaks the spectral interior of this figure. The Ghost appears in armor because during his reign he had conducted a border war against Old Fortinbras, the King of Norway, who threatened the boundaries of Denmark. (In a bitter irony, Fortinbras' son will inherit the kingdom of Denmark from the dying Hamlet Jr., gaining not only what his father had lost to Old Hamlet but the Danish kingdom itself.) The Ghost appears to Horatio and the watches with his visor up. The body armor, like the human skull an emblem of contain-ment, identifies his role as warrior-king. In his final visitation, 3.4, the apparition appears in a quite different form, this time, according to the Q1 stage direction, "*in his night-gown*." In this later scene, Q2 and F1 have the ghost entering just *after* Hamlet says "a king of shreds and patches." If this is accurately placed, it is difficult to grasp what Hamlet means by "a king of shreds and patches." How is Claudius "a king of shreds and patches," we wonder? However, if the Ghost is meant to enter just *before* Hamlet's exclamation, as I suspect it is, then Hamlet is describing his ghostly father's night clothes. Regardless of where exactly it enters the scene, if we adopt the Q1 stage direction, as many editors do, we have a softer, but no less definitive ghost delimiting the limitless dead. At the very least, having the Ghost enter in a nightgown powerfully conveys its fading presence, his being lost to mem-ory, which is his ostensible reason for returning in 3.4—"to whet," he says, his son's "almost blunted purpose."

This straining attempt to contain the infinite is not merely incidental in *Hamlet*. The Ghost returns to earth from a "prison-house," of course, an image that Hamlet picks up in 2.2 when he meditates on the various forms of containment that the world presents to him, beginning with the claim that Denmark is a prison. He confesses to Rosencrantz and Guildenstern that "I could be bounded in a *nutshell* and count myself king of *infinite space*." Later in this scene Hamlet re-expresses this idea, figuring the human body as a container of the uncontain-able. Hamlet admires the "*infinite* . . . faculties" expressed in the finite, animal form of man—this creature, he will remark in F1's 4.4, endowed "with such large dis-course, / Looking before and after." Man remembers and anticipates, unlimited by temporality, moving freely back and forth. Existential containment reappears in 5.1 when Hamlet talks with and of skulls, particularly Yorick's, this "fellow of *infinite jest*." In these instances a container—a prison-house, the world, Denmark, a nutshell, the form of the human animal (and later the grave and the vessel of the brain, the skull)—is said to comprehend the incomprehensible: infinite space, infinite faculty, and infinite jest.

A terrible anxiety over confinement accompanies this crowded imagery, an anxiety arising from the fact that these images are reductive rather than expansive. They present us with increasingly restrictive rather than liberated space. To the degree that the skull epitomizes this restriction, it locates the experience of reality within the confines of the human head, the seat of thought, memory, feeling, and desire. This inward-directedness marks a radical break with the absolute, unquestioning faith in God that Shakespeare's generation inherited from the Middle Ages. As a recent critic remarks, *Hamlet* is "a play poised midway between a religious past and a secular future." This "secular future" necessarily implies a loss of the worldview Shakespeare's generation held. To be sure, Hamlet cites the Everlasting's prohibition against self-slaughter, and he declines to kill Claudius while the King is praying, so as not to send him to heaven. These seem to reflect an orthodox mindset. But other evidence points in a different direction. Hamlet is far removed from a medieval worldview in his construction of death as an infinite secret, "the undiscovered country, from whose bourn / No traveler returns." It is not nothingness—oblivion—that paralyzes Hamlet but rather something after death, decidedly not Heaven, unknown dreams that may come—these stop him. Dreading death rather than viewing it as a blessed relief from the agonies and indignities of this life, Hamlet breaks sharply with the past. It is not surprising, then, that *Hamlet* is marked by an obsession with death, with comprehending it.

Hamlet's father, a dead man talking, contradicts Hamlet's claim in 3.1 that death is a country from which no man returns. The Ghost repeatedly crosses and recrosses that existential bourn, appearing twice before the action commences and then twice more before the end of the first act. The membrane between the quick and dead is permeable. Hamlet's father crosses it, and so does his son, only in the opposite direction, from the living to the dead and back.

To condition him for death—for his role as dead son—in 1.4, Shakespeare has young Hamlet cross with his father into the region of the dead and return from that terrible place. At the end of this scene, father and son walk offstage together, leaving behind Hamlet's cautious and cautioning witnesses. Hamlet's companions had tried to restrain the desperate prince, afraid of where the Ghost may lead him. But Hamlet threatened to make a ghost of any one of them who got in his way.

When father and son return to the stage in 1.5, the famous Cellarage Scene, one is visible, the other invisible. Father and son prank Hamlet's friends as the Ghost, now underneath the stage, demands that Horatio and Marcellus swear not to tell anyone what they have seen. Hamlet and his friends move to the place from which the voice comes. But by the time they get there, the Ghost has moved beneath them to the other side of the stage and cries again, "Swear." As they move toward the voice, Hamlet calls his father a "boy" and a "truepenny" (an honest fellow). Once again, the Ghost shifts his position. As Hamlet, Horatio, and Marcellus follow, Hamlet calls his father an "old mole" and a "worthy pioneer" (a soldier who digs beneath enemy lines to lay mines). Hamlet Sr. moves freely but unseen beneath the stage, "here and everywhere, *hic et ubique*." Together father and son are masterful players, manipulating the material stage with astonishing dexterity, performing a kind of vertical *pas de deux* with remarkable success. Their rapt audience can only clumsily follow, nearly speechless.

From this crossing with his father, Hamlet acquires a psychic liberation no other character, except the Ghost, can claim. The terrifying doubt about the Ghost's nature and mission is missing in this early encounter. "It is an honest ghost," Hamlet assures his friends, "that let me tell you." Father and son, dead and quick, enter the Cellarage Scene of 1.5 with complete trust in each other. The satisfying interaction that had presumably eluded them while both were alive now allows them to comprise an exquisite reciprocal whole. Not only ghoulish pranksters and dance partners, father and son are in this scene friends perhaps for the first time, talking confidently across the boundary of the stage floor, which now represents that bourn that separates those alive at Elsinore from those conveyed to the undiscovered country beyond or below.

As a corollary to this perfect moment, Hamlet is forever attempting to couple heaven and earth. In this effort, he often employs hendiadys, a rhetorical figure remote from us yet familiar to Shakespeare, meaning literally "one through two," in which "two substantives, or sometimes a substantive and a genitive or adjective [are] connected by a conjunction to express a single, complex idea." *Hamlet* contains a large number of hendiadys, sixty-six in all, more than in any other of his plays, many of which suggest a link between the invisible and the visible, as in "angels and ministers of grace." Others, such as Hamlet's reference to "the book and volume of my brain," seem to link something material and finite ("book") with a concept that if not infinite is unlimited ("volume") in the sense of an unspecified amount. The use of hendiadys in *Hamlet* is perhaps the chief means whereby Shakespeare attempts to contain infinity within finite limits, to encase heaven in earth.

But the reach of *Hamlet* is not limited to heaven and earth. As in 1.5, Hamlet also "couples hell." *Hamlet* conjoins, that is, every stage of the existential paradigm—Heaven and Earth and Hell (or, if not Hell itself, then purgatory, or some version of the underworld). *Hamlet*—from its staging to its complex moral, ethical, and intellectual concerns—is vertically arrayed. We move from the ramparts of Elsinore to the cellarage and the grave of Ophelia and up again to the scaffold where Hamlet's body is taken in the final scene of the play.

The vertical axis of *Hamlet*—heaven, earth, and underworld—intersects with a linear, durational axis in which events in the drama unfold over time. In 2.2, for instance, Hamlet enters reading a book. Polonius asks, "What do you read, my lord?" Hamlet wearily replies, "Words, words, words." Hamlet is presenting this "grave" councilor, whom he will shortly dispatch to his grave, with the durational pattern, word after word after word. All speech, dramatic as well as nondramatic, is linearly composed, syllables coupled together to form words, words joined to make phrases, phrases to make clauses, clauses coupled into sentences, sentences extended to speeches.

The vertical and lateral organization of the play is important from a structural perspective. Looking for Hamlet, we confront a host of elements that anticipate modern conceptions of language and meaning. These modern conceptions develop from principles articulated by the Swiss linguist Ferdinand de Saussure (1857–1913), in the first decade of the last century, as Europe hovered on the precipice of the cataclysmic First World War. Saussurean linguistics is complex and its implications far-reaching, but a brief synopsis of its basic principles here might help us understand why Hamlet remains so important in our own time. Saussure's most fundamental and radical claim is that language is an artificial rather than a natural system. That is, meanings don't inhere in words because of a natural connection of sounds with things and concepts, but rather meanings are a product of convention, an agreement implicit among members of a language community to apply, in Saussurean terms, signifiers to signifieds. There is, structural linguistics insists, nothing of "dogness" in the word "dog." We call a dog a dog because we tacitly agree to do so. Language is artificial and conventional rather than divinely ordained. As Juliet says, "That which we call a rose / By any other word would smell as sweet."

Of course, it doesn't follow from the recognition of artificiality that language can be significantly altered by individual speakers. We manipulate language only within established parameters of meaning. We might indicate a "dog" by any number of metaphors or other figures of speech but we cannot willy-nilly call a dog a cat and still communicate an intended meaning. Yet, because language is artificially rather than divinely commissioned, it is preeminently a game, and as such it encourages play. Shakespeare's age was acutely aware of the pleasures of playing with language. Indeed, perhaps more than any period in the history of the language, Elizabethans reveled in linguistic artifice, endlessly exploiting the myriad ways words and sentences can be truncated, distorted, paralleled, dressed up, and made ornately beautiful.

Hamlet the play revels in the kind of verbal games that point to the artificiality and arbitrariness of language systems. Hamlet the character is supremely talented at such play, as we see in his first appearance before the audience. Having granted Laertes permission to return to Paris, Claudius, Hamlet's uncle-father, turns his attention to the prince: "But now, my *cousin* Hamlet, and my *son*" (emphasis mine). Hamlet's reply, his first words in the play, puns on the linguistic affinity of the concepts of likeness and gentleness: "A little more than *kin*, and less than *kind*." Claudius follows with the question, "How is it that the *clouds* still hang on you," to which Hamlet replies, "Not so, my lord, I am too much in the *sun*," punning on his being the late King's, not Claudius', son. His mother then asks him to "cast thy *nighted* color off," which puns on Hamlet's aristocratic identity. She notes that it is "*common*" for fathers, like all things, to die. "Ay, madam," Hamlet replies, "it is *common*," referring to base-ness. If so, she asks, "Why *seems* it so particular with thee?" "'*Seems*,' madam?" Hamlet says, "nay, it is. I know not '*seems*'." Shakespeare here is advancing with casual brilliance a field of verbal affinities that suggest Hamlet's grievance. Though he may stand in the sun, his color—his cloak—is nighted, dark. All fathers must die, but in this case, his own, singular father has died. The common is particular to Hamlet. He asserts that appearances—forms, gestures, vestments of mourning—mean nothing to him, finishing this great first encounter with the claim of interiority. "But I have that within which passes show, / These but the trappings and suits of woe."

The unparalleled involvement of Hamlet in words places *Hamlet*—which introduces some 600 new words to the language—at the cusp of a new and disturbing worldview, a secularism that denies the view of language that words have some natural relation to their meanings. Like Juliet, Hamlet is well aware that if we called a rose by any other word, it would smell as sweet. Of course, many if not all of Shakespeare's plays revel in word play, but in *Hamlet* the density, complexity, and self-referential nature of its verbal ingenuity reflects, to a degree not found in other linguistically brilliant works—*Love's Labors Lost*, for example—a preoccupation with subjectivity, the encased mind.

As dexterously as Hamlet manipulates language, one linear dimension trips him up. Hamlet seems to be pathologically bad with time, the most subjective of all experiences. Admonished to remember his father, he seems uncertain how long ago his father died. Was it two months ago? Or "a little month?" Or a month passing with "wicked speed?" Or is it a matter of "two hours," as he insists to Ophelia in the "Mousetrap" scene of 3.2, to which she replies with a correction. "Nay, 'tis twice two months, my lord." We remember Hamlet's complaint at the end of 1.5 that "The time is out of joint /—O cursed spite, / That ever I was born to set it right!" In the play's final scene, he will grapple with linearity, with the fact that two things can't occupy the same place in time. In F1, he tells Horatio, "If it be now, 'tis not to come. If it be not to come, it will be now. If it be not now, yet it will come." Hamlet's analysis of time—past is not present is not future—reminds us of the collapse of time in the rushing world of the Macbeths, as in Lady Macbeth's "I feel now / The future in the instant." As with them, so with Hamlet the present portends a catastrophic future. It cannot nor will it come to good.

For his part, Hamlet Sr. is bounded, or more precisely re-bounded, in time. His first words are "Mark me." Not only hear me, he says to Hamlet, but see me visible before your eyes wearing my armor. Regardless of where he resides in the nether world, whether in Catholic purgatory or some more nebulous region—a question that has concerned critics for hundreds of years—he would not risk returning to his son were he at peace in death. His visits are anxious and furtive. He comes from a place of torment where, if we saw its secrets, our hairs would stand out like quills "of the fretful porpentine." "I am thy father's spirit," Hamlet Sr. tells his son in 1.5,

> Doomed for a certain term to walk the night,
> And for the day confined to fast in fires
> Till the foul crimes done in my days of nature
> Are burnt and purged away. But that I am forbid
> To tell the secrets of my prison-house.

"Confined to fast in fires" of his "prison-house," the ghost of Hamlet's father underscores the point that, even in the place of the dead, identity is inseparable from containment. Accordingly, his return to earth can be manifested only in forms of containment: a suit of armor or a night shirt. As I suggested earlier, the prison-house where the Ghost resides in the nether world anticipates, even prompts Hamlet's obsession with the world, with Denmark, as a prison.

In the famous soliloquy in 3.1, Hamlet expresses a desire to transgress the boundary separating him from the dead and, at the same time, a fear of committing that transgression. He earlier complained that the Almighty had set his canon against suicide, and had accompanied his father into the region of the dead in 1.5. Yet, here in the 3.1 soliloquy, he fears death's imminence. Even though—perhaps because—he had ventured into this region, he is overcome with dread. Hamlet pauses at the threshold of death, fear paralyzing the will and making him resolve to bear those ills he knows, rather than to fly to others he knows not of. Here at this precipice, contemplating whether to be or not to be, Hamlet reverses his father's anxieties. If Hamlet Sr. both desires becoming bounded and yet seems furtive and uncomfortable among the living, appearing in vestments on the battlements of Elsinore only to flee back to the confines of his prison-house with the crowing of the cock, his son desires and fears becoming unbounded, resolving to bear the burdens of this life rather than face the unknown.

In the final scene of the third act, Hamlet the prankster spills the first blood of the play by dispatching Polonius, who has hidden himself behind the arras in the Queen's chamber. Hamlet kills the old man and then abuses his memory with ugly puns drawn from the stench of a rotting corpse to be eaten by politic worms. Asked where he has hidden Polonius' corpse, he tells the King that he may seek him in heaven or hell, "but if indeed you find him not within this month you shall nose him as you go up the stairs into the lobby." Hamlet's quip about nosing Polonius in the lobby and his subsequent discourse on maggots—"your worm is your only emperor for diet: we fat all creatures else to fat us, and we fat ourselves for maggots. Your fat king and your lean beggar is but variable service, two dishes to one table"—anticipate his encounter with the smelly skulls of 5.1.

Act Five, Scene 1 of *Hamlet* presents us with old skulls, empty vessels of interiority, present absences, silent and distant speakers; the second scene offers fresh kills, newly butchered bodies—which language has recently abandoned—silent now, at rest. Strewn about the stage in a ghastly spectacle, Claudius, Gertrude, Laertes, and of course Hamlet are just beginning the process of decomposition that will in time reduce them to human remains, chopfallen skulls that a joking clown might toss about.

Reduced to material remains, the cast of *Hamlet* call out to the near and distant future. In 1607, only four years after *Hamlet* appeared in print, and four years after Queen Elizabeth died, one of the most savage of all revenge plays, *The Revenger's Tragedy*, was published. It opens with the brutal revenger, Vindici, holding the skull of his murdered mistress, Gloriana. No one in 1607 could hear the name Gloriana and not think of the late Queen. Thirteen years earlier, Edmund Spenser had given Elizabeth the name of "Gloriana" in his monumental epic poem *The Fairie Queene*, an enormous enterprise that, if completed, would have filled a dozen books or more. In the April Eclogue of his *Shepheardes Calender*, published in 1579, he had celebrated her as a goddess without blemish: "No mortal blemish may her blot." That same year smallpox threatened her life. She survived but was so scarred that she wore makeup half an inch thick. Spenser gave England Queen Elizabeth as a timeless virgin goddess benevolently governing her grateful subjects. *Hamlet* supercedes this idealized image with the graphic reality that *The Revenger's Tragedy* then exploits in the name of the skull, Gloriana. It is not Elizabeth as idealized youth that endures into the seventeenth century but rather Elizabeth as skull. In effect, *Hamlet* buries the Spenserian Elizabeth in the horrors of mortality. This becomes her future in *The Revenger's Tragedy*, a detached skull, a present absence.

Hamlet's contemplation of the skull of Yorick, Vindici's contemplation of the skull of Gloriana, do more than present us with emblems of mortality. These moments stand as milestones in the process of internalizing reality, of turning all meaning inward, of coming to believe that nothing is good or bad but thinking makes it so. In the distant future, the incessant operation of the mind that thwarts Hamlet's action in a waste of words also paralyzes his distant child, T. S. Eliot's J. Alfred Prufrock, who, mired in thought, an infinite brain trapped in a finite skull, is unable to get off the sofa to meet the faces that he must meet. Prufrock will deny that he is Hamlet—"I am not Prince Hamlet, nor was meant to be"—but, of course, he really is. The earliest images of Hamlet, which predate Shakespeare, depict the character holding an orb in his hand representing dominion over the world. It's a potent, prescient image, for the globe that Amleth holds will become the skull Hamlet clutches. The transformation of this sphere into a death's-head will stand for a redirection of attention inward toward self-referentiality, doubt, embodiment and a preoccupation with mortality. Hamlet will become the axis of a gravitational field that has held us in orbit for centuries, from which we cannot escape. There will be dissenting voices, of course, but that's to be expected. With Horatio's benediction, "Goodnight, sweet Prince, / And flights of angels sing thee to thy rest," Shakespeare bequeaths to the future the Melancholic Prince as a dead son by which the future will define itself.

FOUR

DEAD SON HAMLET

With good reason we think of *Hamlet* as a play about dead fathers. Not only does Hamlet's father haunt the play, but so does Old Fortinbras and, in fact, all fathers who have passed on. "But you must know your father lost a father," Claudius tells Hamlet in 1.2, "That father lost, lost his, and the survivor bound / In filial obligation for some term / To do obsequious sorrow." What Claudius says about nature itself, "whose common theme / Is death of fathers," is certainly true of *Hamlet*. To underscore the point and reinforce this important theme, Hamlet kills Polonius in the third act, robbing Ophelia and Laertes of *their* father, thus making Laertes a mirror of Hamlet, the son of a murdered father. "Old Hamlet's ghost," Stephen Greenblatt writes in *Hamlet in Purgatory*, doomed to walk the night, "has now lasted some four hundred years, and it has brought with it a cult of the dead that I and the readers of this book have been serving." The theme of dead fathers echoes Shakespeare's life: his own father, John, died in 1601, very close to the composition of *Hamlet*.

But, in fact, dead fathers fade as the drama unfolds. Hamlet's father figures in the first act four times, twice by report and twice on stage, but he appears only once thereafter, in 3.4, when he returns in his nightclothes, a king of "shreds and patches"—suggestive of a decaying presence—to plead with his son not to forget. "This visitation," he says, "is but to whet thy almost blunted purpose." Clearly, Hamlet Sr. is irrevocably fading from his son's mind. The Ghost never appears again, and by the fifth act, only the faintest trace of him remains. In his meditation on skulls in 5.1 Hamlet thinks of lawyers, land developers, courtiers, high-born women, a jester, but never explicitly of his dead father.

In the place of forgotten fathers *Hamlet* presents us, in the end, with dead sons: Laertes and Hamlet. Horatio and Fortinbras are witnesses to the slaughter of innocents. Horatio's final remark to his friend—"Goodnight, sweet Prince, / And flights of angels sing thee to thy rest"—is a benediction for a dead boy. The pain of losing a son was certainly still fresh in Shakespeare's mind when he wrote *Hamlet*. His only son Hamnet (or Hamlet—the names were virtually interchangeable for Elizabethans), Judith's twin, had died in early August 1596.

Why did Shakespeare take up this play, with its ancient history when he did, if not for the death of his son? Perhaps it was convenient, an old play from the 1580s that Shakespeare and his company saw potential profit in reviving. But it must have been more than that. One has to suspect that such a brilliant creation as Hamlet, one that would shape the future, was accompanied by some deep, cathartic experience that we will never fully recover. In any case, Shakespeare was probably in London when the news reached him that eleven-year-old Hamnet was gravely ill or already dead in Stratford-upon-Avon. We don't know the cause of young Hamnet's death, whether it was a swift or lingering illness, or perhaps even an accident that took him away. It was August, high summer. Maybe the boy drowned swimming in the Avon that flows under Clopton Bridge at the foot of the hill below Shakespeare's boyhood house on Henley Street.

If Hamnet's sickness was slow in taking him, perhaps Shakespeare learned of the crisis in time to make the three-day trip by horseback west from London through Oxford to his home. If he was already dead, it would be three days before the news reached Shakespeare and another three for the return trip, a minimum of six days before the boy could be buried with his father in attendance.

We do know that Hamnet was buried in Stratford on August 11, though there's no way to know whether Shakespeare made it home by that Saturday. This loss must have been devastating to Shakespeare on many levels. Hamnet, his only son, was the presumptive heir to the fortune his father was then amassing as a London poet and playwright of enormous success and acclaim. The boy Hamnet would carry the Shakespeare name—bolstered by the granting in 1596 of a coat of arms to Shakespeare's father, John—into the future. Apart from any dynastic interests, Hamnet's death must have been emotionally crushing. We have been taught to think that parents in Shakespeare's age were not close to their children in the same way that we are today. So many children died in infancy and childhood that parents couldn't invest emotional energy in loving their children.

But this is true only in the aggregate. In the particular, substantial evidence exists to the contrary. Montaigne's essay "On the Affection of Fathers for their Children" is largely about the relations between fathers and sons—all of Montaigne's children but one daughter died in infancy. Montainge (1533–92) is concerned with matters of inheritance and the distribution of wealth, of course, but he's remarkably modern in his attitude toward parental love. He himself tasted "the rod only twice during all my childhood, and that was but lightly." Montaigne believed in being especially careful with sons since boys "are born less to serve and [their] mode-of-being is freer: I would have loved to make their hearts overflow with openness and frankness."

To Montaigne, the beating of boys was stupid brutality. "I have never seen a caning achieve anything except making souls more cowardly or more maliciously stubborn," Montaigne writes. And later, "even if I were able to make myself feared I would rather make myself loved," he says, inverting the Machiavellian formulation that it is better to be feared than loved.

Shakespeare's friend and rival, Ben Jonson, who loved The Master "just short of idolatry," grieved the death of his son, Benjamin, in a tender poem. In terms immediate and poignant, the pain of grief is almost as palpable today as it must have been when Benjamin, a Hebrew name meaning "child of my right hand," died of plague in 1603. Grief comes through a deeply wounded yet composed father, who frames his sorrow in somber couplets. He asks his son to speak from the place of the dead:

> Rest in soft peace, and, asked, say, "Here doth lie
> Ben Jonson his best piece of poetry."
> For whose sake, henceforth, all his vows be such
> As what he loves may never like too much.

"As what he loves may never like too much." Jonson is promising never again to invest emotional energy in a child he might lose at any moment. Contrast this with Shakespeare's take on loving that which will, sooner or later, be lost to death. "This thou perceiv'st," he wrote in the couplet of sonnet 73, "which makes thy love more strong, / To love that well which thou must leave ere long." Though Shakespeare urges us to love deeply because we must lose everything to time, except the poetry itself, for that same reason Jonson urges us to withdraw, or rather, to attempt withdrawal of parental love and care, not to love well precisely because the pain of loss is too great to endure. Shakespeare and Jonson advocate opposite positions— engagement and disengagement; still both must have loved intensely their dead sons, Hamnet and Benjamin. It is difficult to imagine otherwise.

In fact, the play *Hamlet* and the character Hamlet are in profound ways attempts to exorcise the supremely painful experience of the death of a son. This exorcism would occupy Shakespeare beyond *Hamlet*, off and on for the remainder of his career. Dead sons are conspicuous in later plays. In *Macbeth*, Banquo's son Fleance escapes his butchers, but Macduff's son isn't so lucky. He is hacked to death on stage in front of his mother. When Macduff learns that his children have been slaughtered, he vows to avenge this outrage. But first he must confront pain. "I must," he says "feel it as a man."

The most emblematic instance of a dead son after *Hamlet* is Prince Mamillius from *The Winter's Tale*, the product of the final phase of Shakespeare's dramatic evolution, the Romance. Shakespeare's Romances—*Pericles*, *Cymbeline*, *The Winter's Tale*, and *The Tempest*—take the viewer from loss to recovery. Characters presumed dead are found to be alive, children are returned to parents, brothers reunited with sisters; peasants are princes; flower children, princesses. Though the Romances are defined by this miraculous pattern, defying the inevitable pattern of life, they make concessions to time. In *The Winter's Tale*, Leontes' virtuous Queen Hermione, whom he had condemned to death on the false charge of adultery, is miraculously restored to him. Her statue comes alive on stage, but it is not the young queen he had ruined sixteen years before. She's an older woman, lovely but no longer youthful.

Hermione is returned to Leontes, but his son is not. The boy-prince Mamillius is, in fact, the only member of the royal family of Leontes not to be rescued from death. Mamillius, as if in a delirium, utters among his last words, an evocative line snatched from an old saying: "There was a man . . . dwelt by a churchyard."

The Winter's Tale anticipates the pain of the loss of this young prince early in the play when Leontes asks his guest Polixenes, King of Bohemia, whom Leontes secretly suspects of fathering Mamillius, "Are you so fond of your young prince as we / Do seem to be of ours?" The word "seem" is pregnant to us, echoing Hamlet's "'Seems,' madam—nay it is," but its import escapes Polixenes, whose reply allows all the complexity of how a father responds to a son, a king to a prince, to be lost. The boy is a totalizing presence, one that focuses upon himself all fatherly feeling, a catalogue of powerful emotions:

> He's all my exercise, my mirth, my matter,
> Now my sworn friend and then mine enemy,
> My parasite, my soldier, statesman, all.
> He makes a July's day short as December,
> And with his varying childness cures in me
> Thoughts that would thick my blood.

Such is the effect of sons upon fathers. The joy Polixenes takes in his living son only heightens the effect of Leontes' subsequent loss of Mamillius. This rumination prepares us for the unspeakable pain of the son's loss.

Indeed, there is evidence that almost immediately after Shakespeare's *Hamlet* was produced England registered the impact of Hamlet as son. A remarkable increase of male babies named "Hamlet" occurred in the decade following *Hamlet*. Why did people start naming their sons Hamlet after 1603? It may have been a vogue independent of Shakespeare's play, of course, but that's improbable. Except for the profound and diffuse influence of Shakespeare's Hamlet, it's hard to think how otherwise to explain this demographic anomaly. The increase of babies christened "Hamlet" in the years following, if it's real, argues that Shakespeare's play, with its emblematic dead son, exerted a profound influence upon the national psyche.

Critic Barbara Everett expands dead son Hamlet to the Continent. "Young Hamlet, as it were all Europe's 'Elder Son,'" she writes, is "the white hope of history [who] grows up to find that he has grown dead." In *Ulysses*, James Joyce treats Hamlet in a similar vein. In a brilliant riff on Shakespeare, Hamlet seeps into the slipstream of Joyce's language, becoming the plot of a conversation about fathers and sons involving the characters Stephen Dedalus, Buck Mulligan, and John Eglinton in the National Library of Dublin. Stephen carefully directs Hamlet's infiltration of the conversation: "When Rutlandbaconsouthamptonshakespeare or another poet of the same name in the comedy of errors wrote *Hamlet* he was not the father of his own son merely but, being no more a son, he was and felt himself the father of all his race, the father of his own grandfather, the father of his unborn grandson who, by the same token, never was born for nature. . . ." This wildly recursive logic effects mental gymnastics in Buck Mulligan as he listens. "Himself his own father, Sonmulligan told himself. Wait. I am big with child. I have an unborn child in my brain. Pallas Athena! A play! The play's the thing!"

"Hamlet, the black prince, is Hamnet Shakespeare," Stephen says, echoing his earlier remark that "the son [is] consubstantial with the father." And earlier still: "[S]o through the ghost of the unquiet father," Stephen says, "the image of the unliving son looks forth."

I don't mean to infantilize Hamlet. Burbage, the first Hamlet, was in his thirties when he played the part, and many actors succeeding him have played the role far beyond the time when they could pass for young men. The great Restoration actor Thomas Betterton (1635–1710) played Hamlet on the London stage for forty years, well into his seventies. What links Joyce's characters and Hamlet is in fact precisely what is *not* childlike about them, their facility with language. Montaigne thinks that a child becomes lovable when it can hold a conversation, when it's no longer an infant (from the Latin *infans*, a thing without language). "I am incapable," Montaigne writes, "of finding a place for that emotion which leads people to cuddle new-born infants while they are still without movements of soul. . . ." And then: "A true and well-regulated affection should be born, and then increase, as children enable us to get to know them; if they show they deserve it, we should cherish them with a truly fatherly love, since our natural propensity is then progressing side by side with reason." The ability to reason through language is what triggers fatherly affection. In this sense is Hamlet farthest from infancy and most like a son. Shakespeare's Hamlet, this is to say, is the son that Montaigne would have loved deeply, and whose death he would have grieved even more deeply.

Grief for dead Hamlet mirrors Hamlet's mourning for his dead father, of course. The idealization of the father is transferred to the idealization of the son. Just as the ghost of Hamlet's father haunts *Hamlet*, young Hamlet haunts the future. Throughout the generations that inherit this play over four centuries,

Hamlet the character is never thirty or, as his mother says, "fat and scant of breath." He is the epitome of tortured youth—dark, trim, and handsome, an idealized young man whose death generations will grieve.

If children should not die before their parents, we all of us outlive Hamlet, just as Shakespeare outlived Hamnet. And then we are outlived by Hamlet, who's resuscitated and resurrected in succeeding generations. The history of the play's reception is the search for a young man lost; but not merely a character in a play. Hamlet is more than a character; he rather becomes a projection of an internalized version of ourselves onto the character, or the character onto ourselves. Burbage's gratuitous "O, O, O, O—" in the First Folio, a primal expression of grief at the loss of himself and the Hamlet he was playing, launches the greatest drama ever written into future generations that will often construe Hamlet, consciously and unconsciously, as its own fading or already faded youth. He will be regarded with the deepest feelings of greatness and loss, a grief so wrenching as to cause, at times, the most shocking confessions, outpourings of grief. The future is left, in the words of Macduff, who has just learned that his wife and children have been butchered, to "give sorrow words."

Jacques Derrida's reading of the sacrifice of Isaac says much about Shakespeare's relationship to *Hamlet*/Hamlet. Demanding that Abraham kill his son, Isaac, God is anticipating his own sacrifice of his son Christ. In both instances "absolute responsibility" to kill the son locks the killing father in a prison-house of silence. They "must remain hidden, secret, jealous . . . ," Derrida writes. He contrasts the silent obedience of the sacrificing father with the tragic hero's ability to talk. "The tragic hero . . . can speak, share, weep, complain. He doesn't know the dreadful responsibility of loneliness. . . . Abraham can neither speak nor commiserate, neither weep nor wail. He is kept in absolute secret."

In the sacrifice of Hamlet, Shakespeare is likewise silent, secret. We know nothing of what it meant for him to sentence this incomparable prince, following so closely his own son's death, to the status of the skull. What must it have felt like to kill Hamlet, one naturally wonders, to condemn this beautiful and compelling creation, this great son, to death, thus reenacting the death of Hamnet? The Abrahamic Hamlet, the tragic hero, speaks volumes; his creator is a mute enigma, on whom we foist an unbearable burden of responsibility to shape the future.

Hamlet as dead son is a master trope of the play, a conceptual framework capable of focusing enormous intellectual and emotional energies, available to all readers and viewers at all times, but by no means engaged by all people at all times. As we shall see, the Romantic Movement will react profoundly and universally to Hamlet as a dead son. Hamlet will stand as the premier emblem of unrealized promise. Among the moderns, the development of analytical methodologies of interpretation will suppress the wrenching grief unleashed by conceiving of Hamlet as doomed youth, but these methodologies themselves—especially those associated with psychoanalytic approaches to *Hamlet*—will regularly return us to the Prince as a child. But this reaction to Hamlet—as the figure of a dead son containing reality within the confines of the skull—will not appear immediately. For the generation that came of age during the Restoration, when London theaters were reopened after the fall of the Cromwellian regime, through the eighteenth century, Hamlet will be a problematic figure. On the one hand, they will recognize the dark brilliance of the character; on the other, they will find his hesitation to act, his solipsism, his entrapment in thought as inimical to their own cultural and philosophical values. For them, if Hamlet is a child, he is an unruly one whose behavior they are inclined to rebuke. It is to this dissenting age that we now turn our attention.

THE MAN IN BLACK
GALLERY ONE

Figure 1A

Though undated, this sketch is probably the earliest extant representation of Amblett, the character that will evolve into Shakespeare's Hamlet. He bears a crown—in the Danish sagas Amblett/ Amleth/ Hamblet lives to rule Denmark—along with a royal scepter and sword. The globe is a representation of dominion; Amblett literally holds the world in his hand. The image is suggestive of Hamlet's effort to contain all levels of existence: "I could be bounded in a nutshell and count myself king of infinite space," he says to Rosencrantz and Gildenstern. Amblett's emblem of dominion will become Hamlet's distracted globe, and then the empty crown, the death's head, in the Graveyard Scene of *Hamlet*. Illustration courtesy of the Royal Library, Copenhagen.

Figure 2A

In this illustration from 1597, Amblet lacks the royal scepter but the crown is prominent, as is the sword. Again, the globe he holds represents worldly dominion, the containment of power within the grasp of the ruler. To the chain around his neck will later be added the pendant of the Order of the Elephant, Denmark's highest merit, formalized in 1693 by King Christian V. In many English productions of Shakespeare's play, this pendant is the Order of the Garter. Illustration courtesy of the National Library of Sweden.

Figure 3A   John Philip Kemble, by Sir Thomas Lawrence (1801)

Lawrence depicts Kemble (1757–1823) as Hamlet in the 5.1 Graveyard Scene at the height of the Romantic Movement. Missing are the gravediggers and Horatio, as Kemble, departing from the iconic posture of Hamlet gazing on the skull, stands utterly alone staring up into space behind the viewer. He holds the skull familiarly by his side, his thumb inserted through one of its sockets. The horror of the death's head is attenuated, however, with the pate turned to the viewer, creating a visual effect similar to the orb in the Danish sketches. Kemble wears a plumed hat, a cape, sash and sword, shirt open, with a pendant (Order of the Elephant?) hanging at his chest. Though Kemble played Hamlet with restraint, suppressing the wild passion favored by Romantic commentators, his princely visage is the essence of Romantic dejection. In the background, the battlements of Elsinore rise into a sky that is either lightening or darkening. By permission of the Harvard Theatre Collection.

Figures 4A and 5A   Left, Herbert Beerbohm Tree (1854–1917); right, E. H. Sothern (1859–1933)

Both the Englishman Beerbohm Tree and the American Sothern were popular Victorian Hamlets. Here, similarly dressed, they appear in a stock gesture more typical of Hamlet in the Graveyard Scene. These gestures would seem clownish but for the fact that the skulls they hold are chop-fallen, jawless, a much more graphic representation with the death's head than among the Romantics. Sothern is wearing the medallion of the Order of the Elephant. Beerbohm Tree courtesy of Harry Rusche; Sothern courtesy of Michael A. Morrison Collection.

SARAH BERNHARDT

Figure 6A Sarah Bernhardt (1844–1923)

In Paris, on May 20, 1899, the 54-year-old Sarah Bernhadt—acting as producer, director, and starring in the lead role—launched one of the most influential *Hamlets* in history. With extensive scene changes, the Bernhardt *Hamlet* ran more than five hours. Bernhardt radically altered tradition by staging the play with fewer cuts—885 lines—than typical of any earlier period, restoring Fortinbras, "The Mousetrap," Hamlet's encounter with Claudius after the murder of Polonius, the Graveyard Scene, and many smaller moments that were commonly excised. Bernhard produced a retro-*Hamlet*, one stripped of Romantic brooding, that emphasized not the effeminate, thought-plagued prince of inaction, but rather Hamlet the Revenger, capable of extraordinary violence and indeed brutality, thus recalling the Hamlets of Thomas Betterton and Richard Burbage. Ironically, it was a female Hamlet who returned a masculine man of action to the stage tradition. Here, Bernhardt taunts a chopped skull to bite her finger. Illustration courtesy of Michael A. Morrison Collection.

Figures 7A and 8A Right, Laurence Olivier (1907–1989); below, Mel Gibson (1956–)

At right, Olivier, playing the role against type as a blond, nestles the front-on ghastliness of the skull. The Olivier pose—the missing jaw, the missing teeth, the shrunken fascia, the oblong nasal and optical sockets of the skull—is unsettlingly intimate. Below, Mel Gibson in the 1991 film production of the play by Franco Zeffirelli follows Olivier in expressing intimacy with the skull. Photographs courtesy of Michael A. Morrison Collection.

FIVE

CONTRARIANS
AT THE GATE

The establishment of the Royal Society on November 28, 1660—the year London theaters were reopened after being closed under the repressive Cromwellian Interregnum—marked a turning point in the intellectual and cultural history of England. Its weekly meetings were intended to promote "Phisico-Mathematicall learning." Among its founding members were the astronomer and architect Christopher Wren (1632–1723), who would design the new St. Paul's Cathedral to replace the old one destroyed in the Great Fire of 1666; the chemist Robert Boyle (1627–91), who conducted experiments in the properties of air and gasses, and advocated "corpuscularism," an early version of particle theory; and the Scottish nobleman Sir Robert Moray, an early freemason who promoted experimental philosophy and secured a royal charter for the Society; and the polymath Robert Hooke (1635–1703), whose experiments with the microscope led to his coining of the term "cell" for the biological units on which life is built. The great Sir Isaac Newton (1643–1727) became the Society's president in 1710.

The Royal Society formalized scientific inquiry and thus introduced a new and powerful shaping force to the cultural and intellectual life of England, ushering in the Age of Reason. Almost immediately, the Society's interests and methods were construed as a threat to traditional religious belief. Scientific inquiry was the source of man's downfall, tempting him to advance above what God had intended. In Book Nine of Milton's *Paradise Lost*, published only seven years after the founding of the Royal Society, the serpent tempting Eve addresses the forbidden tree, aligning science with the source of original sin, as forbidden fruit:

> O Sacred, Wise and Wisdom-giving Plant,
> *Mother of Science*, Now I feel thy Power
> Within me clear, not only to discern
> Things in their causes, but to trace the ways
> Of highest Agents, deem'd however wise.
>
> (my emphasis)

The architects of the Age of Reason weren't atheists, but a new vision of God was necessary to accommodate rational inquiry. Deism, which conceptualized God as clock-maker rather than personal agent, the power that built the universe according to fixed laws which the Age of Reason was busily discovering, served as the dominant religious belief and practice among Protestants for much of the eighteenth century. Deists distrusted religious fervor, what they called enthusiasm (from the etymological sense of God coming inside one). To them, the passionate belief in a personal relationship with God amounted to madness.

However opposed scientific inquiry was to the old order, the new interest in rational methodology spread through the culture, even to the study of Shakespeare. The earliest efforts at systematic scholarship produced the first reliably accurate texts of Shakespeare's works. Separating Shakespearean wheat from chaff, eighteenth-century editors essentially fixed the canon as we know it today. Nicholas Rowe in his 1709 edition of the plays supplied logical scene and act divisions as well as stage directions, where they had been lacking. Alexander Pope's famously flawed 1723 edition (second edition 1725) followed; Pope's mistakes were corrected by Lewis Theobald in *Shakespeare Restored* (1726), in which he systematically exposed Pope's many misreadings and errors of judgment, for which he incurred Pope's wrath, who cast Theobald as the dullard hero of *The Dunciad* two years later. Theobald must have been hurt, but he was undeterred and produced his far superior edition of Shakespeare's works in 1733–34. Other editions by Thomas Hanmer (1744) and William Warburton (1747) followed. The second half of the century saw editions by Samuel Johnson in 1765 and George Steevens' first in 1773. Edward Capell's important ten-volume edition of 1768 provided the first detailed collation of early printed texts and a consideration of Shakespeare's sources. The century concluded with the magisterial edition by Edmond Malone, which, posthumously published in 1821, took up twenty-one volumes.

It's not surprising that these developments took place during the period known broadly as the Enlightenment. And yet its guiding principles—reason, symmetry, harmony, and restraint—paradoxically blinded many commentators to the brilliance of *Hamlet*. In an age devoted to establishing definitive texts of Shakespeare's plays, some of the best minds were sharply critical, indeed censorious, of his most famous work. This is because to many commentators of the time *Hamlet* wasn't a reasonable play, Hamlet not a reasonable character. To them the play was a wonderful but nonetheless hugely flawed work. It violated not only the pseudo-Aristotelian Unities of Action, Place, and Time (which demanded that a successful play must have a logical structure with a beginning, middle, and end; occur in one place; and span no more than one day), to which eighteenth-century critics were committed, but it also travestied decorum, juxtaposing comic and tragic scenes, intermingling bawdy and lofty, killing the innocent along with the guilty. For John Dryden, principal architect of a new aesthetics that championed classical virtues, especially restraint and decorum, the Player's speech recounting the killing of Priam pandered to low-minded audiences. "What a pudder is here kept," Dryden wrote, "in raising the expression of trifling thoughts!" He continued: "Wise men would be glad to find a little sense couched under all these pompous words; for bombast is commonly the delight of that audience which loves poetry, but understands it not: and as commonly has been the practice of those writers who, not being able to infuse a natural passion into the mind, have made it their business to ply the ears and to stun their judges by these noises." Similarly, in his 1711 *Essay on the Genius and Writings of Shakespeare* (1711), John Dennis, one of the most influential critics of the period, wrote that because "the Good and the Bad [perish] promiscuously in the best of Shakespeare's Tragedies, there can be either none or very weak Instruction in them: For such promiscuous Events call the Government of Providence into Question, and by Scepticks and Libertines are resolv'd into Chance."

Four decades later, in an anonymous commentary on *Hamlet*, the author roundly criticized Shakespeare for failing to adhere to standards of taste and unity set down, so he supposes, by the ancients. The antics of the Gravedigger Scene were simply embarrassing. Shakespeare's "incoherent Absurdity will forever remain," he wrote, "an indelible Blot in the Character of our Poet; and warn us not more to expect Perfection in the Work of a Mortal, than Sincerity in the Breast of a Female." Returning to its Danish sources, another anonymous writer in the February 15–17, 1757 issue of the *London Chronicle* assumed a similarly dismissive attitude. This writer prefers the story of Amleth, in which the hero kills his uncle and escapes, over Shakespeare's play in which the hero dies in the course of exacting his revenge. "If Shakespeare had not deviated [from the pattern of the Danish story], he would perhaps have given the finest Scenes of Terror in the last Act that ever have been imagined: and then a Subject that opens so nobly would have been grand also in the Close. As the Play now stands, the Innocent, contrary to Tradition, fall with the Guilty . . . and the World is left to judge which is worst [*sic*], the Fencing of the Actors, or the folly of the Poet in introducing it."

To the essayist, poet, and novelist Oliver Goldsmith (*Works*, 1765), Hamlet's "To be or not to be" soliloquy seemed childishly indulgent and illogical, inviting a lengthy critique based upon the claim that "there is not any apparent circumstance in the fate or situation of Hamlet that should prompt him to harbour one thought of self-murder; and, therefore, these expressions of despair imply an impropriety of character." For Goldsmith, Hamlet is an indulgent, misguided youngster whose "whole chain of reasoning seems inconsistent and incongruous." Though less dismissive, Samuel Johnson (*Preface to Shakespeare*, 1765) shared much of Goldsmith's reaction to 3.1, treating Hamlet like an unruly boy especially cruel to girls. Hamlet, he wrote, "plays the madman most, when he treats Ophelia with so much rudeness, which seems to be useless and wanton cruelty." Hamlet's sins are laid at the foot of Shakespeare himself. "The poet," Johnson concluded, "is accused of having shewn little regard to poetical justice and may be charged with equal neglect of poetical probability." Hamlet's decision in 3.3 to kill Claudius "[w]hen he is drunk, asleep or in his rage, / Or in th' incestuous pleasure of his bed, / At game a-swearing, or about some act / That has no relish of salvation in 't"—this was especially troubling. Like others of his time, Johnson found in this moment the depth of the play's barbarism. It was "too horrible to be read or to be uttered," Johnson wrote.

My point is that for Goldsmith and Johnson, Hamlet is a son. Immature, rebellious, disrespective, but nonetheless a son. Goldsmith scolds Hamlet's sad introspection. Hamlet has no real reason to despair. He's not yet grown into rational maturity. He muses brilliantly on death but doesn't understand what it means to die; he's all talk. Hamlet doesn't understand what it means to damn someone to Hell. In some eighteenth-century commentators the Abrahamic

Hamlet, the child sacrificed by his father, is incipient. In his summary remarks on Hamlet in his 1793 fifteen-volume edition of *The Plays of William Shakespeare*, George Steevens, for example, scolded the boy and his creator, acknowledging in passing that Hamlet is a sacrificial son. "Hamlet cannot be said to have pursued his ends by very warrantable means; and if the poet, *when he sacrificed him at last*, meant to have enforced such a moral, it is not the worst that can be deduced from the play" (my emphasis).

The most famous and outspoken contrarian of the eighteenth century wasn't an Englishman but a Frenchman, François Marie Arouet de Voltaire (1694–1778). Sneering at Shakespeare from the lofty perch of the Enlightenment, Voltaire, who lived for a time in England but never really mastered English, admitted in his *Lettres philosophiques* (1733, translated into English the following year as *Letters Concerning the English Nation*) that "Shakespeare boasted a strong, fruitful Genius: He was natural and sublime." Voltaire wouldn't allow anything more: "[Shakespeare] had not so much as a single Spark of good Taste, or knew one Rule of the Drama." Shakespeare wrote "monstrous Farces, to which the Name of Tragedy is given." *Hamlet* is a ghastly travesty of the Rules of Drama. The author of *Candide* seems curiously deaf to Shakespeare even at his best. Voltaire mocked 5.1, where "two Grave-Diggers make a Grave, and are all the Time drinking, singing Ballads, and making humourous Reflexions . . . on the several Skulls they throw up with their Spades." The "ridiculous Incident" of the Gravedigger Scene appears in a play marked by anachronisms, Voltaire complained. Cannons are fired to celebrate the marriage of Claudius and Gertrude and during the duel between Hamlet and Laertes, though Hamlet is set "in the Ninth Century, before the invention of the Cannon. This little inadvertency," Voltaire continued, "is not more remarkable, than that of making Hamlet swear by St. Patrick, and appeal to Jesus our Savior, at a time when Denmark knew no more of Christianity than of powder and cannon." Voltaire returned to his criticism of 5.1, suggesting that such a comic moment has no place in tragedy. But here even his translator, referring to himself in the third person, parenthetically disagreed—"he [the translator] takes the part of the Grave-diggers. He wishes them to be preserved, as the respectable monuments of a singular genius."

It is not the case, as this suggests, that the neoclassical age universally decried Hamlet's character. Indeed, commentators challenged the complaint that *Hamlet* violates dramatic decorum. In 1709, Nicholas Rowe, the first great editor of

Shakespeare's works, drew upon the similarities of Hamlet and the story of Orestes who kills his mother, Clytemnestra, for murdering his father, Agamemnon. Rowe assumed that Hamlet believes his mother is complicit in his father's murder but admired Hamlet for stopping short of killing Gertrude in retaliation. "Hamlet is represented with the same piety toward his father, and resolution to revenge his death, as Orestes," Rowe noted. "He has the same abhorrence for his mother's guilt, which, to provoke him the more, is heighten'd by incest: But 'tis wonderful art and justness of judgment, that the Poet restrains him from doing violence to his mother." In "one of the most outstanding contributions to Shakespeare criticism of the eighteenth century," George Stubbes, in his "Some Remarks on the Tragedy of *Hamlet*" (1736), set out to examine "*Hamlet*, one of the Pieces of the greatest Tragick Writer that ever liv'd . . . according to the Rules of Reason and Nature, without having any regard to those Rules established by Arbitrary Dogmatising Criticks, only as they can be brought to bear that Test." Others respond with grief. In 1784, while acknowledging the character's flaws, William Richardson called Hamlet "an object not of blame, but of genuine and tender regret."

This devotion to pseudo-Aristotelian notions of structure and decorum deeply affected Restoration and eighteenth-century productions of *Hamlet*, in ways that we would find atrocious. With the reopening of the theaters in 1660, William Davenant wasted no time in bringing *Hamlet* to the stage, with Thomas Betterton in the lead. The most famous diarist of the period, Samuel Pepys reported seeing *Hamlet* at the theater in Lincoln Inn Fields on August 24, 1661, "done with scenes very well." The elaborate staging of the Restoration *Hamlet*—Davenant introduced moveable scenery to the London stage—extended the running time of the already bloated drama and thus required major cuts to arrive at a playable length. Hamlet's advice to the players is understandably expunged. But beyond accommodations to stage time, many cuts in the Restoration *Hamlet* are concessions to the taste of the age. Davenant dutifully followed the requirements of his patent to eliminate all elements of "prophaneise and scurrility" from his production. Betterton didn't say of man "how like a god" in his 2.2 conversation with Rosencrantz and Guildenstern. Neither did he include Hamlet's threat to kill Claudius when "he is drunk, asleep or in his rage," so as to send the usurping King to Hell, the moment that Johnson found so painfully indecorous. But other elements having nothing to with religion or morality were expunged. Aspects of

Hamlet's character that register indecision, obsessive thought, and melancholy were cut. Hamlet's 2.2 soliloquy beginning "O, what a rogue and peasant slave am I" was "shorn of every hint of irresolution and self-reproach." Betterton's Hamlet is no "dull and muddy-mettled rascal"; he does not accuse himself of being a coward, of being "pigeon-livered" and lacking gall. Hamlet's 3.1 "To be or not to be" soliloquy was so well known that it couldn't be sacrificed, but much else that indicated Hamlet's "sensitivity and intellectuality" was removed. As in many productions to follow, Davenant cut Hamlet's 4.4 soliloquy beginning "How all occasions do inform against me," thus eliminating any sense that Hamlet is paralyzed by "thinking too precisely on th' event."

The cumulative effect of these alterations is to present a Hamlet suited to Restoration tastes, "cleansed of crudity, on the one hand, and complexity on the other." The overall result, one viewer reported, was an edifying spectacle of "virtue represented on stage with its proper ornaments." Restoration sensibilities do not register an interest in Hamlet as a victim of subjectivity, habitually relocating reality within his own human brain. In keeping with the character of the age, the awkwardly formed and portly Betterton played Hamlet as a man of action never diverted for very long from his mission of avenging his father's murder and setting things right in Denmark.

While *Hamlet* escaped the fate of *Macbeth* and *Measure for Measure* and other Shakespearean plays that were more radically revised during the Restoration, the Davenant Hamlet is nevertheless a travesty of the character. Stripped of psychological complexity, skepticism, and obsessive thought, the Restoration Hamlet would leave us cold today, but in its time, Betterton's Avenging Prince was universally praised. His final appearance in the role, on September 20, 1709, at age 74, brought to a close a version of *Hamlet* that had dominated the stage for more than forty years.

David Garrick succeeded Betterton as the next great Hamlet. Like Davenant, Garrick suppressed or eliminated scenes and passages that he felt violated decorum. His Hamlet doesn't call his father a "truepenny" or a "mole" or place him in the cellarage. His Ophelia makes no mention of Hamlet appearing to her in disarray, his "stockings fouled, / Ungartered and down-gyved to the ankle." Hamlet's meeting with the players was time-consuming and perhaps gratuitous, so Garrick all but eliminated this material, cutting directly, after an intermission, to Hamlet's "To be or not to be" soliloquy. One viewer remarked that the audience knew this speech as well as the Lord's Prayer. Rather than abusing Ophelia, Garrick treated her with "gentleness and delicacy" and "real tenderness." As Davenant had, he cut Hamlet's intention to send Claudius to Hell. Garrick, whose remarkable ability to shift moods in an instance transfixed audiences in his encounters with the Ghost, eliminated most of Shakespeare's fifth act, including, at least in many productions, the Gravedigger Scene. This streamlined, tidied-up *Hamlet*, stripped of its improprieties and breaches of decorum, ruled the English stage for another three decades, supplying thousands of viewers with a sanitized version of the character, purified of moroseness, misogyny, madness, and much of the interiority that Shakespeare had so carefully crafted. Together, Betterton and Garrick gave English audiences more than seventy years of Hamlet as a man of action who sets about the task of revenge with little delay or reflection.

As a way of setting the stage for the next chapter, which explores Hamlet's reception in the Romantic Movement, let me conclude by attempting to place the eighteenth century's ambivalence over Hamlet within the larger philosophical and intellectual context of the Enlightenment. Published over two years, 1734 and 1735, Alexander Pope's *An Essay on Man* appears at the height of the English neoclassical period. It is a seminal work. Recasting Milton's famous Invocation to Book One of *Paradise Lost*, Pope's mission is to "*vindicate* the ways of God to Man" (my emphasis). The four verse epistles that comprise the *Essay* place mankind in relation to the rest of creation. "Know then thyself," Pope wrote, quoting Socrates, "presume not God to scan; / The proper study of mankind is man."

The important word here is "study." Pope's aim is to extend the thrust of rational inquiry, the obsession of his age, to man himself. By "study" Pope doesn't mean the kind of self-analysis we see in Hamlet. Rather, he wants to study mankind in context. To do so, he adopts the concept of the Great Chain of Being to show man his place in the order of creation—below God and angels but above the beasts. All creation exists in this vertical configuration, held together in a *concordia discors*, literally "harmony in discord," a concept he borrowed from Horace. "All subsists," Pope writes, "by elemental strife." This tension holds every element of creation in a vital suspension, as life is constantly recycled through various forms. "Look round our World," Pope writes, "behold the chain of Love,"

> Combining all below and all above.
> See plastic Nature working to this end,
> The single atoms each to other tend,
> Attract, attracted to, the next in place
> Form'd and impell'd its neighbor to embrace.
> See Matter next, with various life endu'd,
> Press to one center still, the gen'ral Good.
> See dying vegetables life sustain,
> See life dissolving vegetate again:
> All forms that perish other forms supply,
> (By turns we catch the vital breath and die)
> Like bubbles on the sea of Matter born,
> They rise, they break, and to the sea return.

This logic reminds us of Hamlet's meditations on the fate of Alexander and Caesar, to be sure. What's different is Pope's tone. To him, the process of life falling into decay from which life is reborn is the design of a divine plan, "the chain of Love." For Hamlet, on the other hand, it's the inevitable loss of the individual mind and personality to oblivion that matters. Mortality swallows up the unique being—Yorick, Alexander, Caesar, Hamlet—taking us all, great and small, to an undiscovered country from which no traveler returns, leaving behind only skulls and bones for the living to contemplate.

For Hamlet the radical skeptic, this is not good, nor can it come to good. For Pope, however, this is the very affirmation of hope, which "springs eternal in the human breast," and of faith in a divine creator. Man is not an absolutely unique creature trapped in the endless processes of the mind, where nothing is good or bad but thinking makes it so. Rather, he is a being uniquely placed in relation to other phenomena. So

> Nothing is foreign: Parts relate to whole
> One all-extending all-preserving Soul
> Connects each being, greatest with the least;
> Made beast in aid of Man, and Man of Beast;
> All serv'd, all serving! nothing stands alone;
> The chain holds on, and where it ends, unknown.

What's important in the study of man is to recognize our place in this chain of being, the farthest reaches of which we cannot fathom. "No eye can see, / No glass can reach! from Infinite to thee, / From thee to Nothing." This realization must necessarily lead to humility, even for vaunted scientists. Pope imagines a world of "Superior beings, when of late they saw / A mortal Man unfold all Nature's law, / Admired such wisdom in an earthly shape, / And shew'd a NEWTON as we shew an Ape."

Our ability to reason distinguishes us from the lower orders. It is a blessing that enables such endeavors as the investigation of the universe, and yet it is also a curse. Those beings placed below mankind, lacking his ability to reason, are free of a terrible anxiety that consciousness produces. "The lamb thy riot dooms to bleed today," Pope writes, "Had he thy Reason, would he skip and play? / Pleased to the last he crops the flow'ry food, / And licks the hand just raised to shed his blood." But neither is man in all ways materially superior to the lower orders. Why doesn't man have a microscopic eye? "For this plain reason, Man is not a Fly."

"Plac'd on this isthmus of a middle state," man is distinct from higher and lower orders of being, but he is inseparable from his own kind, from the society in which he lives. Man's "jarring int'rests of themselves create, / Th' according music of a well-mix'd State." His "partial ill is universal Good." It is not his peculiar experience, therefore, that matters: "the Universal Cause / Acts not by partial, but by gen'ral laws." Our awareness of our place in the plenitude, in the fullness of creation, leads inescapably to the conclusion, repeated several times in the *Essay*, that "Whatever is, is right." There can be no more forceful challenge to Hamlet's relativism than this claim.

Scientific inquiry is the engine of Pope's optimism, directing his thinking outward, as it were, from individual consciousness to the general experience of the species. The recognition of our place in "this isthmus of a middle state" is a check to excessive pride, on the one hand, and to excessive self-loathing, on the other—both of which Hamlet, lacking Pope's perspective, has in abundance. If Pope's "study" is outwardly directed, Hamlet's "study" is inwardly directed, endlessly analyzing the facets of his own consciousness. To be sure, Hamlet acknowledges the chain of being. "What a piece of work is a man," he exclaims to Rosencrantz and Guildenstern, "how noble in reason; how infinite in faculties, in form and moving; how express and admirable in action; how like an angel in apprehension; how like a god; the beauty of the world, the paragon of animals." But he immediately removes himself from this uplifting context. To him, man is only "a quintessence of dust." He takes no delight in man or woman.

Such pessimism is inimical to Pope, and yet there is much in the *Essay on Man* that seems Hamlet-like. Man, Pope writes, is "a being darkly wise and rudely great." He warns that science must avoid "tricks to shew the stretch of human brain"; he speaks of our early recognition of "the lurking principle of death" that becomes "the Mind's disease." And in some instances—Hamlet might serve as a case in point—men "swell'd to Gods, confess ev'n Virtue vain." These faults, which result from a failure to achieve and maintain a rational perspective, are the hallmarks of Hamlet's character. He knows no happiness because he cannot see himself in proper relation to all else. His isolation results in emotional chaos—doubt, fear, and sadness—with which the Romantic Movement, which I consider next, will closely identify. *Hamlet* rather than *An Essay on Man* will shape the sensibilities of the generation that comes of age at the close of the eighteenth century.

SIX

HAMLET AMONG THE ROMANTICS

A BRIEF HISTORY OF GRIEF

The eighteenth century's devotion to reason faded as the Romantic Movement took shape at century's end. In poetry, this new age was inaugurated by the publication in 1798 of *Lyrical Ballads*, a collection of poems by Samuel Taylor Coleridge and William Wordsworth that explored the emotional response to life in a radically new kind of poetry freed from the constraints of symmetry and decorum that had dominated the previous age. Romantic poetry emphasized the value of emotion over thought, finding truth in the experience of the heart rather than the head. In the famous Preface added to the second edition of the *Lyrical Ballads* in 1800 (expanded in a third edition of 1802), Wordsworth stated that his purpose was "to choose incidents and situations from common life, and to relate or describe them, throughout, as far as possible, in a selection of language really used by men." Accordingly, Wordsworth rejected as artificial the poetic diction and forms, principally the couplet, favored by the generations of Pope and Johnson, in favor of simpler, more authentic forms such as the lyric and ballad stanza. "Low and rustic life was generally chosen," Wordsworth wrote, "because in that condition, the essential passions of the heart find a better soil in which they can attain maturity, are less under restraint, and speak a plainer and more emphatic language, because in that condition of life our elementary feelings co-exist in a state of greater simplicity, and, consequently may be more accurately contemplated, and more forcibly communicated." The poet stands in contrast to the scientist, who "seeks truth as a remote and unknown benefactor; [who] cherishes and loves it in his solitude." For the poet, truth is much closer at hand. "The poet, singing a song in which all human beings join him, rejoices in the presence of truth as our visible friend and hourly companion." This truth is apprehended by emotions rather than reason. "All good poetry," Wordsworth famously declared, "is the spontaneous overflow of powerful feelings . . . recollected in tranquility."

As the Romantic Movement takes shape, a radically different valuation of Hamlet emerges. Hamlet is increasingly idealized and internalized as an expression of profound grief for the passing of youth. The Romantics internalize Hamlet, just as Hamlet internalizes reality in F1. For them, he is youth transient and tragic, lost to time.

The first writer to register this new interpretation of Hamlet is not English but German. In *Wilhelm Meister's Apprenticeship* (1795–96) Johann Wolfgang von Goethe inaugurated a new subgenre of the fast-developing, relatively young form of the novel: the bildungsroman, or coming-of-age novel. The protagonist Wilhelm is a developing actor and producer who has only recently become acquainted with Shakespeare. Immediately, he conceives Hamlet as a blood relation. As Wilhelm's disillusionment with life and the theater deepens, he is drawn to the Melancholic Prince, whom he figures as a stepbrother, Shakespeare being his surrogate parent.

> His friend Shakespeare, whom with the greatest joy he acknowledged as his god-
> father, and rejoiced the more that his name was Wilhelm, had introduced him to
> a prince, who frolicked for a time among mean, nay, vicious companions, and who
> notwithstanding his nobleness of nature, found pleasure in the rudeness, inde-
> cency and coarse intemperance of these altogether sensual knaves. This ideal like-
> ness, which he figured as the type and the excuse of his own actual condition, was
> most welcome. . . .

In Meister's identification with Hamlet we have a virtually complete and succinct Romantic take on the character. The paternal identification confirmed by the patronymic coincidence—William and Wilhelm—casts the young actor Wilhelm as Shakespeare's stepson, Hamlet's surrogate brother. It is as brothers to Hamlet that a young generation of Englishmen and Europeans at the turn of the nine-teenth century will, in part, define itself. But Hamlet is only superficially a sibling to the Romantics. Even in Goethe's seminal novel, Hamlet is something deeper, closer than a brother. He is an idealized version of the self. In the martyred Hamlet, Meister finds his "ideal likeness" and "the type and excuse of his own actual condi-tion," a perfect young man of noble nature beset and doomed by vicious, rude, inde-cent, and coarsely sensual knaves; a virgin sacrificed in a den of debauchery.

As Wilhelm studies Hamlet, a kind of mourning mixed with empathy charac-terizes his growing attachment. "I . . . conceived that I was penetrating quite into the spirit of the character, while I endeavoured as it were to take upon myself the load of deep melancholy under which my prototype was labouring." As he learns more and approaches closer to the heart of the matter, he has no doubt that he will "by and by become one with my hero." This idealization completely suppresses the darkest aspects of Hamlet's character: his brutalization of Ophelia, his killing of Polonius and his denigration and mockery of the old man's corpse, and his dis-patching of Rosencrantz and Guildenstern. Behind these troubling features Wilhelm attempts to recover what he can of Hamlet's essential character, looking to find Hamlet before the murder of his father was discovered and the terribly dis-figuring burden of revenge fell upon him. Wilhelm concludes that "[p]leasing in form, polished by nature, courteous from the heart, [Hamlet] was meant to be the pattern of youth and the joy of the world." Given the impossible circumstances that confront him, Hamlet's reluctance to act is not only understandable but heroic, the source of his tragic stature. Hamlet is a costly jar in which an oak tree is planted; the roots expand, the jar is shivered. This is an odd metaphor but an apt one, since Hamlet himself repeatedly presents us with containers—prisons, wards, confines, skulls, a nutshell: "A lovely, pure, noble and most moral nature, without the strength of nerve which forms a hero, sinks beneath a burden which it cannot bear and must not cast away." Wilhelm's responses to Hamlet become more elegiac as he comes closer to a full understanding of the character. Wilhelm's sentimental, idealized grief might then be seen as a reflection of Goethe's lament for something lost. This lost something is perhaps the lost youth of the middle-aged writer himself—Goethe was forty-seven when he completed the novel—resurrected in Wilhelm Meister.

In terms of familial relations, if Hamlet is nominally a brother to Wilhelm, he is stepson to Goethe himself, with Shakespeare standing in the relation of brother to Goethe, fulfilling relationally Goethe's mentor Johann Herder's call for a German Shakespeare. This may be to extend the familial network too far, but there can be no doubt that, in time, Hamlet will stand in a profound way for the soul of nineteenth-century Germany. Germany saw itself as the Melancholic Prince. In 1844 Ferdinand Freiligrath published a remarkable poem titled "Hamlet," which begins with the line "Deutschland ist Hamlet." It followed an 1842 poem by Albert Knapp titled "Deutschland ist Hamlet." Like Hamlet, one commentator noted, Germans "have been deeply absorbed with the occupation of the mind and the cultivation of the heart, even to a forgetfulness of the world." Like Hamlet, they have "lost delight" in existence and grown "skeptically embittered against the world, life, and mankind." Gifted with the "qualities for esteeming human worth," he wrote, "we excited ourselves into misanthropy, and with such a vocation for active service in the world, we indulged in *weltschmerz*— a passive universal suffering."

In 1815, the hugely influential lectures on Shakespeare by the German critic and philosopher August Wilhelm Schlegel (1767–1845), published in translation as *Lectures on Dramatic Art and Literature*, became available to English readers. "*Hamlet*," Schlegel remarked, "is singular in its kind: a tragedy of thought inspired by continual and never-satisfied meditation on human destiny." *Hamlet* as a tragedy of thought is a distinct contrast to Goethe's idealizing of the character. For Schlegel, Hamlet is a victim of chronic thinking. Necessarily, then, "Hamlet has no firm belief either in himself or in anything else, from expressions of religious confidence [in the 1.2 soliloquy, for example] he passes over to skeptical doubts." Schlegel notes Hamlet's relativism in 2.2: "there is nothing either good or bad, but thinking makes it so."

Goethe, on the one hand, and Schlegel, on the other, provide the two dominant Romantic views of Hamlet—as the ideal young prince ruined by a vile, corrupt world, and as the thought-plagued melancholic. These are not necessarily exclusive views, of course—one may incorporate a Goethean idealism into a darker view of Hamlet as tormented thinker. Still, they are distinctly different interpretations of the character.

These two conceptions of Hamlet were channeled to the English Romantics by Samuel Taylor Coleridge (1772–1834). Coleridge advanced the understanding of Hamlet a step beyond Goethe and Schlegel by arguing that Hamlet's fundamental problem is the imbalance of thought and action. In Hamlet, Coleridge writes, Shakespeare

> seems to have wished to exemplify the moral necessity of a due balance between our attention to the objects of our senses, and our meditation on the working of our minds—an *equilibrium* between the real and imaginary worlds. In Hamlet this balance is disturbed: his thoughts and the images of his fancy are far more vivid than his actual perceptions, and his very perceptions, instantly passing through the *medium* of his contemplations, acquire, as they pass, a form and colour not naturally their own.

> The effect of this overbalance of the imaginative power is beautifully illustrated in the everlasting broodings and superfluous activities of Hamlet's mind, which, unseated from its healthy relation, is constantly occupied with the world within, and abstracted from the world without—giving substance to shadows, and throwing a mist over all commonplace actualities.

For the first time, a writer explicitly says what becomes a commonplace of Hamlet studies, that Hamlet's problem is his inability to act. In Hamlet thought so dominates that it precludes the necessary duty he must perform—the avenging of his father's murder. The effect of this "disproportionate mental exertion" Coleridge identifies as *taedium vitae*, "which necessitates exhaustion of bodily feeling."

By considering the relationship between thought and action, Coleridge introduces a reading of Hamlet that underlies virtually all modern (and postmodern) positions on the play, one that hinges upon a belief that reality is a matter of perception, of thought; nothing is either good or bad, as Hamlet says, but thinking makes it so. For Hamlet the final reality, Coleridge suggests, is a function of the mind, and the mental exertion required to construct this reality takes an enormous toll on the disposition, exhausting what Coleridge terms "bodily feeling."

According to notes taken by an attendee of Coleridge's important but never published Twelfth Lecture on *Richard II* and *Hamlet*, delivered in January 1812, the poet praised Hamlet as Shakespeare's "finest conception and working out of a character." But Hamlet is also a lesson in the debilitating results of thought. "Shakespeare wished to impress upon us the truth that action is the great end of existence—that no faculties of intellect however brilliant can be considered valuable, or otherwise than as misfortunes, if they withdraw us from or render us repugnant to action, and lead us to think and think of doing, until the time has escaped when we ought to have acted."

Coleridge advances our understanding of Hamlet by, first, removing the robe of idealism that Goethe had cloaked him in and, second, stressing the conflict between thought and action, taking us considerably closer to our modern belief in the preeminence of individual consciousness, or, better, the inability to escape or get beyond consciousness. But, like Goethe, he vests much importance in Hamlet as a figure of loss, the focus of the writer's own psychic bereavement. At the conclusion of Coleridge's lecture on Hamlet, a listener remarked to the diarist Henry Crabb Robinson that Coleridge had delivered a satire on himself, to which Robinson replied, aptly, that it was not a satire but an elegy. Robinson suggested that Coleridge's response to Hamlet is really grief for himself, something absent or dead within him.

"I have a smack of Hamlet myself," Coleridge famously remarked later in life. Like Goethe, Coleridge is internalizing the character. Coleridge, too, knows Coleridge as the refraction of Hamlet. Coleridge must be fundamentally understood as an elegist, it has been argued, a man plagued as Hamlet was by a melancholic mourning. Watching Shakespeare sacrifice Hamlet as Abraham had offered up Isaac, Coleridge sees the sacrifice of his own self, a youth of enormous desire and capacity lost with age (a loss accelerated, in Coleridge's case, by drug addiction) that makes Coleridge's remarks on Hamlet an elegy for the self.

A reaction similarly located in a sense of loss, bereavement, and melancholy is found in William Wordsworth, Coleridge's sometime friend and collaborator, the author of the manifesto of English Romanticism in the *Lyrical Ballads*. In 1812, the same year that Coleridge delivered his lecture of Hamlet, Wordsworth remarked to Crabb Robinson that he, Wordsworth, was "one of the happiest of men." This state of mind, however, would prove unsustainable. In the same year, Wordsworth was devastated by the deaths of his six-year-old son Thomas and his five-year-old daughter Catherine, losses from which he never fully recovered. Indeed, grief is a constant strain in the poetry of this "happiest of men." Much earlier, in "Ode: Intimations of Immortality"—prefaced with the aphorism, "Child is Father of the Man"—Wordsworth had powerfully mourned the passing of youth. In the fifth stanza of the "Ode," Wordsworth alludes to Hamlet while describing the growth of the newborn through youth:

> Heaven lies about us in our infancy!
> Shades of the prison-house begin to close
> Upon the Growing Boy
> But he beholds the light, and whence it flows,
> He sees it in his joy
>
>   * * *
>
> At length the Man perceives it die away,
> And fade into the light of common day.

"Shades of the prison-house" echoes a passage in 1.5 of *Hamlet*, when Old Hamlet tells his son that he is forbidden "To tell the secrets of my prison-house." But, significantly, Wordsworth figures the inmate as youth rather than age, presenting us, as it were, with Hamlet Jr. rather than Hamlet Sr., in effect, transferring the experience of the parents to their children. Brooding Wordsworth felt a special affinity for "Hamlet the soliloquist of mortality," in whom the poet found a model for the inadequacy of his own grief, as expressed in "The Vale of Esthwaite": "I mourn because I mourn'd no more." Wordsworth's repositioning of Hamlet Sr.'s experience—imprisoning the young man rather than the old one—offers a new context for this generation of English intellectuals as they age, returning to the figure of a young man dying, an experience we must mourn, as Man, Wordsworth writes, watches youth "die away / And fade into the light of common day."

To be sure, Wordsworth resists mourning in the "Intimations" ode; even in old age vestiges of youth, the essence of which can be appreciated only in age, survive:

> O joy! That in our embers
> Is something that doth live,
> That nature yet remembers
> What was so fugitive.

Thus,

> We will grieve not, rather find
> Strength in what remains behind;
> In the primal sympathy
> Which having been must ever be;
>
>   * * *
>
> In the faith that looks through death
> In years that bring the philosophic mind.

The problem is this: the philosophic mind cannot help but be ever mindful of human suffering, of inevitable loss and the anticipation of death. The very passage in which Wordsworth turns away from grief is itself deeply elegiac, a lament for all that must inevitably pass.

"Whether is fled the visionary gleam?" asks Wordsworth, only a few short years before he lost two children, "Where is it now, the glory and the dream?"

For Coleridge, Hamlet is a version of himself as he once was—or might have been. For Wordsworth, Hamlet is the child that is the father to man. Two things are happening here simultaneously: Following Goethe and Schlegel, Coleridge institutionalizes for the English Romantics Hamlet as a version of the lost self. At the same time, Wordsworth's Hamlet exchanges roles with his simpatico father. This means, paradoxically, that Hamlet, the Western world's collective dead son, is also its collective dead father. Hamlet appears to the future at once both dead son and dead father.

Later Romantics also evince a radical and painful identification with Hamlet. "This is that Hamlet the Dane," William Hazlitt writes in *Characters of Shakespeare's Plays* (1818), "whom we read of in our youth, and whom we may be said almost to remember in our after-years." Hamlet's thoughts, he continues,

> are as real as our own thoughts. The reality is in the reader's mind. It is we who are Hamlet. This play has a prophetic truth, which is above that of history. Whoever has become thoughtful and melancholy through his own mishaps or that of others; whoever has borne about with him the clouded brow of reflection, and thought himself "too much i' the sun"; whoever has seen the golden lamp of day dimmed by mists rising in his own breast, and could find in the world before him only a dull blank with nothing left remarkable in it; whoever has known "the pangs of despised love, the insolence of office, or the spurns that patient merit of the unworthy takes"; he who has felt his mind sink within him, and sadness cling to his heart like a malady, who has had his hopes blighted and his youth staggered by the apparitions of strange things; who cannot be well at ease, while he sees evil hovering near him like a spectre; whose powers of action have been eaten up by thought; whose bitterness of soul makes him careless of consequences, and who

goes to a play as his best resource to shove off, to a second remove, the evils of life by a mock representation of them—this is the true Hamlet.

Hazlitt's Hamlet begins life in this paragraph as a kind of Everyman—"It is we who are Hamlet"—universal, timeless. Yet as his meditation continues, as more and more particulars accrue, as "thought" and "melancholy" and "mishaps" "cloud the brow"; as the world becomes to the speaker "a dull blank with nothing left remarkable"; as the mind sinks and "sadness cling[s] to his heart like a malady"; as his hopes are blighted and youth staggered and he comes to see himself bitterly as nothing, as he turns, a melancholic figure, to the theater where he sees "the evils of life" mocked in a play—the Hamlet we see at the end of this passage is less Everyman than he is a version, one feels, of Hazlitt himself, of this particular man differentiated from others by the specifics of loss. The dead Hamlet is really the young man, now dead, that the forty-year-old Hazlitt once was. He is no longer the universal Hamlet of "we" but an internalized, particularized Hamlet of "I." This replication of Goethe's and Coleridge's internalization of Hamlet as doomed youth reasserts, again, the Romantic notion of the self as the center of things.

"Reality is in the reader's mind," Hazlett writes, echoing Hamlet in 2.2, "staggered by the apparitions of strange things."

The reaction to Hamlet as the soul of suffering is particularly intense among Europeans at the end of the Romantic period. To Fyodor Dostoevsky, writing in 1838, the encounter with Hamlet threatens to tear his soul to pieces: "Hamlet! Hamlet! When I think of his moving wild speech, in which he resounds the groaning of the whole numbed universe, there breaks from my soul not one reproach, not one sigh. . . . That soul has been so oppressed by woe that it fears to grasp the woe entire, lest so it lacerate itself." There is an important difference, or reversal, I should say, here: Dostoevsky's reach is outward, from the self to the universe, coupling, as Hamlet repeatedly does, earth to heaven to hell, here to there, inside to outside. The enormous psychic expense figures itself as a grief so overwhelming that it can allow nothing to escape from it. It's a black hole that threatens to swallow everything. The soul can't afford to "grasp the woe entire," or else grief would lacerate the soul. Hamlet's appalling misery is both particular and universal, limited and delimited, personal and cosmic.

Voltaire had dismissed *Hamlet* as "a vile and barbarous drama, which would not be tolerated by the vilest populace of France, or Italy," but half a century later his countryman Hector Berlioz responded very differently. Berlioz was emotionally and psychologically consumed by *Hamlet*, under whose influence he labored for much of his life. Indeed, *Hamlet* would inspire some of the composer's greatest work. He described attending his first performance of the play in 1827, with the Irish actress he would later marry, Harriet Smithson, playing Ophelia. "[T]he melancholy, the heart-rending griefs, the weeping love, the cruel irony, the black meditations, the heart-breaks, the madness, the tears, the mourning, the catastrophes, the sinister accidents of *Hamlet* . . . the black clouds, the icy winds of Denmark"—all this "was too much," he confessed. At the third act, Berlioz felt an iron hand grip his heart and he said to himself "with complete conviction: 'Ah, I am lost.'" Insomniac, he wandered the streets of Paris in a "nervous condition like an illness which only an outstanding doctor could give an adequate account." On occasions, at the end of this lengthy period of meanderings, he fell into "a deep, death-like sleep"—spending one night unconscious in a corn field, another in a field in the middle of the day, still another in the snow on the banks of the frozen Seine, and still another in a café.

At the time of his encounter with Hamlet Berlioz didn't understand a word of English.

A "nervous condition like an illness which only an outstanding doctor could give adequate account." For Dostoevsky and Berlioz, as for countless thousands of others, the wild emotions Hamlet triggers—the delirium, the frantic grief, the *weltchmerz*—amount to something like true mental illness. The "outstanding doctor" Berlioz appeals to can only be a physician of the mind, a specialty that had not yet been developed. The future will dwell extensively upon the question, where and when is Hamlet mad? Indeed, the development of psychology and, later, psychiatry will sustain an interest in the play as a fundamental record in annals of the distracted globe.

SEVEN

"THIS DISTRACTED GLOBE"

HAMLET AND MELANCHOLY

On Friday, January 18, 1760, Lawrence Shirley, fourth Earl of Ferrers—a descendent of the Earl of Essex, whose uprising had exploited Shakespeare's acting company in the staging of *Richard II*—summoned his capable steward, John Johnson, to his estate near Ashby-de-la-Zouch in Leicestershire. Ferrers ordered Johnson to his knees, shouted, "Your time is come—you must die," and shot him.

Ferrers assaulted Johnson in an alcohol-induced, paranoiac rage. When sober, he seems to have been a likable man, sensible and decent; drunk, he was a brute. But as an earl he was a man of enormous privilege. He owned estates in Leicestershire, Derbyshire, and Northamptonshire, and held a seat in the House of Lords. For years Ferrers had kept a high-born mistress, Margaret Clifford, who must have been a dissolute soul, with whom he had four children, all girls. Though he maintained his relationship with Clifford long after his marriage ended—she was at his estate that Friday when Ferrers shot Johnson—he wasn't about to marry her. He needed sons, and so he seized a better opportunity nearby; he married the sixteen-year-old daughter of Sir William Meredith of Cheshire.

Ferrers brutalized his young wife so egregiously that she returned to her family in terror and disgrace. The wealthy and upstanding Meredith promptly appealed to the House of Lords for a separation of his daughter from the violent and cruel Ferrers. Not only did the Lords grant the separation, they also ordered Ferrers to provide for Meredith's daughter's maintenance for the rest of her life. This payment—a form of alimony, really—would come from rents from Ferrers' estates.

Parliament appointed his steward Johnson, a man "distinguished for the regular manner in which he kept his accounts, and his fidelity as a steward," to oversee these forfeitures. Delusional and enraged, believing that Johnson was colluding with his ex-wife's family to ruin him, Ferrers determined to kill the man.

Gravely wounded, Johnson managed to rise to his feet and beg not to be further harmed. Lost in a brandy fugue, Ferrers helped carry Johnson to a bed, washed his wound, and summoned a surgeon. Telling the surgeon that Johnson was more frightened than hurt, the earl retired to his apartment and took to his cups again. While Johnson lay dying, Ferrers drank himself into new fits of rage. During one of these he attacked the wounded man a second time, threatening to shoot him through the head. Later that night Ferrers assured the terrified household that he, Ferrers, would not be arrested, that he had just cause for shooting Johnson. And besides, Johnson wasn't badly hurt.

In the middle of the night, the surgeon—who had risked his own life coming into a mansion occupied by a drunken, paranoid maniac—bundled Johnson in a chair and had him carried home, where he died in his own bed the next morning.

News of Johnson's murder spread quickly through the village. A crowd gathered on the lawn of the estate. The forty-year-old earl appeared at the window several times and ranted at the villagers below. Later that day, a heavily armed Ferrers was cornered in his stables as he mounted a horse, preparing to flee. Faced with no possibility of escape, Ferrers surrendered, was arrested, and confined in the Tower of London. His trial before the House of Lords in April 1760 was one of the most sensational events of the century. Ferrers defended himself vigorously and articulately on the grounds of insanity, though he seems to have mounted this defense to mollify his disgraced family. But the Lords determined that he was aware of the gravity of his act and, on the eighteenth, the body that had granted the separation and ordered the maintenance of Mary Meredith, found him guilty of murder. The Lords unanimously condemned Ferrers to death.

On May 5 Earl Ferrers—the last of its members the House of Lords condemned to die as a common criminal—was taken from the Tower to Tyburn in a carriage, through crowds so dense that the trip of a few miles took two and a half hours. Ferrers was having a very bad day. Twice he asked to stop for a drink, but was convinced that that wouldn't be a good idea. At Tyburn, the condemned man, dressed all in white, walked to the scaffold fitted, for the first time in history, with a trap floor, a device English theater had used for many years with great success. Dropping the condemned man would snap his neck, meaning instant death.

Presumably, Earl Ferrers didn't know of this innovation. Until then, the method of hanging involved pushing the condemned man off the edge of the scaffold, or hauling him up by the neck. At Tyburn he stood calm and composed in a white suit as a white hood was pulled over his head. He listened as the Twenty-third Psalm was read but declined to recite it himself. He stood silent while his arms were bound, and the noose tightened at his throat. At the sheriff's sign, Earl Ferrers was dropped into eternity. The body was left hanging for an hour, then cut down and taken to Surgeon's Hall where it was eviscerated, and, as prescribed, displayed in the viewing room. Three days later, the remains were released to friends for interment.

Ferrers would be of no particular interest to us but that, the night before he was executed, he asked that *Hamlet* be read to him. This is a surprising request, certainly not the kind of reading that would take one's mind off his dire situation. Indeed, his extraordinary circumstance confers a special importance on this choice. Samuel Johnson famously remarked that "when a man knows he is to be hanged in a fortnight, it concentrates his mind wonderfully."

What was Ferrers looking for in *Hamlet*? Perhaps he found a connection between his own circumstance and Hamlet's. At his trial he had mounted a defense of insanity, but admitted his guilt privately to his intimates. Maybe in the drunken Danish court Ferrers saw a place for himself, for his own besotted life. Perhaps in Hamlet's brutal treatment of Ophelia and Gertrude, Ferrers saw mirrored his abuse of his own wife. Perhaps Ferrers saw in Hamlet's killing of Polonius a version of his rash attack on Johnson. Maybe he turned to Hamlet as a model of resolve and courage in the face of death. No matter how drunk he could get in the Tower, after all, he couldn't have passed over the meditation on skulls in 5.1. Ferrers must have anticipated that moment when he would enter the company of those successful and high-born individuals whose skulls the Clown and Hamlet toy with.

What specific reflections came to Earl Ferrers in his final night, we can't, of course, know. Reality for Ferrers, as for Hamlet, was subjective and contingent. We can't know what he was thinking or feeling. But we can fairly deduce that in Hamlet Ferrers saw a version of himself, which is to say, a man suffering from genuine mental disease. *Hamlet* is, clearly, the record of a disturbed mind, though there is ample method to it. Whether we are talking about alcoholism or depression or mania or any combination of these, or any of the myriad other mental disorders, *Hamlet* is a play about a distressed mind. Evidence for this is overwhelming: Twice Hamlet threatens suicide, the first time, in 1.2, even before he learns that his uncle has murdered his father. Then follow other signs of what today we recognize as manic-depressive or bipolar disorder. Hamlet ruthlessly abuses the largely guiltless Ophelia. He verbally attacks his mother and in the same scene murders Polonius. He launches off onto tangents of too-precise thought—considering, for instance, how a beggar may make a progress through the guts of a king. He himself admits his own distractedness. Just before the duel with Laertes in 5.2, he says

> What I have done
> That might your nature, honor and exception
> Roughly awake, I here proclaim was madness.
> Was't Hamlet wronged Laertes? Never Hamlet!
> If Hamlet from himself be ta'en away,
> Then Hamlet does it not; Hamlet denies it.
> Who does it then? His madness.

Looking back through the play, this admission of madness seems as genuine as it is obviously convenient to the circumstance.

Let's take a closer look at manifestations of Hamlet's mental instability. In his first soliloquy, even before he has confronted the ghost of his murdered father and been burdened with the account of that murder and the responsibility to avenge it, Hamlet presents himself as suicidal. Before he turns with revulsion to his mother's marriage, he yearns to obliterate himself:

> O that this too too [sullied] flesh would melt,
> Thaw and resolve itself into a dew,
> Or that the Everlasting had not fixed
> His canon 'gainst self slaughter.

He suffers a generalized malaise, an exhausted contempt for all things, for *every-thing*, a posture of world weariness congenial to the young.

> How weary, stale, flat and unprofitable
> Seem to me all the uses of this world!
> Fie on't, ah fie, 'tis an unweeded garden
> That grows to seed, things rank and gross in nature
> Possess it merely.

This self-destructive motif resurfaces in Hamlet's most famous meditation:

> To be, or not to be—that is the question;
> Whether 'tis nobler in the mind to suffer
> The slings and arrows of outrageous fortune
> Or to take arms against a sea of troubles
> And by opposing end them; to die: to sleep—
> No more, and by a sleep to say we end
> The heartache and the thousand natural shocks
> That flesh is heir to: 'tis a consummation
> Devoutly to be wished.

Hamlet's suicidal impulses spring in part from his sense of unfulfilled prom-ise, a cue that Coleridge and others seem to respond to. This must include the painful realization that Hamlet's uncle has thwarted his ambitions, usurped from him the crown of Denmark. His distress, his imbalance, is compounded by encounters with the Ghost that, in its final appearance in the play, is seen only by Hamlet. The Ghost selectively presents itself. This is a cruel twist that has the effect of making Hamlet appear mad to his mother. Returned home from the uni-versity for his father's funeral, directionless, perhaps hallucinating at times, eventu-ally bearing the terrible burden of grief compounded with the demand of revenge, Hamlet sees himself as a manifestation of existential, indeed cosmic, failure and loss. When he spews a bitter stream of misogynistic taunts at Ophelia, claiming "It"—his hatred of himself and women—"hath made me mad," he is telling at least a partial truth; there's no doubt that here and elsewhere Hamlet is genuinely unhinged.

But not always. I don't want to obscure or obfuscate or underestimate Hamlet's self-possessed craft—his controlled manipulation of guises, his skill at *appearing* mad. His character, as I discussed in an earlier chapter, is deeply rooted in the tradition of feigned madness. For both Saxo's Amleth and Belleforest's Hamblet, the assumption of an "antic wit," as Hamlet calls it, is essential for their survival, a mask behind which they hide and scheme, sharpening staves with which to ensnare and kill their enemies. Examples of the wise fool are everywhere, dating back in Greek tradition to Odysseus, who fakes madness to avoid going to Troy, and in Roman tradition to Lucius Brutus, who feigned foolishness as a means of escaping the danger from Tarquin, who had murdered his brother. Indeed, the name "Brutus," like "Hamlet," etymologically suggests foolishness or dullness, while the character's circumstance, like Hamlet's, suggests that this foolishness is a form of wisdom, a cover to allow the character time to strategize.

In Christian tradition we can trace the figure of the wise fool to Paul's remarks to the Corinthians: "Has not God made foolish the wisdom of the world? For since in the wisdom of the world, through its wisdom did not know him, God was pleased through the foolishness of what was preached to save those who believe" (1 Cor. 1: 20–21). And later: "For the foolishness of God is wiser than man's wisdom, and the weakness of God is stronger than man's strength" (25). Christians are willing to be persecuted here on earth because they know that bliss follows; that for the label of fool in this life they will receive in exchange the wisdom of eternity. In the humanist movement, Erasmus' seminal work on the history of folly, *Encomium Moriae* (1511), whose title translates as "The Praise of Folly," evokes the tradition through the etymological correspondence of "More" and "*mores*," meaning in Latin black and stupid and late. Erasmus announces in the dedicatory letter to his English friend Thomas More, who became Henry VIII's lord chancellor in 1529 and was executed in 1535 for refusing to sign the Act of Supremacy, that he, More, is as far from foolishness as his name is close to it. More, of course, refashioned this amalgam of wisdom and folly in his own life—he planted mulberry trees in his yard, and his coat of arms featured a black face, "mulberry" and "black" sharing the etymology *mores*. In his own *Utopia*, which in many ways is an answer to Erasmus' *The Praise of Folly*, More fashioned the protagonist's name, Raphael Hythlodeus, which may be interpreted as "a trilingual pun," a compound of Hebrew, Greek, and Latin roots—*Raphael* from the Hebrew meaning "God heals"; *Huthlos*, from the Greek meaning "through the nonsense"; and *deus*, from the Latin for God. God heals through the nonsense of God. This yoking of wisdom and folly so resonated among humanists that they literalized it, bringing "fools" into their households to share their quotidian lives (see figure 7.1).

Shakespeare incorporates the oxymoron of wise folly with the remarkable history of stage fools, dating back to the Commedia dell' Arte, to create *Twelfth Night*'s Feste and Lear's scourging fool, characters who enjoy the immunity provided by the guise, and who speak wisely through riddles. The chronology of Shakespeare's fools may be significant. The first reported performance of *Twelfth Night* occurred

THE FAMILY OF SIR THOMAS MORE

Figure 7.1 The More household, from a sketch by Hans Holbein the younger, with Henry Patenson, More's "fool," fourth from right, standing. Author's collection.

on February 2, 1602; so the play may have been written as late as 1601, at about the same time as *Hamlet*, perhaps a little later. And then Lear's fool, Shakespeare's most brilliant and sophisticated example of the type, comes six or seven years later. If the melancholic Jaques of *As You Like It* (1599), though not technically a fool, is in some ways a prototype of Hamlet, then Hamlet may be the pattern of Shakespeare's later fools.

The wise fool may be, this is to say, the deepest aspect of Hamlet's character. In fact, there is good reason to portray him as just that: Ophelia describes him showing up when she is sewing, disheveled, giving every appearance of being crazy, every bit the fool. Hamlet's ancestors, Amleth and Hamblet, pretend to be chickens, flapping their arms wildly. This isn't quite Shakespearean. His Hamlet bursts through "with his doublet all unbraced, / No hat upon his head, his stockings fouled / Ungartered and down-gyved to his ankle." He has come to her as a ghost, "Pale as is his shirt, his knees knocking each other." And Ophelia sees to the heart of this antic. Hamlet's look is "so piteous in purport / As if he had been loosed out of hell / To speak of horrors." Taunting her, Hamlet has come to her chamber in the ghostly guise of his father.

For Hamlet, folly is a craft practiced to achieve an end. He tells Guildenstern, "I am but mad north-north-west. When the wind is southerly I know a hawk from a handsaw," cryptically suggesting that he is not really insane. It has been argued that Hamlet's pretending to be mad is gratuitous since, unlike his ancestors in Danish myth, Hamlet has nothing to fear from Claudius since the new King doesn't suspect Hamlet's knowledge of his father's murder. But I disagree. Claudius, having killed Old Hamlet, might be predisposed to kill again, and, if so, Hamlet, the principal challenger to the crown, would be his obvious target. (Indeed, after Polonius' death, Claudius does send Hamlet to England with orders to have him killed.) Subtle evidence indicates that Hamlet has all along suspected that Claudius killed his father. When Old Hamlet tells him that his own brother dispatched him, Hamlet cries, "O my *prophetic* soul! My uncle!" (my emphasis).

Hamlet prudently assumes the guise of madness as both a means of preempting a strike from Claudius and of buying time to plot revenge. At the end of his meeting with the Ghost in 1.5, Hamlet makes his friends swear that they will not betray him:

> Here as before: never—so help you mercy,
> How strange or odd some'er I bear myself

(As I perchance hereafter shall think meet
To put an antic disposition on)—

      * * *

. . . . That you know aught of me. This do swear,
So grace and mercy at your most need help you.

Feigning madness, Hamlet acquires a strategic advantage, like his previous itera-
tions using the guise of madness to gain time.

From his first words in 1.2, "kin" and "kind" and "sun"—pointing to what's
familial and alien, common and cloudy—Hamlet the wise fool stands these concepts on their heads. His brilliant sophistication makes a simpleton of Claudius,
playing upon him as upon a stringed instrument. The blundering Polonius—just
smart and sinister enough to get himself killed—understands that Hamlet's replies
are pregnant, that there's method in this madness, wisdom nesting in folly. His is a
"happiness that often madness hits on, which reason and sanity could not prosper-
ously be delivered of," Polonius says. As in Saxo and Belleforest, in *Hamlet* Hamlet
becomes a scourge who will effect a great bloody cleansing of the Danish royal
household.

Hamlet, though, will not play the fool through to the end. He assumes the
guise of fool only to discard it as he approaches death. In the Closet Scene,
Hamlet's father, in his last appearance, is visible only to him, not to his mother.
This cruel deception makes Gertrude think that Hamlet is, in fact, mad, that he is
hallucinating. But Hamlet insists the opposite is true. Here, he begins to shed this
wise-fool identity as he assumes a new avatar as scourge and minister, the avenger
of his father's murder. "It is not madness / That I have uttered," he tells his mother,
challenging her to "bring me to the test." By the fifth act Hamlet has become something greater—and less—than the wise fool.

If the putting-*on* of folly places Hamlet within the framework of the wise fool
tradition, the putting-*off* of this identity marks Hamlet as tragic hero. In the end,
what is lost in Hamlet's transition from clown or fool to hero is precisely the keen
wit with which Hamlet had combated his enemies—Claudius, Gertrude,
Rosencrantz and Guildenstern—earlier in the play. Hamlet shares this devolution
with Shakespeare's Prince Hal, who sacrifices his verbal facility as he rises to
become Henry V. The young waggish prince who had sparred with the great
Falstaff, renounces him in *2 Henry IV* with "I know thee not old man. Fall to thy
prayers." This cold rejection kills the old man. Hal is more than he was in his

younger days, when he drank too much and walked on the wild side, but he is less too. He tells his new wife, Katherine, the princess of France, that "I am glad thou canst speak no better English, for if thou couldst, thou would find me such a plain king that thou wouldst think I sold my farm to buy my crown."

Like Henry V, Hamlet undergoes a diminution of wit as he approaches the fulfillment of his destiny. In 5.1, the gravedigger is so far superior to Hamlet in wit, so like Hamlet himself in the first act, that Hamlet succumbs to this sharper mind and tongue. "How absolute the knave is!" Hamlet says, "We must speak by the card, or equivocation will undo us." We can't imagine such a capitulation in the early stages of the play, where Hamlet is so completely superior to his interlocutors. But if he is losing his flashy antic wit and disposition, he is gaining a new, restrained, sober (and sobering) way of knowing and speaking. Hamlet now comprehends the darkest truths of mortal nature; he confronts death head-on, as he pursues life through death and decay into remains—skulls, loam, dust—in an infinite cycle of decomposition, all things returning inevitably to this primal state and condition. In a short time, Hamlet will join the dead in silent rest, prompting four centuries of speech in others.

If Hamlet plays the fool for strategic and tactical purposes, however, at other times he exhibits genuine mental and emotional distress. In the last scene Hamlet explodes in a crescendo in which he's both supremely wise and insanely violent at the same time. By all expectations the underdog, Hamlet out-duels Laertes, presumed to be his superior at sword play, hitting him twice early in the bout. He then wisely—there's more than luck to this—declines a drink from the poisoned wine cup offered by his mother. She's not so clever. He then orders the doors closed—the final of his many attempts at containment—and attacks Claudius, killing him twice. He had killed Polonius by mistake. He had dispatched Rosencrantz and Guildenstern by fiat, as it were. By the altering of a letter, by executive order. Now, in the final scene he's completely engaged, not so much with words as action, fighting not by proxy but by himself. Blood and vomit wash the stage. Such violence is madness, of course.

Beneath the layers of studied postponement, deliberate obfuscation, dazzling wit—all surface play—Hamlet is brilliantly deranged. This is why a man so desperate as Ferrers turned to Hamlet in his last days. To find Hamlet, we must look to mental illness. Behind, beyond, and within the Prince's pretended madness, his "antic wit," a truly distracted globe spins. Caught in a horrible situation, Hamlet's doubting nature and his learned skepticism combine with a peculiar habit of "thinking too precisely on the event" to plunge him, at times, into madness. Horatio senses the potential that Hamlet might be carried over the edge into madness very early in the play. He rightly warns Hamlet not to follow the Ghost, which might "tempt you toward the flood, my lord,"

> Or to the dreadful summit of the cliff
> That beetles o'er his base into the sea,
> And there assume some other horrible form
> Which might deprive your sovereignty of reason
> And draw you into madness?

Shakespeare's age was just beginning to probe the disturbances of the mind. Its understanding of mental illnesses would have ascribed Hamlet's symptoms to melancholy, one of the four so-called humors, based on an ancient theory of physical and mental equilibrium derived from the physical theories of second-century AD Greek physician Galen. Fully codified in the Middle Ages, the theory associated blood, phlegm, choler, and black bile with four elements—earth, air, fire, and water—and four qualities—dry, cold, hot, and wet. These humors were, in turn, associated with four temperaments:

Humor	Temperament
Blood (warm and moist)	Sanguine
Phlegm (cold and moist)	Phlegmatic
Choler (hot and dry)	Choleric
Black Bile (cold and dry)	Melancholic

The theory held that as long as the body maintained an equilibrium among these humors, the individual remained healthy, but as soon as one humor emerged as dominant over the others, illness resulted.

By the Elizabethan age, melancholy had attracted enormous attention. In 1586, a prolific commentator on health matters, Timothy Bright, had published a hefty tome titled *A Treatise of Melancholy* that treated melancholy as a genuine sickness, and in the generation following Shakespeare, Robert Burton's masterpiece, *The Anatomy of Melancholy* (1621, enlarged 1651), treated the disease not only as a person-specific malady but a sickness afflicting whole societies, one that ruined faiths and states. After a lengthy "Letter to the Reader" surveying the general folly of modern governments and the presentation of his own ideal government, Burton presents his work in three "partitions"—the first devoted to the nature, causes, and symptoms of melancholy; another on the cures for melancholy; and a third on two special forms of the disorder, caused by love and religious fervor.

Burton is acutely aware of the pain and pervasiveness of depression. His narrator, Democritus Junior, is the spiritual descendant of the Greek philosopher Democritus (460–370 BC) who propounded the first theory of atomism, the belief that matter was not the result of metaphysical forces acting in some sort of concert, but rather the result of the random collision of tiny particles of matter, atoms, which were too small to observe, too obscure to have any logic about them, the sort of curious, Hamlet-like subdividing of thought that anticipates chaos theory. The ultimate application of atomism to Shakespeare is the famous dictum I'll paraphrase as follows: given infinite time, an infinite number of monkeys hammering randomly at an infinite number of computers, one of them will—must—write *Hamlet*.

At once profound and absurd, Democritus became known as the Laughing Philosopher. While his counterpart Heraclites is said to have reacted to the world's folly, inanity, and mendacity with tears, Democritus laughed. Burton's Democritus Junior recalls the original Democritus not only in his detached and droll view of life but also in the prolix and copious nature of his thinking. Incorporating Democritus' atomism in its title, Burton's *Anatomy* shares much with Shakespeare's *Hamlet*, especially if we are mindful that Hamlet is a university student. Students, Democritus notes, are especially vulnerable because their lives are characteristically sedentary and devoted to study. They dote because they are negligent, having no tools to apply to tasks, such as painters, smiths, and husbandmen have. They dote also because they are excessively contemplative, which "dries the brain and extinguisheth natural heat," a sense registered in Coleridge's mention of excessive thought exhausting 'bodily feeling.'" "Hard students" are susceptible to an uncommon variety of common and exotic illnesses, including "gouts, catarrhs, rheums, cachexia, bradiopepsia, bad eyes, stone, and colic, crudities, oppilations, vertigo, winds, consumptions, and all such diseases as come by overmuch sitting." Scholars, typically "lean, dry, ill-colored . . . lose their wits and many times their lives, and all through immoderate pains and extraordinary studies." The best scholars are often "silly, soft fellows" who suffer "dotage, madness and simplicity" and are "subject to all casualties, and hazards." "Striving to be excellent, to know all, they lose health, wealth, wit, life and all." The primary cures for study-induced melancholia, according to Democritus, are activity and fresh air.

Figure 7.2 Dürer's Melancholia, 1514. By permission of the Metropolitan Museum of Art.

Although Burton makes no overt reference to *Hamlet*—despite apparent verbal echoes from Shakespeare's plays in the *Anatomy*—Hamlet generally fits Burton's diagnosis of melancholy quite well. He's doting, excessively introspective, negligent, studious. Returned from Wittenberg to attend his father's funeral (and to claim his throne?), Hamlet is most familiarly the melancholic student.

The future will focus on melancholy as Hamlet's definitive malady. Among the Romantics, as is apparent from an earlier discussion, the reaction of Goethe, Coleridge, Wordsworth, Hazlitt, and others is focused upon the mental distress they see in Hamlet. Victor Hugo, writing in 1864, made the case most forcefully and with great passion. "Like the great spectre of Albert Dürer" (see figure 7.2), he wrote,

> Hamlet might be named "Melancholia." Above his head, too, there flits the disemboweled bat; at his feet are science, the sphere, the compass, the hour-glass, love; and behind him, at the horizon, a great and terrible sun, which seems to make the sky but darker.

EIGHT

HAMLET AMONG THE MODERNS

Writing in the shadow of Goethe and Schlegel, Coleridge and Hazlitt, the Victorians of England and America offered little new, it seems to me, to the interpretation of Hamlet. With some exceptions—Edgar Allan Poe, for example, anticipated a major issue of twentieth-century commentaries by cautioning readers that Hamlet is not a person but a fictional character—the Victorians give us detailed explications of the play, typically not confronting the great problems and challenges of the work. A close reading of *Hamlet* is the business of Victorian critics, and a kind of hiding place where they see the trees but not the forest. I offer this lengthy summary by Sir Edward Strachey, published in 1848 as *Shakespeare's Hamlet, an Attempt to find the Key to a Great Moral Problem by Methodical Analysis of the Play*, to illustrate the sentiments of an age. Admittedly unfair to one degree or another, it is, however, an efficient method of representing mainstream thought and attitudes of the time.

Having determined that Hamlet has "a natural aptitude to reflect his father's [noble] image," Strachey writes:

> Birth and the court have given him the feeling and the manners, the quick sensibilities, and the quiet self-possession of a gentleman; the camp has called forth in him not only personal courage, but that soldier's intuitive sagacity which, on any sudden emergency, at once takes in the whole field of circumstances, and decides on the right thing to be done; and in the philosophic school of

Wittenberg he has not only acquired the best intellectual culture, but learnt to understand and meditate on the springs of human life, thought and action, in all their forms. He has a love of humour and sense of the ridiculous, and a keen wit, what though mainly arising from the superabundant activity of the intellect, may perhaps be somewhat attributable to the enjoyment with which, as a child, he listened to the fun of Yorick, his father's jester: an affectionate and dutiful son, not only to his high-minded father, but to his weak though fond mother, he ever treats her with respect and tenderness, though he is painfully alive to the degradation she has sunk herself to by her unprincipled folly; he is a devoted lover; and a man for whom religion is not a theory or form, but a practical guide of the heart and conscience. His temper is naturally irritable and passionate, as might be expected with one who was at once a prince, and the only child of a foolishly fond mother; but his irritability is for the most part kept carefully under control, and when for a moment it breaks out, it is speedily repressed with remorse and self-condemnation, and manly entreaty for pardon from him it has attacked. And connected with this yielding to passion, is Hamlet's habitual royalty of will, which gives a tone to his whole character, and without recognizing which, it is impossible adequately to understand him:—he is not simply Hamlet, but "Hamlet, Prince of Denmark."

This is the Victorian Hamlet, tidied up to suit nineteenth-century precepts of the ordered life—a well-bred and mannered young man, soldier and scholar, brave and sagacious, felicitous, passionate but capable of self-restraint, an honorable lover and man of faith, dutiful to his noble father and obedient to and indulgent of his deeply flawed mother: the model son and prince, in Ophelia's words, "[t]he glass of fashion." No madness here, no violence, no misogyny, no suicidal despair, nothing dark or nihilistic or internalized. It's clear, despite his subtitle's claim, that for Strachey there is no real moral problem in Hamlet. To him, Hamlet is a thoroughly good chap, working hard to remain decent and balanced under trying circumstances.

While mainstream English and American criticism of the Victorian period was normalizing Hamlet, in Germany a "battle-royal" was brewing between critics who, on the one hand, might be termed subjectivists, and those who, on the other, might be termed objectivists. Both camps were concerned with explaining the inconsistencies and anachronisms in the Hamlet character—primarily, and most importantly, the fact that he delays acting even when enjoined by his dead father to avenge his murder.

Following Goethe and Schlegel, the subjectivists looked to the character himself for an answer to the question, Why does Hamlet delay? They located Hamlet's inaction in his own personality, pointing to his final soliloquy (4.4) when he says, "I do not know why yet I live to say this thing's to do." The subjectivists insist that it's in Hamlet's nature to think rather than act. The objectivists countered with the fact that Hamlet indeed *does* act, often and at times violently. To them, the question why he does not kill Claudius as soon as he is convinced of the Ghost's veracity— thus saving the lives of Polonius, Ophelia, Gertrude, Rosencrantz and Guildenstern, Laertes, and Hamlet himself—is a separate issue. Perhaps the situation Hamlet faces is too complex to be solved by simply killing Claudius. Killing Claudius, after all, wouldn't necessarily result in Hamlet gaining the crown and peace settling upon the state. It might do little or nothing to weed the garden of Denmark. The problem with "objective" theories is that they have little or no foundation in the text of the play. Nowhere does Hamlet mull the consequences of regicide; nowhere does he express a desire to put Claudius on trial for his crime.

For all their shortcomings, the "objectivists" have the virtue of attempting to free Hamlet from the thrall of sentimentalism cast by Romantic critics. At least putatively, they subject the character to analysis from a detached perspective, based in method rather than emotion, one that employs something resembling scientific inquiry.

The effort to develop a "scientific" approach to interpreting Hamlet, one based in method rather than emotion, would become the common denominator of twenti-eth-century commentaries—and the groundwork for literary analysis as we know it today. We can trace the origins of this break with the Romantic past to the series of seminal essays on Shakespeare's four major tragedies—*Hamlet, Othello, King Lear,* and *Macbeth*—by the eminent Oxford Professor of Poetry A. C. Bradley, published in 1904 as *Shakespearean Tragedy.* Dismissing as irrelevant to his endeavor such matters as Shakespeare's life, the development of his genius, "the genuineness, sources, texts, interrelations of his various works," Bradley sought to present a "dramatic appreciation" of these plays, a goal he could achieve only by means of a close reading of the texts—"to compare, to analyze, to dissect."

Bradley dismissed the Goethean strain of "sentimental" interpretation, which sees Hamlet as "lovely, pure and most moral," a young man crushed by a task to which he is not adequate, a precious vase destroyed by a calumnious, depraved culture. This interpretation, he pointed out, was not "the Hamlet who scarcely once speaks to the King without an insult, or to Polonius without a gibe." The Goethean Hamlet doesn't account for the desperate and violent man who, he wrote,

> hearing a cry behind the arras, whips out his sword in an instant and runs the eavesdropper through; the Hamlet who sends his "school-fellows" to their death and never troubles his head about them more; the Hamlet who is the first man to board a pirate ship, and who fights with Laertes in the grave [of Ophelia]; the Hamlet of the catastrophe, an omnipotent fate, before whom all the court stands helpless, who, as the truth breaks upon him, rushes on the King, drives his foil right through his body, then seizes the poisoned cup and forces it violently between the wretched man's lips, and in the throes of death has force and fire enough to wrest the cup from Horatio's hand ("By heaven, I'll have it") lest he should drink and die? This man, the Hamlet of the play, is a heroic, terrible man.

Bradley's Hamlet is a man of action, quite capable of rash and violent acts, which leads Bradley to reject, as well, the Schlegel-Coleridge theory of Hamlet as a character plagued by irresolution. The belief that in Hamlet "the energy of resolve is dissipated in an endless brooding on the deed required," in fact "degrades Hamlet and travesties the play." Bradley speculates about Hamlet as if he were a real person, with a life prior to the drama itself. His Hamlet was never a man of such an introspective nature that he was habitually irresolute. The "Schlegel-Coleridge view," Bradley writes, is "fatally untrue" because it implies "that Hamlet's procrastination was the normal response of an overspeculative nature confronted with a difficult practical problem."

Rather, according to Bradley, Hamlet's tendency to delay action is rooted in psychology, what Bradley terms "morality"—the terrible shock to his psyche not so much from his father's death as from his mother's remarriage. Bradley points out that the "sickness of life" and "the longing for death" comes in his first soliloquy ("O, that this too too [sullied] flesh would melt"), *before* the Ghost reveals that he has been murdered by his brother. Rather than his father's death, it is mother's remarriage—"not for any reason of state, nor even out of old family affection, but in such a way that her son was forced to see in her action not only an astounding shallowness of feeling but an eruption of coarse sensuality, 'rank and gross' "—that plunges Hamlet into a sea of despair. This new union violently poisons Hamlet's mind. Anticipating later psychological interpretations, Bradley's Hamlet can never look on any woman the way he had before; his scourging of Ophelia in 3.1 is a generalized misogynistic attack on all women.

Returning to Renaissance tradition, Bradley identifies the disturbance of Hamlet's mind caused by the shock to his psyche as melancholy, which he distinguishes from dejection or insanity. Bradley concurs with what he calls the modern "pathologist" who "emphasiz[es] that Hamlet's melancholy is no mere common depression of spirits," but rather a form of "mental disease." "It would be absurdly unjust," he concedes, "to call *Hamlet* a study of melancholia, but it contains such a study." If this distinction seems obscure, Bradley attempts to clarify his meaning by reaching out to the common experience of the play's readers/viewers over the centuries into his own time, stressing the universal reach of pathological depression but carefully distinguishing it from madness: a madman can't be a tragic hero.

Mental illness is one source, if not the only source, of Hamlet's universal status. To Bradley, this is precisely what links Hamlet with the masses of men: "The man who suffers as Hamlet suffers—and thousands go about their business suffering thus in greater or less degree—is considered irresponsible neither by other people nor by himself: he is only too keenly conscious of his responsibility. He is therefore, so far, quite capable of being a tragic agent, which an insane person, at any rate according to Shakespeare's practice, is not." Melancholy—great depression of spirit and mind—is the cause of Hamlet's "inaction," as well as "his almost savage irritability on the one hand, and on the other his self-absorption, his callousness, his insensibility to the fates of those whom he despises, and to the feelings of those whom he loves."

Locating Hamlet's problem internally, as a condition of the mind, Bradley advanced an unmistakably modern conception of Hamlet, one that in many ways anticipates the light to be shed upon the character by later developments in psychology and psychoanalysis. In doing so, he tacitly endorses Georg Wilhelm Fredrich Hegel's view of *Hamlet* as the supreme example of "modern" (as opposed to "classical") drama, one driven not so much by ethical or moral necessity but rather by, in Hegel's words, "the particular personality, the inner life of Hamlet." But Bradley stepped back from the precipice of radical modernity (and postmodernity). In fact, while taking our understanding of Hamlet far beyond his predecessors, Bradley was in the end fairly conventional. He conceived of *Hamlet* as a "religious" play. As the action moves inexorably toward the catastrophe, we have "the feeling" that Hamlet's life is "in the hands of Providence." Though in no specific sense is *Hamlet* a "religious drama," it is, according to Bradley, more so than any of Shakespeare's tragedies, informed by the "intimation of a supreme power concerned in human evil and good." This would seem starkly at odds with his discussion of Hamlet as a man suffering from the hopelessness of depression.

With the advent of the formal study of psychology in the second half of the nineteenth century, Hamlet's mental condition, not surprisingly, becomes increasingly of interest to commentators. Bradley provides a case in point. In a character for whom reality is a product of internal experience, psychology—and later psychiatry—offers a rich and ever-widening avenue of approach to the doomed Prince.

Since the eighteenth century, psychology as a discipline had been recognized as a branch of philosophy concerned with the operation of the mind. But it was not until the second half of the nineteenth century that significant empirical developments occurred. In 1875 Wilhelm Wundt, the father of experimental psychology, established the first laboratory devoted to learning and memory in Leipzig. In 1883, the Englishman Francis Galton, a cousin of Charles Darwin, published his groundbreaking investigation into mental differences among individuals, *Inquiries into Human Faculty*. Comparative studies of learning followed, with Lloyd Morgan's *Animal Life and Intelligence*, published in 1890, and E. L. Thorndike's *Animal Intelligence* in 1911. Published in 1890, William James's monumental *Principles of Psychology* is the jewel in the crown of the fast-developing study of the mind.

Given the growth of psychology in the final decades of the nineteenth century, it's hardly surprising that Bradley, writing in the early 1900s, wasn't the first modern commentator to identify Hamlet's problem as a form of mental disease. In 1876, the physician and psychologist Ernest Onimus, who did groundbreaking work in the use of electricity in medical treatments, argued in his *La Psychologie de Shakespeare* that "Natures like Hamlet's are early thoughtful and suffering; they are all nerves, enthusiastic at one moment, depressed at another, according to circumstances. . . . [They] are misanthropes, kindly or morose, sympathetic or sneering, often rude and suspicious but capable of fine repartees and keen wits." "Hamlet," Onimus wrote, "would never become really mad, but only more rational" as he descended into misanthropy.

A decade later, A. O. Kellog, in *Shakespeare's Delineations of Insanity, Imbecility and Suicide* (1886), considered Hamlet's mental condition to be somewhere along the fine line between madness and sanity, where a supreme state of understanding and insight is achieved. Kellog smugly proclaimed that

> Shakespeare recognized what none of his critics, not conversant with medical psychology in its present advanced state, seem to have any conception of; namely, that there are cases of melancholic madness of a delicate shade, in which the reasoning faculties, the intellect proper, so far from being overcome, or even disordered, may, on the other hand, be rendered more active and vigorous, while the will, the moral feelings, the sentiments and affections, are the faculties which seem alone to suffer from the stroke of disease.

Kellog focuses upon the maniacal aspect of Hamlet's character, which—rather than distracting the mind—intensifies the clarity with which it comprehends the world.

As these examples illustrate, the language of the last decade of the nineteenth century was still heavily impressionistic and ornate, not yet supplanted by the technical idiom of modern psychoanalysis and the institutionalization of literary criticism that would come about with time. Nevertheless, remarkable insights into the mental condition of Hamlet appeared on the eve of the new century. Writing in 1894, E. K. Chambers, the great historian of the Elizabethan stage, offered an impressively subtle interpretation of Hamlet's mental condition, one that acknowledges the importance of the study of the mind, the mind looking at the mind, investigating itself. This is an inward turning that neatly reflects Hamlet's own inwardness.

"Psychology," Chambers wrote, "knows no rigid dividing line between the sane and the insane." To claim that Hamlet is frankly insane is to misrepresent him, "to put his actions in a quite different category from those of other men. That would [be] to divest [Shakespeare's] work of humanity and leave it meaningless." Hamlet is not merely suspended between madness and the pretense of madness, according to Chambers. Rather, the two states are implicated in one another—reciprocal, inseparable. Hamlet "plays the madman to prevent himself becoming one." Chambers anticipates the claim of Bradley and many others that a true madman can't stand as a tragic hero.

Psychology offered new ways of understanding Hamlet, especially regarding the relationship between Hamlet and his parents. In a 1917 essay, "Mourning and Melancholia," published while the Great War devoured young men of Europe, Sigmund Freud articulated the psychological mechanisms—identification, projection, and transference—that underlie Hamlet's complex relations with his newly dead father. Though he mentions Hamlet only once in "Mourning and Melancholia," and then in passing, Freud's essay recalls Hamlet at every turn. Freud theorizes that the melancholic's reaction to the loss of the loved object, particularly feelings of anger and reproach, "are shifted away" from the lost love object "on to the patient's own ego." That is, Hamlet puts his anger over the loss of his father onto himself. In opposition to mourning, as Freud writes early in the essay, melancholia involves "a profoundly painful dejection, cessation of interest in the outside world, loss of the capacity to love, inhibition of all activity, and a lowering of the self-regarding feelings to a degree that finds utterance in self-reproaches and self-revilings, and culminates in a delusional expectation of punishment." The melancholic, he adds, experiences "an extraordinary diminution in his self-regard, an impoverishment of his ego on a grand scale. In mourning it is the world which has become poor and empty; in melancholia it is the ego itself." In a heightened state of self-criticism, the melancholic patient "describes himself as petty, egoistic, dishonest, lacking in independence, one whose sole aim has been to hide the weakness of his own nature." Hamlet's 3.1 self-critique to Ophelia exactly registers Freud's observation:

> I could accuse me of such things that it were better my mother had not borne me.
> I am very proud, revengeful, ambitious, with more offences at my beck than I have
> thoughts to put them in, imagination to give them shape, or time to act them in.
> What should such fellows as I do crawling between earth and heaven? We are
> arrant knaves—believe none of us.

One can't help but see in Freud's idea of transference Hamlet's state of mind in the first soliloquy. Indeed, the imagery of decay, disgust, bestiality, and incest that oozes from Hamlet's meditation in 1.2—"things rank and gross in nature . . . a beast that wants discourse of reason . . . increase of appetite . . . incestuous sheets"— is remarkably similar to that of his father, in his first postmortem encounter with his son in 1.5: "Shameful lust . . . Lewdness . . . lust . . . prey on garbage . . . the Royal bed of Denmark . . . a couch for luxury and damned incest."

Along with evidence already cited, the similar imagery in these two speeches may be seen as evidence of the transference that Freud attributes to the melancholic. This transference depends upon "an *identification* of the ego with the abandoned object," Freud writes. "Thus the shadow of the object [falls] upon the ego, and the latter"—the ego—"[can] henceforth be judged by a special agency"—the ghost of Hamlet's father—"as though it were an object, the forsaken object."

This psychological reintegration of father and son, enacted in the great of 1.5, sets the stage very precisely for viewing Hamlet Sr. as an "abandoned object," lost to death. "Melancholia borrows some of its features from mourning, and the others from the process of regression from narcissistic object-choice to narcissism," Freud writes. "Narcissism"—a concept that fits Hamlet like a glove—"bleeds through [the melancholiac's] suicidal meditations."

HAMLET AND OEDIPUS

Even before "Mourning and Melancholia," Freud had laid the groundwork for the most enduring and influential vein of psychoanalytic criticism of Hamlet in what was originally a footnote to *The Interpretation of Dreams* (1900). "Shakespeare's *Hamlet*," Freud wrote, "has its roots in the same soil as *Oedipus Rex*." Freud went on to sketch out the lineaments of the Oedipal reading of Hamlet, a reading that has become one of the bastions of Hamlet criticism. Freud noted that, contrary to general assumptions about Hamlet since Goethe, the Prince is *not* incapable of action. On the contrary, Hamlet is very active. Only in the peculiar task of avenging the murder of his father is action thwarted. This, Freud reasoned, is because Claudius is "the man who shows him the repressed wishes of his own childhood realized." The resulting paralysis is accompanied by "self-reproaches, by the scruples of conscience, which remind him that he himself is literally no better than the sinner whom he is to punish." Concomitantly, the Oedipal complex explains Hamlet's "distaste for sexuality" and his abuse of women, Gertrude and Ophelia.

The complete elaboration of the Oedipal reading of Hamlet fell to Freud's protégé, Ernst Jones, whose investigation grew over four decades into the seminal book *Hamlet and Oedipus* (1949). In making this case, Jones returns us to Hamlet as a child, and speculates what the Prince had experienced when he was very young. This gambit earned Jones opprobrium. Subsequent commentators point out that Hamlet is a character in a play and, so, didn't have a childhood. But Jones, in a chapter titled "Tragedy and the Mind of the Infant," insists that it is precisely in the projected childhood of Hamlet that the secret to his thought and action lies. Early in this putative childhood Hamlet wanted to kill his father to possess entirely the love of his mother. The prototype for this contest between father and son for the affection of the mother, Freud had located in the character of Oedipus, who, in Sophocles' play *Oedipus the King*, killed his father and married his mother. As summarized by Jones, the Oedipal Complex involves "the resentment felt by a boy towards his father when the latter disturbs, as he necessarily must, his enjoyment of his mother's exclusive affection. This feeling is the deepest source of the world-old conflict between father and son, between the younger and the older generation," a conflict rooted in the boy's awakening sexual attraction for the mother. "When the attraction exercised by the mother is excessive," Jones writes, "it may exert a controlling influence over the boy's later destiny." In boys who successfully resolve this conflict, the logic supposes, desire is dissipated through "normal" attachments to women, and the transference of sexual attraction to women of his own generation. However, "if the awakened passion undergoes an insufficient 'repression,' then the boy may remain throughout life abnormally attached to his mother." On the other hand, when "the aroused feeling is intensely 'repressed' and associated with shame, guilt, and similar reactions the submergence may be so complete as to render the person incapable of experiencing any feeling at all of attraction to the opposite sex; to him all women are as forbidden as his mother." The boy, according to Jones, may become deeply misogynistic or homosexual.

The father, therefore, must be understood as his son's rival, one that at some unconscious level the son wishes to eliminate: "The unimpeded train of thought in the unconscious logically culminates in the idea, or rather the wish, that the father (or his substitute) may disappear from the scene, i.e. that he may die." According to the Oedipal reading of Hamlet's character, Hamlet has only partially succeeded in transferring his sexual desire from an unhealthy attachment to Gertrude to a healthy attraction to Ophelia. With his father's death and his mother's remarriage, Hamlet is suddenly reminded of his mother's sexuality; what was repressed now violently returns to the surface in feelings of disgust and grossness, which Hamlet gives voice to in his first soliloquy, feelings that are both particular and general. The entire world is "an unweeded garden / That grows to seed, things rank and gross in nature / Possess it merely." Hamlet recalls his mother's sexual attachment to his father. "Why, she should hang on him / As if increase of appetite had grown / By what it fed on." Now that Claudius has taken the position of his dead father in his mother's bed, "Hamlet is stunned by the effect of the internal conflict thus re-awakened." His distressed unconscious manifests itself in new revulsion and hostility toward his mother, which is projected most violently toward Ophelia in 3. 1 when he rails against her in language fraught with terms of corruption and disease, obsessed with duplicity and deceit. Hamlet offers Ophelia a plague for a dowry should she marry. He knows that no woman can be faithful to a man, that women turn men into "monsters"—a reference to the crown of horns that cuckolds were traditionally depicted as wearing; that women wear two faces, one that God gave them and another that they paint for themselves; that women are vain and frivolous; they "jig" and "amble" and "lisp" and nickname God's creatures; they make their wantonness their ignorance. The effect of this tirade is to drive Hamlet "mad." He concludes with a veiled threat to murder Claudius and/or Gertrude: "Those that are married already—all but one—shall live."

The Oedipal reading represents a major development in the search for Hamlet. It provides an explanation for Hamlet's melancholy unavailable to pre-Freudian critics. Nevertheless, to some, the Freudian approach was misleadingly reductionist. "To it, the flower is nothing but a differentiated root," wrote Harold Goddard, one of Shakespeare's most perceptive interpreters, in *The Meaning of Shakespeare* (1951), "and the tragic mysteries of Hamlet nothing but his infantile fantasies in disguise." Instead, Goddard offered a more discerning interpretation of parent-child relations in *Hamlet* by seeing Hamlet as but one in a series of Shakespearean characters who labor under the scrupulous watch of a father or father figure who demands obedience. In this tradition Goddard places Romeo, Prince Hal, and Brutus, characters who "speak" to Hamlet from earlier in Shakespeare's drama. Romeo's heart told him to love Juliet and embrace the Capulets as in-laws, but the voice of the father demanded that he continue the hereditary quarrel, and Romeo obeyed the father. Hal's soul told him to remain in the fecund, life-affirming milieu of Falstaff and company, but his father—not only Henry IV but the more powerful surrogate father of the State—demanded that Hal reject Falstaff on the path to the throne of England and the butchery that follows. Hal, like Romeo, obeyed. Brutus' heart and soul compelled him to avoid involvement in national destiny, but Cassius, a surrogate for the father-function of history, reminded Brutus of another Brutus who had expelled a tyrant. Cassius in effect demands that Brutus duplicate that act, regardless of Brutus' desire to study and contemplate. Brutus obeyed. "Each of these men," Goddard writes, "wanted to dedicate himself to life. Romeo wanted to love. Hal wanted to play. Brutus wanted to read philosophy. But in each case a commanding hand was placed on the man's shoulder that disputed the claim of life in the name of death." Each resisted the name of death for a while but, in the end, capitulated.

From this perspective, Hamlet's delay is anything but a sign of weakness. It is rather a sign of great, tragic strength that Hamlet resists his father's command to avenge his death. "It shows his soul is still alive and will not submit to the demands of the father without a struggle." To this list of sons struggling to resist might be added the tortured Angelo from *Measure for Measure*, a play written shortly after *Hamlet*. Installed as a surrogate ruler by the absentee Duke of Vienna, who disguises himself as a priest—a *father*—Angelo is burdened with the daunting assignment to wrench the chaotic city of Vienna into order, a task that he, like Hamlet, sees himself as inadequate to undertake. Having this onus foisted upon him, Angelo becomes a vicious man, to be sure. But he is also an exquisitely perceptive, self-aware man tormented by dark demons of the soul, and thus much closer to Hamlet than Romeo, Brutus, or Hal.

THE QUESTIONABLE SHAPE OF THE GHOST

GHOST: List, list, O list,
            If thou didst ever thy dear father love—
HAMLET: O God!
GHOST:—Revenge his foul and most unnatural murder!

With this awful demand, framed as a test of Hamlet's love for his father, and pivoted upon an unsettling ambiguity—the Ghost refers to himself in the third person, commanding Hamlet to revenge "his" (rather than "my") unnatural murder, thus raising the possibility that the Ghost and Hamlet's father aren't exactly synonymous—the Ghost in *Hamlet* propels a vast dramatic movement that ends in the slaughter of the final scene. Shrouded in indeterminacy, the Ghost inaugurates a pattern of action that is, in the end, bloodily unambiguous, as starkly "real" as silent corpses.

The questionable issue of the Ghost necessarily concerns the issue of religion, specifically the degree to which the apparition is to be seen in the light of Protestant or Catholic belief. This uncertain question, in turn, is inseparable from the larger issue, touched upon elsewhere in this book, of Shakespeare's own religious disposition. In fact, Shakespeare in his plays seems not to register a clear set of orthodox beliefs, either Catholic or Protestant, it seems to me, and *Hamlet* can be construed as a religious work only in the vaguest sense, that the workings of Providence direct the action, as Bradley thought, a sense more apparent toward the end rather than the beginning of the action. Shakespeare's family, like all English families, had been Catholic prior to the 1530s, when Henry VIII precipitated the Reformation in England. But many biographers have held the view that the Shakespeares were recusant, persisting in the Catholic faith even through Shakespeare's generation. Some have speculated that the troubles that befell William's father, John, in the 1570s—he fell into debt and stopped attending Stratford council meetings—resulted from his clinging (or returning) to the old faith. Shakespeare himself, it has been suggested, served as a tutor to the children of a Catholic family during the "missing years" of the 1580s, and, according to one persistent legend, on his deathbed called for a priest to administer his last rites.

On the other side of the ledger, Shakespeare wrote in a period when Protestantism was the official, orthodox practice. He was associated, moreover, with powerful men who supported orthodox practice. Even though his patron, the third Earl of Southampton, came from a deeply Catholic tradition, Southampton was at the center of a sphere of powerful Protestants led by the Earl of Leicester.

In some ways Shakespeare seems at pains to place *Hamlet* within the framework of orthodox Protestantism. Like Marlowe's Dr. Faustus, Hamlet and Horatio (perhaps Rosencrantz and Guildenstern too) are or have been students at Wittenberg University, which, since the time of Martin Luther, had been the axis of European Protestantism. This Protestant mooring is countered, however, by the Ghost of

Hamlet's father, who apparently comes to the witnesses from purgatory, that place in Catholic belief where souls were purged of sin before being admitted to heaven. "I am thy father's spirit," he tells his son,

> Doomed for a certain term to walk the night
> And for the day confined to fast in fires
> Till the foul crimes done in my days of nature
> Are burnt and purged away.

He is expressly forbidden "to tell the secrets of my prison-house." Prison-house is a particularly appropriate description of Catholic purgatory. The conflict, as we shall briefly see, is important because Protestants and Catholics conceived the spirit world in significantly different ways.

Hamlet's anxiety about the Ghost is evident after Horatio describes its appearance the previous night, that is, even before Hamlet confronts the apparition. "All is not well," he muses, "I doubt [suspect] some foul play." When the Ghost first materializes before Hamlet and the three other witnesses, there would seem to be no doubt that it is real; multiple people see it. Yet its nature and motive are far from clear. Hamlet immediately recognizes that it may be either "a spirit of health or a goblin damned," its "intents wicked or charitable." Hamlet sees that the figure "com'st in . . . a questionable shape," by which he means that it appears to invite interrogation, but the secondary meaning of "questionable," reinforcing the uncertainty of its nature, can't be ignored. If all were known about the Ghost, there would be no need to question it. Voicing concerns that were widely held in Renaissance England, Horatio fears that the revenant, dressed in the menacing vestments of war, may be attempting to drive Hamlet to madness or suicide. Horatio is aware that his age associates ghosts with dangerous and frightening landscapes, preeminently cliff tops above heaving surf:

> What if it tempt you toward the flood, my lord,
> Or to the dreadful summit of the cliff
> That beetles o'er his base into the sea,
> And there assume some other horrible form
> Which might deprive your sovereignty of reason
> And draw you into madness?

Horatio urges Hamlet to consider the horrible possibility that cliffs put "toys of desperation / Without more motive into every brain / That looks so many fathoms to the sea / And hears it roar beneath."

Is the Ghost good or evil? Is it bent on ruining young Hamlet, or is it rightly intent on prompting noble conduct in this untested son of nobility? Is the Ghost's motive to damn or save Hamlet? The answers to these questions are crucial in the search for Hamlet. Because the killer of Amleth's father is known to all, the Danish saga doesn't require a ghost to reveal this information. The Ghost enters the Hamlet narrative in the old play of Hamlet from the 1580s. In his *Wit's Misery* of 1596, Thomas Lodge describes a character who "looks as pale as the Visard of the ghost, which cried so miserably at the Theatre, like an oyster-wife, 'Hamlet revenge.' "

The Ghost in *Hamlet*, said to have been performed by Shakespeare himself, seems in earlier versions to have been an unproblematic bogey man staged to horrify the audience with "Hamlet, revenge." But Shakespeare rejected the stereotypical ghost, creating instead the evocative, plaintive, remonstrative yet deeply unsettling and indeterminate figure that Hamlet, Horatio, and the sentinels confront.

In the early twentieth century, as interest in Hamlet's mental state deepened, the Ghost for the first time became the subject of intense scrutiny, precisely because of its uncertain nature. In 1915, as Europe entered the second year of slaughter—an experience that would forever alter the spiritual, intellectual, and psychological disposition of the Western world—Charlotte Carmichael Stopes, an amateur antiquarian and historian of Warwickshire, pointed to an obvious problem with the Ghost. Considering the pivotal 3.4 when Hamlet viciously harangues his mother in her chamber and murders the eavesdropping Polonius, Stopes noted that the Ghost appearing to Hamlet alone, not to his mother, suggests that it is, in fact, a hallucination. "Was this the real objective ghost [Hamlet] had seen with Horatio?" she asked. "Or a subjective ghost evolved from his own inner consciousness? I am inclined to think it was the latter." She goes on to say, "that a concrete vision, born of memory, rose from his excited brain. It told him nothing that he did not know. His mother saw nothing save Hamlet's countenance, she heard nothing save Hamlet's excited words." Bradley had pointed out that Elizabethan spiritualism allowed that ghosts had the ability to appear selectively, visible to one but not another. But Stopes is the first commentator, as far as I know, to press the more radical interpretation of the scene as evidence that Hamlet is hallucinating.

The year after Stopes presented her reading of the Ghost in 3.4, the great textual critic W. W. Greg cast even greater doubt upon the nature of the Ghost and its motives. Greg pointed out that Claudius sits through the dumb show, which reenacts the murder of Hamlet's father, without reacting to what is depicted. It is only when this action is reproduced in "The Mousetrap" immediately following the dumb show, which in effect presents a second test of Claudius' guilt, that the King abruptly calls for the lights. Yet "The Mousetrap", Greg notes, "adds nothing new whatever" to the representation of the murder of Hamlet Sr. If Claudius is guilty of murdering Old Hamlet by pouring poison in the ear, as the Ghost tells Hamlet, why does Claudius sit through the depiction of that murder during the dumb show without reacting? The dumb show doesn't affect Claudius, Greg reasons, because he didn't in fact kill Hamlet Sr. in the manner the Ghost details in 1.5. "[T]his immediately leads," Greg writes,

> to a far more important conclusion. If the King did not murder his predecessor by pouring poison into his ears, then the account of the affair given by the Ghost to Hamlet is untrue—in other words, the Ghost's narrative is not a revelation from the dead but a figment of Hamlet's brain.

But if the scenario in which Claudius poisons Hamlet's father is nothing but a projection of Hamlet's own disturbed mind, then why does Claudius respond to "The Mousetrap"? When Claudius finally interrupts the play scene, he does so not because he sees his own guilt depicted on stage, Greg asserts, but rather because Hamlet is now behaving in a "wild and menacing" manner. Hamlet, we might speculate, is silently raving at this point, perhaps waving his arms like a chicken, as his prototypes had, or flitting about the stage with some other business, signaled, as the English actor William Charles Macready (1793–1873) thought, by Hamlet's remark, "I must be idle."

Greg's case needed strengthening if it was to persuade. Most obviously, he had to solve one very obvious problem with the hallucination theory: the fact that in the first act the Ghost appears to four witnesses on multiple occasions. The only possible explanation, short of the Ghost being in fact real, was to posit a kind of collective hysteria among these witnesses. Bernardo, Marcellus, the scholar Horatio, as well as Hamlet must be projecting the same hallucinated figure. Greg attempted to show that this was possible because these witnesses are themselves unreliable, terrified, or simply gullible. This was to become a seminal moment in the history of the Ghost.

In November 1917, John Dover Wilson, an inspector for England's Board of Education and the Board of Munitions, settled in for a long train ride from his home in Leeds to Sunderland to attend to some trouble among union workers. He had missed the express train, and so was obliged to board a "stopping train" that would take four hours to deliver the thirty-six-year-old Wilson to Sunderland. Finding an empty compartment, Wilson opened *The Modern Language Review* and read "Hamlet's Hallucination," in which Greg expanded and buttressed his argument. Then he read it again. And again. And again—six times before he reached his destination. The Cambridge-educated Wilson, who chafed that in the fourth year of World War I he still had not been "'released' for war service,"—that he was not allowed to join the fight against the Germans— immediately found a new focus for his life's work. He would prove Greg's hallucination theory wrong.

And to the satisfaction of much of the scholarly community, he did. His article refuting Greg was published and a new and productive career launched. Refuting Greg would be only the start of a very long journey into Shakespeare. Dover Wilson became a star of Shakespeare studies, especially *Hamlet*. Over the next two decades, he produced a body of work ranging from groundbreaking textual studies to the editorship, with Sir Arthur Quiller-Couch, of the Cambridge edition of the plays (1921–66) to important critical interpretations of Shakespeare plays. He was appointed Reader in Bibliography at Cambridge in 1932, and a Leverhulme Fellow in 1933–34, which provided a year free of other duties during which he completed *What Happens in Hamlet*, a work whose origins can be traced to a long train ride through the night in the company of Greg's "Hamlet's Hallucination." Though now dated, Wilson's body of work, especially regarding *Hamlet*, has not been entirely superceded.

Eighteen years after that train to Sunderland, in a dedicatory epistle prefacing his *What Happens in Hamlet* (1935), Wilson remembered that fateful trip. The dedicatory epistle, commonplace in Shakespeare's day, with its fawning deference and hyperbolic praise of its dedicatee, had long ago fallen out of fashion, so readers of 1935 must certainly have found "The Road to Elsinore / being an epistle dedicatory to Walter Wilson Greg"—whose interpretation of the Ghost Wilson thought wholly mistaken—quaint, to say the least.

From the twenty-first century perspective, its quaintness fades. Deep into a war that was destroying an entire generation of European manhood, Wilson was enduring a crisis of the soul. "Though I did not know it," writes Wilson, "my spiritual condition was critical, not to say dangerous, a condition in which a man becomes converted, falls in love, or gives way to a mania for wild speculation. In a sense, all three destinies awaited me."

"From the first [I] realized that I had been born to answer it." That night he dropped a note in the post asking the editor of *The Modern Language Review* to allow him to respond to Greg's "devilish[ly] ingenious, but damnably wrong article." In time there came from the editor a favorable reply, and Wilson, working initially with the questionable matter of the Ghost in *Hamlet*, launched his remarkable career. Based on his research into Renaissance spiritualism—notably Ludwig Lavater's *Of Ghosts and Spirites walking by Nyght* (1572), Reginald Scot's *Discoverie of Witchcraft* (1584), and *Daemonology* (1597) by the future king of England, James I—Wilson published a flurry of essays refuting Greg's claim that the Ghost is a hallucination.

Greg had doubted that Shakespeare believed in ghosts, but in *What Happens in Hamlet* Wilson argued that this premise was unlikely since the belief in apparitions was almost universal during Shakespeare's time. Interpretations differed significantly, however, and fell, broadly speaking, into three categories. First, the Catholic belief in purgatory—the nether region where the dead are purged of sin in preparation for entry into heaven—allowed that ghosts of dead people actually returned from their prison-house to visit the living. Catholics believed that purgatorial spirits were the only human spirits to return from the dead, and these visitations were uncommon. All other apparitions were either hallucinations or, more commonly, demonic spirits. Protestants, for whom purgatory was a myth, were taught that the dead went to their just reward without passing through any intermediary stage. This meant that ghosts couldn't be the spirits of the departed. There was a remote possibility that a revenant was angelic, but it was far more likely, Protestants believed, that demons assumed human form in order to torment or lead the living to madness and/or damnation. A third body of thought, less common still, held the skeptical view that apparitions were the projections of disordered minds, or even knavish pranks staged to terrify the gullible. This last position, espoused by Scot in *Discoverie of Witchcraft*, was widely denounced after the publication in 1597 of *Daemonologie* by James I, which was explicitly written to refute such skepticism. All three views of the spectral world held that ghosts were more likely to appear to melancholic persons than to others.

Because the Ghost appears to multiple witnesses, there can be little doubt, Wilson argued, that the Ghost of Hamlet's father is "real." Instead, the important question is whether the Ghost means to harm or help Hamlet. The crucial test of the matter comes in 3.4, the Closet Scene, in which the Ghost appears to Hamlet and to us, of course, but not to Gertrude. It enters in the midst of Hamlet's shending of his mother, when his comparison of Claudius and Old Hamlet has turned Gertrude's eyes inward on her soul where she sees "such black and grieved spots / As will not leave their tinct" (F1). The Ghost's appearance is timely but not so timely, it should be noted, as to save the hapless Polonius.

Hereafter, from Gertrude's point of view, everything that Hamlet does seems patently insane. Having turned his attention from the killing of Polonius to his mother, who has every reason to fear for her own life, Hamlet sees his father's Ghost and abruptly breaks off his attack at "—a king of shreds and patches." Gertrude, of course, can't know what has caused this sudden distraction. "Alas, he's mad!" she cries. The Ghost chastises Hamlet with "Do not forget! This visitation / Is but to whet thy almost blunted purpose." The apparition calls attention to the effect Hamlet's distraction is having upon Gertrude: "But look, amazement on thy mother sits!" he says. He asks Hamlet to "step between her and her fighting soul." Hamlet obeys, turning back from the apparition to his mother: "How is it with you, lady?" But Gertrude has greater cause to ask that question of her son: "Alas, how is't with you, / That you do bend your eye on vacancy / And with th' incorporal air do hold discourse?" For all she knows, Hamlet is in the grips of a visual and auditory hallucination. "Whereon do you look?" she asks. "On him, on him!" he replies, "Look you how pale he glares." The Ghost seems to be registering, at this point, emotional distress, because Hamlet asks the Ghost not to look at him, because by this "piteous action" the apparition might unnerve Hamlet, take him out of the scourging mode. If so, "[t]hen what I have to do / Will want true colour, tears perchance for blood."

"To whom do you speak this?" Gertrude asks. Only now does Hamlet realize what his mother is *not* experiencing. "Do you see nothing there?" he asks. "Nothing at all," she says, adding emphatically, "yet all that is I see." Hamlet asks if she hears nothing. "No," she says, "nothing but ourselves." Unbelievably, the Ghost exits silently, making no attempt, by word or gesture, to rescue his son from this terrible situation, one guaranteed to make him out to be a madman.

In light of what has happened thus far in this encounter, what follows—Hamlet's three attempts to leave the room only to return to berate her to repent and turn away from the filthy sty where she indulges her gross appetite, to "go not to my uncle's bed," to "assume a virtue, if you have it not"—only intensifies the impression of a deranged man. Gertrude understandably wonders if Hamlet is now delusional, though he swears that he is not mad. The bitter obscenities that follow, however, are likely only to confirm the opposite impression for one who hasn't seen or heard the Ghost. "Let not the bloat King," Hamlet says,

> tempt you again to bed,
> Pinch wanton on your cheek, call you his mouse
> And let him, for a pair of reechy kisses,
> Or paddling in your neck with his damned fingers,
> Make you to ravel all this matter out
> That I essentially am not in madness
> But mad in craft.

Hamlet's demand—that his mother not let on that Hamlet is pretending madness—will certainly be heeded. The terrible irony of the moment is that Gertrude is now convinced that her son is insane. And Hamlet, urging her to endorse his ongoing "madness," is ironically the author of this strategic blunder, one that will bring about the deaths of so many.

The devastating impression that Hamlet is psychotic, if only for a few moments, has been entirely created by the Ghost, who entered the scene, as I mentioned, not in time to prevent Hamlet from becoming a murderer but in the perfect time and circumstance to make him out to be a madman. Of that moment when the action of *Hamlet* takes a definitive turn toward tragic inevitability, the murder of Polonius might seem less definitive than the end of 3.4, when Hamlet departs his mother's chamber for all appearances a lunatic.

Given his belief in the "reality" of the Ghost, John Dover Wilson is strangely unmindful of the import of this final, and thus deeply consequential, reunion of the royal family. Wilson sees the selective appearance of the Ghost in 3.4. as evidence of Gertrude's infidelity, but he offers no comment on the manner and degree to which Hamlet's perceived madness will shape things to come. The sinister implications of the Ghost's final encounter with his wife and son—that the Ghost is a demonic spirit orchestrating the catastrophe of the play—may simply have been too radical for Wilson to entertain, even though his own evidence drawn from Renaissance sources practically cries out for such an interpretation.

The radically revisionist view of the Ghost as a malevolent figure intent on ruin would be left for a later scholar-critic, Eleanor Prosser, to present. First published in 1967, her *Hamlet and Revenge* stands as a milestone in *Hamlet* studies, marking a major development in the history of *Hamlet* criticism. Prosser considers Renaissance spiritualism in greater detail than did Wilson. Both Protestants and Catholics agree that ghosts are, more likely than not, evil spirits, though both faiths allowed for the remote possibility of benevolent visitations, Protestants in the case of angelic intercession, Catholics in the case of purgatorial return, the only possibility for a true return of the dead. How would a person of 1600, confronted with an apparition, decide whether it was "a spirit of health or goblin damned?" Prosser offers a checklist of pertinent considerations.

When did a specter appear? Any time, any day except Sunday. If at night, especially near or at midnight, then it was certainly demonic. Any spirit that departs at daybreak is likely evil.

Where? Ghosts might appear anywhere, but evil spirits haunted graveyards, crime scenes, battlefields, gallows, prisons, ruined cities, old houses, and castles— places associated with violence or death. Their fondness for mines and precipices is especially significant for Hamlet, since Horatio warns Hamlet that the Ghost may lead him "to the dreadful summit of the cliff," and later appears under the stage, in the cellarage.

To whom? Ghosts could appear to anyone, but evil spirits often haunt the simple and credulous, innocent children, murderers, tyrants, and magicians. They are, as Wilson had noted, especially attracted to melancholics.

What might be its strategy? Subterfuge was a valuable device. Evil spirits routinely "exhort us to virtue to gain authority."

What does it look like? It might appear in the shape of a man or beast. Angels and demons alike were luminous figures, but demons were shrouded in shadow or haloed in flickering lights.

Do ghosts speak? Yes, but only when spoken to. Angels and purgatorial souls speak with gentle and musical voices; demons' voices are "rough, harsh and loud."

The purpose of the visitation? Gentle purgatorial souls could return only to perform God's will, or "to aid and encheer" the living. Angry demons were bent on wrecking havoc, bringing destruction, death, and damnation.

This synopsis makes clear the overwhelming likelihood that the Ghost of Hamlet's father is, from the perspective of Shakespeare's audience, a malevolent spirit, one whose effect is predictably disastrous. Considering the play from a Christian perspective, Hamlet's mission of revenge—to which he is directed by the Ghost—must in fact be morally unacceptable, despite our very real sense that to persist in delay, to do nothing, is worse than doing something, however tardy. Volumes of evidence adduced from Renaissance sources reflect the disposition that revenge was the work of God not man, that no good could come of it, either for the avenged, of course, or for the avenger, or for the society to which they belong.

Because it makes sense of Hamlet's descent into madness (as opposed to the guise of madness), his abuse of Ophelia, his murder of Polonius, his haranguing of his mother, the killings of Rosencrantz and Guildenstern, and much else that is troubling and out of step with Hamlet as righteous hero, Prosser's thesis is tempting.

The problem is that when taken to its logical conclusion—that the Ghost is evil and that Hamlet's revenge damnable—it reduces one of the world's greatest tragedies to a fable, to an exemplum of moral weakness. Prosser, however, is careful to forestall this conclusion. While tradition may point to warnings that the Ghost is evil, the dramatic situation is not entirely clear. The Ghost, after all, reveals a terrible truth that must be addressed, lest evil go undetected. We are left with a vital uncertainty, an ambiguity that elevates Hamlet's predicament to tragic dimensions. "If we could unequivocally pronounce the host a demon and its command a damnable temptation, the tragedy would be destroyed," she concedes. "We cannot, and as a result are caught up in Hamlet's dilemma"—the question whether the Ghost is an instrument of good or evil. "The warnings have not made us pull back and condemn his vow to take revenge; they have made us aware of the intolerable alternatives he faces. . . . To retreat into patience would be to acquiesce in the evil. But, as both Hamlet and the audience . . . know, to act may be to couple Hell."

In order to preserve Hamlet's status as a tragic hero, Prosser, moreover, must cast him as something other than the instrument of the Ghost. "The command to murder [Claudius]," she concludes, may be "as malign as we sense it to be," but "Hamlet himself is responsible for his descent into savagery." Hamlet is endowed with free will; his decisions are his own, his fate the result of a very difficult choice, one that will destroy many lives, including his own. But would it have been better not to act? Obviously not. To ignore the Ghost's command to avenge his murder, to leave vengeance to God, might be the morally correct choice, one insisted upon by virtually every commentator in Shakespeare's time; but it's difficult to imagine how that would have produced a tragedy for Hamlet, much less a great one.

Still, the bloody spectacle of the final scene is a stark reminder of the cost of Hamlet's decisions. It can't be tidied up with accounts, however sincere, of Hamlet's tragic stature, not even with the mitigating contextual circumstances such as Hamlet's brief reign as king, Horatio's poignant benediction, and Fortinbras' according Hamlet's corpse soldier status. "Hamlet's revenge," Prosser writes, "has led him to wanton and meaningless slaughter. He may have ultimately won the battle within himself, but he dies with the blood of eight men on his hands, five of them innocent victims, helpless bystanders who were pointlessly struck down because they came between two mighty opposites. Hamlet's revenge has led to the destruction of two entire families and to the abandonment of the State to a foreign adventurer."

Surprisingly, Prosser makes no effort to trace the stark horrors of the final scene—whose very dreadfulness proves her thesis—back to the pivotal 3.4 when the Ghost appears to Hamlet but not to Gertrude. Of 3.4, Prosser is mainly concerned with showing that the encounter does not, as presumably it should, drive Gertrude to contrition for her sins. Prosser concedes that the scene "offers further evidence of Hamlet's progressive descent into evil," but that dark path is not her focus.

Neither is what seems to me the all-important question of why the Ghost doesn't appear to both. Prosser raises two possible reasons for the Ghost not appearing to Gertrude: one, that it wishes to protect the widow from the true sinfulness of her actions; and the other, that the Ghost wishes to spare her the knowledge that her new husband is a murderer. Prosser rightly dispels both notions. From a Christian ethical position, there could be no reason to withhold the truth from Gertrude, however painful that truth may be, since "self-knowledge leads to salvation." Furthermore, would the loving husband, "a spirit of grace," deliberately create the illusion that her son is a "lunatic whose words can be dismissed as mere raving?" Wouldn't it be better to reveal that Gertrude is living with a murderer (assuming she doesn't already know this) than to persist in blindly trusting Claudius? But Prosser isn't interested in the impact this selective appearance has on the direction of the action, in shaping Hamlet's future, and the futures of the others who will die off- and onstage. Prosser's conclusion seems patently myopic. The Ghost's final visitation, Prosser says, "has served only one purpose: not to lead Gertrude to Heaven but to leave her to Hell."

Hamlet's final encounter with his father's ghost, though now an irrevocably fading presence, is a last, brilliantly successful direction of the action of the play. Whether Hamlet is hallucinating in the Closet Scene, or is actually confronting the Ghost, the effect is the same. The encounter sets Gertrude up to betray her son. When Hamlet lugs the corpse of Polonius, this "most still, most secret and most grave" councilor, from the room, he believes that he has made an ally of his mother. The perplexed Queen has vowed not to tell anyone what Hamlet has said, and, strictly speaking, she's true to her word. But her actions effectively betray Hamlet, sealing her son's fate as well as her own and others'. She immediately reports the murder of Polonius to her husband, thus removing any doubt that may have lingered in Claudius' mind that Hamlet has to be eliminated. Hamlet, she tells her husband, is as mad as the global forces of nature, the sea and wind when they "contend which is the mightier." Her language spins the event so as to impugn her son's action while effectively suppressing her own complicity—and the King's—in the circumstance that led to the killing of Polonius. She conveys, moreover, no hint of the emotional storm that raged between mother and son in her closet. Her report to Claudius lays the blame squarely on mad Hamlet while honoring Polonius as "the unseen good old man." Hamlet acted in a "lawless fit," and with a "*brainish* apprehension" stabbed him (my emphasis). This seat of Hamlet's rage is the brain, importantly, not the heart.

Though Prosser's reading of 3.4 turns away from the most radical consequences of that scene, those consequences must be explored. Perhaps it's not

Hamlet who avenges the murder of his father, but rather Hamlet's father who, with this one trick, effectively guarantees that he will avenge his *own* murder, reducing the cast of *Hamlet* to his own sorry condition. After all, who among the dead at the end of the play is properly shrived? Who will rest in peace? None, perhaps. All are cut off in the blossom of their sins, "Unhouseled, disappointed, unaneled," as the Ghost says of himself.

If the Ghost's motive has all along been to ruin those he left behind, to accomplish a sort of universal revenge such as Amleth carries out in the Danish saga, then it has succeeded wonderfully. It has scourged Denmark, leaving only a ghastly spectacle of corpses at the feet of a skeleton crew—the historian Horatio and the new king Fortinbras—to remember the past and direct the future. None of Hamlet's rich and tortured questioning, none of his radical internalizing of reality, none of his brilliant antics or his terrible bouts with madness, not even the question of whether to be or not to be—none of this and nothing else can divert the action from such a terrible consequence as this.

Does it finally matter whether the Ghost in 3.4 is in fact a true spirit, either good or evil, or a hallucination? Well, yes and no. No, because the question is entirely unanswerable—the encounter itself yields no discernable answer whether the Ghost is an objective reality or a product of Hamlet's imagination. Yes, on the other hand, because it is a dramatic reality and because the nature of the tragedy is significantly different if the final appearance of the Ghost is a dramatic projection of Hamlet's mind. If this is the case, then *Hamlet* is a tragedy of a very human nature, the struggle of an individual against the demons of the mind. Hamlet's actions are not, except in the loosest sense that we are all on the road to death, the result of fate or Providence. If we believe the Ghost is real, then the tragedy of *Hamlet* takes on cosmic dimensions. It's Greek tragedy, the struggle of a man against fate. It's man contesting hopelessly with the gods, whose ends Hamlet ultimately must serve.

This is not, I think, the case. *Hamlet* is not modeled on Attic tragedy, though it may be thought to share general affinities with Greek drama. We have no formal chorus (though the Ghost may be thought to serve that capacity), no ritual dance and song, no flowing gowns; no *deus ex machina*, no god in the machine, directs *Hamlet*. It is rather, as Hegel said, the supreme modern play. As I have argued, *Hamlet* marks a turning point in the historical process whereby reality becomes internalized. The Ghost is a representation of this process. Because it materializes multiple times before Barnardo, Marcellus, and Horatio in the first act, I find the Greg's theory of collective psychosis incredible. But its final appearance is another thing entirely. If we think of Hamlet Sr. in 3.4 as a hallucination, then the Ghost is a projection of something produced within Hamlet's brain. *Hamlet* is, as Prosser believes, a tragedy of personal choice. But these choices are directed by and through the individual mind, housed within this nutshell that contains infinity. As hallucination, the Ghost represents the internal reality of Hamlet's psyche, a subjective phenomenon projected as objective form.

If manic depression is a frustrated mess, psychosis is a much more serious disorder. It's not that the mind judges things good or bad by its own directives. In the case of hallucination, the mind invents what is not there, and then, as Hamlet does in 3.4, it must decide whether what it conjures is good or bad. If we take the Ghost in 3.4 as a phantasm of the mind, then this is the moment of Hamlet's most extreme mental disturbance, the point at which he becomes completely divorced from "reality." But this is a momentary condition. A mad Hamlet can't be a heroic Hamlet. He must, and he does, recover his sanity in the play's final movement.

Like all claims for *Hamlet*, this one—that Shakespeare meant to indicate that Hamlet is hallucinating in 3.4—is compromised by the problems of the text. No reading of *Hamlet* can be anything other than a confrontation with the text and yet, as we saw in an earlier chapter, there are three significantly different texts of *Hamlet* with some claim to authority, and behind these is a massing play based upon the Danish saga of Amleth/Hamlet. The resulting textual complications and uncertainties are baffling. In the same decade that Stopes and Greg were claiming the Ghost to be a hallucination, J. M. Robertson in *The Problem of Hamlet* (1919) drew attention to the unstable ground on which all readings of the play are made to stand. Focusing attention on the "problem" of Hamlet's delay, Robertson rehearsed the weaknesses in the argument of the Goethe/Schlegel/Coleridge tradition, which saw Hamlet's delay as a result of his psychological disposition, and the weaknesses of a lesser known tradition of German criticism that argued that, given the circumstances of the crime, no adequate means were available to Hamlet for bringing

Claudius to justice. Robertson rejects not only these views; he also dismisses the charge that Shakespeare himself is at fault for Hamlet's otherwise inexplicable tendency to delay acting. All three theories are undone, Robertson argued, by the very fact that *Hamlet* is not "a planned play" but rather "a play of adaptation and adjustment." The stuff of *Hamlet* is inherited material extending back in time to Danish mythology, relatively little of which Shakespeare himself invented. The shape of this material was hardly consistent or logical, which explains why *Hamlet* "is not an intelligible drama as it stands." It is entirely mistaken, Robertson insisted, to treat Hamlet as a work conceived by Shakespeare *ab ovo*, literally "from the egg," as commentators routinely do. The work rather resembles a kind of dramatic palimpsest, a surface on which traces of earlier hands—Saxo, Belleforest, Kyd, and perhaps others unknown—mingle with Shakespeare's to produce, in its ultimate form, a masterpiece characterized by strange anomalous qualities and aspects. Given the fact that the immediate source of *Hamlet* is missing, no reading of the play can reveal an entirely coherent design. Reminding critics of the difficulties of the text, Robertson's argument, if squarely confronted, threatens to nullify all interpretations of *Hamlet*.

Today, Robertson's *The Problem of Hamlet* is remembered principally for providing the impetus for T. S. Eliot's provocative essay, "Hamlet and His Problems," in which Eliot famously claimed that Hamlet "is most certainly an artistic failure," and that Shakespeare was unable to wrest his inherited material into a coherent shape. That is, the work Shakespeare inherited from the Danish sources through the intermediary of the Ur-*Hamlet* was beyond the dramatist's ability to adequately shape and thus produce coherent meaning.

For Eliot, the peculiar inadequacy of Hamlet the character is the inadequacy of the "objective correlative"—"a set of objects, a situation, a chain of events" through which character is adequately expressed. There are no objective means of conveying the deep emotions that torment Hamlet:

> Hamlet (the man) is dominated by an emotion which is inexpressible, because it is in excess of the facts as they appear. And the supposed identity of Hamlet with his author is genuine to this point: that Hamlet's bafflement at the absence of an objective equivalent to his feelings is a prolongation of the bafflement of his creator in the face of his artistic problem. Hamlet is up against the difficulty that his disgust is occasioned by his mother, but that his mother is not an adequate equivalent for it; his disgust envelops and exceeds her. It is thus a feeling which he cannot understand; he cannot objectify it, and it therefore remains to poison life and obstruct action.

We must simply admit," Eliot concluded, "that here Shakespeare tackled a problem which proved too much for him."

The Byzantine complexities of the texts of *Hamlet*, complexities that make any reading of the play contingent and provisional, became the main concern of a host of textual critics in the latter part of the twentieth century. To these commentators, more so than to readers trained in other approaches to literary analysis, an understanding of the transmission of the material of *Hamlet* is of foremost concern. Textual critics have shown us that *Hamlet* is shaky ground, indeed. The usual practice of conflating Q1, Q2, and F1 into a composite text and presenting that as *Hamlet* can't be justified as reflecting Shakespeare's authorial design and intention. The composite *Hamlet* is the work of editors, not the dramatist. When the 1986 Oxford Shakespeare printed two versions of *King Lear*, a similar fate for the various *Hamlets* couldn't have been far behind. The 2006 Arden edition of *Hamlet* prints separately all three version of the play, the 1603 Q1 and the 1623 Folio versions in one volume, the 1604–1605 Q2 version in another. Traditionally, the Arden editions have been the most heavily documented, and thus the most authoritative editions of Shakespeare's plays. If the Arden assumes a position atop the pantheon of scholarly editions of *Hamlet*, as it likely will, then future students of the play will have to make some very difficult choices that were heretofore made for them by editors. Q1 will always occupy something of a niche position, appealing to those attempting to reconstruct an Elizabethan acting version of the play. But the other two versions will require painful sacrifices for directors and actors, teachers and students alike. If we adopt Q2, we will preserve Hamlet's fourth soliloquy but we will lose his remarks on the child acting companies and his profound skepticism that are present only in F1. If we select F1, then we must sacrifice the last of the play's four great set speeches.

POLITICAL *HAMLET*

Until the twenty-first century, the 4.4 soliloquy was routinely cut from productions. This is because it contributed, to be sure, to the impression of Hamlet as a man who still lacked the courage or resolution to bring about his revenge. Throughout much of its stage history, Hamlet was presented as a rather straightforward, if supremely eloquent, avenger, which meant that speeches such as the 4.4 soliloquy that played up his tendency to hesitate, to be paralyzed by thought, were routinely excised. But it also seemed unsettling, I suppose, to have Hamlet dwell, as he does in his final set speech, upon the futility of war. That would be a dimension of his character out of step with any time prior to World War I. Paul Fussell has brilliantly shown how the unprecedented slaughter of innocents in the 1914–18 hostilities forever changed our view of war. Never again, after the horrible specter of trench warfare, after such innovations as the machine gun, the airplane, and poison gas had been introduced with devastating effect, would we see war as the simple display of manly courage, valor, and duty, the unsullied struggle of the forces of good against evil. All wars are ironic, Fussell conceded, but he was able to show that "the Great War was more ironic than any before or since. It was the hideous embarrassment to the prevailing . . . myth which had dominated the public consciousness for a century. It reversed the Idea of Progress." In the aftermath of the largely pointless savagery of World War I, Hamlet's 4.4 soliloquy takes on a new and vital importance. Some parts of it anticipate the great anti-war poetry of Wilfred Owen and Siegfried Sassoon and T. S. Eliot. As a contrast to his own inaction, Hamlet cites ". . . this army of such mass and charge"

> Led by a delicate and tender prince
> Whose spirit with divine ambition puffed
> Makes mouths at the invisible event
> Exposing what is mortal and unsure
> To all that fortune, death and danger dare
> Even for an eggshell.

He ruefully imagines "[t]he imminent death of twenty thousand" of Fortinbras' soldiers

> That for a fantasy and trick of fame
> Go to their graves like beds, fight for a plot
> Whereon the numbers cannot try the cause,
> Which is not tomb enough and continent
> To hide the slain[.]

Eliot's 1922 poem "The Waste Land"—its title drawn from the ghastly spectacle of No Man's Land, the area between the trenches of the First World War where the dead and dying lay—reimagines such pointless butchery, where men died in vast numbers for no reason and to no end. The fifth section of the poem, titled, "What the Thunder Said," is inseparable from the roar of artillery that had only recently ceased and would, with the outbreak of the Second World War, start up again. Tracing Christ's journey with the unknowing disciples on the road to Emmaus, this section opens with images of stunned exhaustion, pain, thirst, and the certain proximity of death.

> After the torchlight red on sweaty faces
> After the frosty silence in the gardens
> After the agony in stony places
> The shouting and the crying
> Prison and palace and reverberation
> Of thunder of spring over distant mountains
> He who was living is now dead
> Who were living are now dying
> With little patience.

Red torches lighting exhausted faces, frosty silences interrupted by sudden thunder, shouts and cries reverberating through prisons and palaces, the specter of the dead and dying—these visions unmistakably recall the unprecedented destruction of the mad war that raged in Europe from 1914 through 1918.

It's not surprising that, in the wake of a war that produced Stalin and Hitler, and prepared the way for Pol Pot and Pinochet, as well as a host of lesser monsters, attention should have turned to the politics of the state in *Hamlet*. While we may be inclined to think of the play as a personal tragedy played out in the context of the family, at mid-century the German playwright Bertolt Brecht, who had worked in an army hospital during the last year of the Great War, reminded us that the forces that shape Hamlet's fate are as much political as they are personal, familial, or spiritual. Indeed, the political nature of the play is precisely the nature of the modern political state. In 1948 Brecht, who had recently fled to Europe from exile in the United States after having testified before the House Un-American Activities Committee, writing under the watchful eye of what he called the "criminal ruling classes," read *Hamlet* as a mirror of "bloody and gloomy" modernity, in a time "of general despair of reason." As was his own age, Brecht saw *Hamlet* framed by war. For Hamlet, the memory of his father's war against Old Fortinbras is fresh, and the possibility of another war pitting yet another generation of Danes against Poles—over "a little patch of ground," the Captain tells Hamlet, "That hath in it no profit but the name"—looms.

In Hamlet's time, as in the post–World War period in which Brecht wrote, the landscape is peopled with spies; the climate demands political loyalty. *Hamlet* opens, tellingly, with a test of allegiance to the State. Bernardo asks, "Who's there?" Francisco challenges him with, "Nay, answer me. Stand and unfold yourself." Barnardo declares, "Long live the King."

The prevalence of eavesdropping, an instrument of state surveillance in *Hamlet*, underscores the political issues at play. I've argued that Hamlet's interiority—"that within which passes show"—signals a relocation of reality. But his interiority can also be seen as a forced retreat from scrutiny. Rosencrantz and Guildenstern are, of course, spies, who would play upon Hamlet as upon a flute, who would know his stops and "pluck out the heart of [his] mystery," sounding Hamlet from his lowest to his highest note. But they are supported by other levels of surveillance closer to home, members of his own family and his intimate circle: Polonius and Ophelia, even his own mother in the Closet Scene.

Perhaps too little attention has been paid to the degree to which Claudius manages the State through surveillance. He's an effective ruler, for sure, neither savage nor ruthless, despite the fact that he acquired his crown by means of fratricide, what Claudius calls "the primal eldest curse." But without hesitating, he exploits everyone within his reach to maintain his power. This is especially true of Polonius' family, whom he enlists in a brilliant but reprehensible—and ultimately unsuccessful—campaign, first to circumscribe and then, when Laertes returns to the action, to neutralize Hamlet. For Claudius, this scrutiny of Hamlet is necessary because he suspects that Hamlet's intent is nothing less than a coup d'etat.

The surveilling State is everywhere evident in the *watching* that pervades *Hamlet*, a motif introduced in the opening exchange among the sentinels Barnardo and Francisco. We start out watching a play that's immediately about watching. The intense level of scrutiny in *Hamlet* forces all characters to assume roles and identities behind which they hide. Discussing a production of *Hamlet* staged in Krakow in 1956, the seminal critic Jan Kott saw not the plight of the individual but the role of political forces in shaping the life of the individual. For Kott, something is indeed rotten in the *state* of Denmark, and Hamlet's Denmark—like Poland in the mid-twentieth century—was, as Hamlet repeatedly says, a prison. In the 1956 Krakow production, Kott saw "only a drama of political crime" that "got at our modern experience, anxiety and sensibility." "Hamlet is mad," Kott wrote, "because politics itself is madness."

The Modern Hamlet is an absurd figure, robbed of humanity, a creature shaped by external forces. Like the other characters, Hamlet's identity is shaped by his position vis-à-vis the State. His identity has been imposed upon him by circumstances he had no part in creating. The book the Krakow Hamlet reads in 2.2 "is not by Montaigne," Kott writes, "but by Sartre, Camus or Kafka." Hamlet is keenly aware of the campaign against him, and he enlists his deeply resonant "antic disposition" as a mechanism of defense, a means of discovering a space beyond the reach of the State where Hamlet himself can hide. His predecessors, Amleth and Hamblet, had done the same thing. Like them, this "madness" registers Hamlet's awareness of the need for partitions, walls, hiding spaces, and secret places, to establish at least the illusion of identity independent of that which is imposed upon him by political circumstances.

Accordingly, productions of Hamlet in post-Stalin Europe present *Hamlet* as "a study of political tyranny," according to Alexander Shurbanov, Professor of English at The University of Sofia, Bulgaria, "easily recognized as the Stalinist repressive regime of the preceding decades." Leon Daniel's landmark 1965 production of the play in Sofia cast the hero as "the only man of conscience [inhabiting] a spiritual void." Hamlet's "noble intelligence was . . . lowered to an indiscriminate neurotic verbal aggression, meant to expose the criminal double-dealings of his environment." He's robbed of everything—his father, his mother, his potential bride, even his final revenge, for in the Daniel production Claudius killed himself "with a scornful pride, thus leaving Hamlet morally and physically helpless in the face of evil. The hero had turned victim." In this vision of the play, "the melancholic prince was transformed into a brave revolutionary waging lonely war for a better world against formidable odds." This *Hamlet* "stunned" its audience; it spoke "about issues that concerned the spectators immediately." The authorities were rightly concerned both because of its "disrespect for authority" and its defiance of "hierarchical decorum." For the next fifteen years, Shurbanov reports, revolutionary Shakespeare ruled the stages of Eastern Europe and the Soviet Union, the most famous instance being Yuri Lyubimov's Moscow *Hamlet*, which toured Europe during the mid-1970s. These productions often depicted the Prince as completely alienated in a world where everyone, even his supposed allies, conspired in his ruin. Perhaps unaware that it was picking up on a thread sewn into the Danish sagas, Jan Maciejowski's 1973 Polish *Hamlet* presented Ophelia as "a sexual opportunist" working as an agent of the State. In the same year, Dinu Cerernescu's Bucharest version gave the audience a Horatio who was, according to Shurbanov, "an arch-villain leading Hamlet by the nose into a trap meant to open the way for a new, more sinister usurpation of the Danish throne by the treacherous foreigner Fortinbras." At times, the drive to render *Hamlet* as a condemnation of the State travestied the work, rendering it merely "a chronicle play devoted to the problem of political power and its mechanisms." A 1981 Bulgarian production presented Hamlet "surrounded by a host of callous timeservers in the grip of an implacable police state." This Hamlet could express his disgust only by "intermittent vomiting and imprecation." As he succumbed to the implacable dictates of the State, he descended into unthinkable "cruelty by torturing and butchering captive animals."

Indiscriminate destruction seems of particular interest in more recent productions. In Kenneth Branagh's 1996 film version of *Hamlet*, for instance, Fortinbras' invading troops are seen making their way across the frozen landscape and then, at the end, smashing their way through Elsinore. Yet, the storming of Elsinore has one virtue missing from modern warfare, and so is of interest for its difference. Fortinbras leads the assault. He risks death with his men, something missing when those who make war merely direct it, for good or ill. Those who instigate modern wars would not be present at the final scene of the play, and so could not possibly achieve the status of the monomaniacal Fortinbras. Dying Hamlet gives Fortinbras his vote for the next king, but if we listen carefully we might hear the cries of mothers and wives whose sons and husbands will be taken off for an eggshell.

As I have said, Shakespeare's Hamlet comes closest to addressing the savage consequences of political decisions in his last soliloquy, which appears only in Q2. Some have found authorial intention behind its absence from Q1 and F1, believing that Shakespeare himself excised the speech because it was redundant and, furthermore, gave Hamlet a resolve that's premature considering his continuing irresolution at the beginning of the fifth act. But I believe that this soliloquy is indispensable because it does reveal new, if subtle aspects of Hamlet's struggle. Consider Hamlet's situation, here at 4.4. A weary man staggering under the weight of his bizarre circumstances, he's alone on stage, though observed by Rosencrantz and Guildenstern from the wings. For a prince who's been so often accused of inaction, much has happened to Hamlet that, in turn, has required of him much reaction. His father dying and his mother remarrying distressed him, but his anguish is deepened when his father's ghost, of all things, appears to him, identifies his killer and charges Hamlet with the burden of avenging the murder. His crown stolen, his mother whored, his friends turned against him, Hamlet has had to struggle with both the ethical and the tactical problems of revenge. He's abused a woman he loves and hates, mounted a skit that proved the identity of his father's killer, passed up the chance to kill Claudius, then murdered an innocent man. Now exiled, on his way over water, he will arrange the deaths of Rosencrantz and Guildenstern, return to Denmark, and bring about a colossal, terrible catastrophe. Hamlet has done much, if not yet that thing the Ghost has commanded. He's now in a very high place, poised to kill again and die, to bring the play to the end.

He does begin his final soliloquy, it is true, on a familiar self-critical note, berating himself for failing to act, comparing himself to a beast which merely sleeps and feeds. If it's not "bestial oblivion" blocking his revenge, then it must be "some craven scruple / Of thinking too much on th' event," returning to the idea that thought—"which quartered hath but one part wisdom / And ever three parts cowardice"—frustrates action. The world is full of action—"examples gross as earth" exhort him. When Hamlet considers the immediate example of the Norwegian army, his attention turns away from himself to the horrors of war. Hamlet's attitude is remarkably ambivalent, his language alternating between admiration for the Norwegian commander, and an awareness of the casual—and pointless—slaughter the ego-driven Fortinbras will precipitate. Hamlet admires this "delicate and tender prince," the son of the king his father had killed, whose spirit is "with divine ambition *puffed*" (my emphasis). Hamlet remarks that Fortinbras will lead twenty thousand men to their imminent deaths, contending for a plot of land "whereon the numbers cannot try the cause, / Which is not tomb enough and continent / To hide the slain."

All this slaughter, droll Hamlet says, "for an eggshell." Claudius is a ruthless tyrant; Prince Fortinbras the casual murderer of innocents. In his apparent revulsion at sending men to die "for an eggshell," Hamlet is the kindred spirit of war-weary Europeans like Brecht and Kott who saw nothing but mendacity, viciousness, and absurdity in their rulers. Hamlet's skepticism and his sense of the absurd rain down like bombshells on modern life, so steeped in the blood of innocents. Though many others must have felt the same way, this sentiment comes from the mind of Shakespeare—there's no apparent connection between this soliloquy and Shakespeare's sources—writing in a time before pavement covered muck, before astringents covered the smell of death, before electricity, modern transportation, medicine, before air conditioners, aspirin, airplanes and rockets, skyscrapers—so much that hides savagery behind the appearance of progress and evolution.

The Moderns, for the first time, recognized and reckoned with political *Hamlet*. And, like Eliot's characters trudging toward Emmaus in "The Waste Land," they were impatient. That's because countless of their numbers—combatants, and the maimed, sickened, and pulverized victims of "collateral damage"—had been sacrificed "for an eggshell," for some misplaced ideology, or The Word from God, or Manifest Destiny, or plain greed and criminality. Heads of state sent innocent people, so often the young and defenseless, to violent deaths. And so we are left wondering how it is possible for Hamlet to admire this apparently ruthless prince who will shortly assume the kingship of Denmark as well as Norway, with Hamlet's dying assent. I don't know the answer to that question, but the question itself is entirely political.

THE MAN IN BLACK
GALLERY TWO

Figure 1B   Richard Burbage (1567?–1619)

Sometime between 1599 and early 1602, the thirty-something Richard Burbage took the stage as the first Hamlet. He seems to have been a portly man, if Gertrude's remark in the final scene that her son is "fat and scant of breath" nods to Burbage's physique and not to the fact that he's sweating, which Shakespeare's age thought of as burning fat. Burbage, the great tragedian of Shakespeare's acting company, Lord Chamberlain's Men and The King's Men, played the lead roles in *Othello* and *King Lear* as well. To the extent that Hamlet's advice to the visiting players can be taken to represent Shakespeare's own directorial preferences, Burbage must have played these roles with a naturalism that would be familiar to modern audiences. Hamlet enjoins the players to "suit the action to the word, the word to the action, with this special observance—that you not o'erstep the modesty of nature. For . . . the purpose of playing . . . was and is to hold as 'twere the mirror up to nature. . . ." By permission of the Dulwich Picture Gallery.

Betterton as "Hamlet."

Figure 2B Thomas Betterton (1635?–1710)

The first great Hamlet after Burbage, Thomas Betterton played the role for more than forty years on the Restoration stage and into the eighteenth century, when Betterton was in his 70s. Having been trained by Sir William Davenant, said to have been the illegitimate son of Shakespeare himself, Betterton was only twice removed from Shakespeare's theatrical traditions and practices. A stout, muscular man, Betterton was widely praised by theater-goers and the literati, including Samuel Pepys, Alexander Pope and Richard Steele. In contrast to the wan, thin, thought-distracted Hamlet of the subsequent Romantic tradition, the Davenant/Betterton Hamlet was rendered through strategic cuts an aggressive avenger. Here, Betterton's strikes the "start" pose at Hamlet's first encounter (1.4) with the Ghost. Note that Betterton performed the role of Hamlet in Restoration dress. By permission of the Folger Shakespeare Library.

Figure 3B   David Garrick (1717–1779)

The famed actor and theater manager David Garrick, dressed in black, strikes the "start"
pose in a 1754 production of Hamlet at Drury Lane (Garrick first played Hamlet in 1742).
The greatest actor of his generation, Garrick was diminutive but gifted with a great voice,
and an ability to create quixotic shifts of mood. He was also cribbed by Enlightenment
principles of decorum. He cut Hamlet's vow to kill Claudius when he's "drunk, asleep or in
his rage / Or in the incestuous pleasure of his bed" and trimmed much else that might
offend eighteenth-century sensibilities, including the graveyard scene, 5.1. But his performances were famously powerful and moving, so much so that they lent themselves to parody.
In Henry Fielding's novel *Tom Jones* (1749), Tom attends a Garrick performance of *Hamlet*
in the company of dullard Partridge, who is completely taken in by Garrick's reaction to the
Ghost. "Nay, you can call me coward if you will; but if that little man there upon the stage is
not frightened, I never saw any man frightened in my life." By permission of the Folger
Shakespeare Library.

EDMUND KEAN.

Figure 4B Edmund Kean (1787–1833)

Following the thirty-four year reign of John Philip Kemble as Hamlet on the English stage, Edmund Kean brought a new passion and quixotic action to the role reminiscent of David Garrick and much admired by Romantic commentators such as Leigh Hunt and William Hazlitt. Samuel Taylor Coleridge, who didn't entirely approve of Kean's Hamlet, remarked that watching him play the role was "like reading Shakespeare by flashes of lightning." Yet Kean could rein in his energies at crucial moments, as in the nunnery scene (3.1) when Kean treated Ophelia with surprising restraint if not gentleness. At the end of their encounter, Kean turned to Ophelia and kissed her hand. He was quite the opposite moments later scene (3.2) when he crawled menacingly toward Claudius while the "Mousetrap" unfolded and gave a triumphant shout when Claudius called for the lights. Kean played Hamlet for two decades. By permission of the Folger Shakespeare Library.

HOW EDWIN BOOTH HIT UPON THE PRESENT MODE OF CARRYING HIS SWORD IN THE GHOST SCENE OF HAMLET.

FRITZ LEIBER
AS HAMLET

Figures 5B and 6B   Left, Edwin Booth (1833–1893); right, Fritz Leiber (1882–1949)

Left: Confronting the Ghost, Edwin Booth holds the sword by its blade, with the hilt forming an apotropaic cross. One widespread story holds that Booth stumbled upon this famous pose by accident. Drawing his sword in rehearsal, it slipped from his hand and he caught it by the blade, realizing instantly how appropriate and powerful the image of the cross was. Many actors, including Sarah Bernhardt and the American Fritz Leiber Sr., at right, followed Booth in using the hilt of the sword as a cross to ward off a possibly evil ghost. By permission of the Folger Shakespeare Library.

Figures 7B and 8B Left, William Charles Macready (1793–1873). Right, Edwin Forrest (1806–1872)

"What mighty contests," wrote Alexander Pope, "rise from trivial things." The English actor Macready introduced some new stage business in the Player Scene (3.2) to explain Hamlet's remark "I must be idle." To Macready this suggested Hamlet's antic disposition. So he pranced and jigged across the stage twirling a handkerchief over his head. Doing this bit in Edinburgh, he was greeted with a vicious hiss from an audience member—Edwin Forrest, America's first tragedian. The subsequent feud between the two actors—the effete, scholarly Englishman and the brawny, populist American—escalated into a conflict between respective national characters, which exploded into deadly violence on the evening of May 10, 1849, at the Astor Place Theater in New York City. While Macready was playing Macbeth inside, outside an angry mob of gangland hooligans, whipped into an anti-English frenzy, descended on Astor Place. The crowd numbering perhaps twenty thousand pelted the theater with stones, smashing windows and littering the lobby with debris. Fearing the worst for the night's performance, authorities had stationed several regiments of militia nearby. When the rabble turned on the soldiers, they responded by firing volleys into the panicked crowd, killing more than thirty men, women and children, and leaving scores more wounded or trampled. It was first time American troops had fired on their own country-men, and probably the greatest violence ever occasioned by Shakespeare. Courtesy of Michael A. Morrison Collection.

Figure 9B Jason Asprey

Asprey as the youthful, fully sexualized Hamlet in the 2006 production of the play by Shakespeare and Company, presents a stark contrast to Burbage, Betterton and other mature Hamlets of tradition. Asprey recalls Adonis, whom Shakespeare memorably rendered in his 1593 Ovidian erotic poem, *Venus and Adonis*. Photograph courtesy of Kevin Sprague, Studio Two.

Figure 10B   Rebecca Hall

By the time Sarah Bernhardt mounted her 1899 production of *Hamlet*, more than 50 women had played the Prince. In 1881, E. P. Vining claimed that Hamlet's propensity to delay was the result of the fact that he "was born lacking in many of the elements of virility"—that, in effect, Hamlet was a woman trapped in a man's body. As preposterous as this may seem, over time the character has undergone a marked feminization. Here Rebecca Hall, in the 1997 Theatre Nomad production, asserts female sexuality in the posture of male aggression. Photograph by Sarah Ainslie; courtesy of Theatre Nomad.

NINE

POSTMODERN HAMLET

*T*he *Merchant of Venice* opens with melancholic Antonio, the merchant
of Venice, lamenting to his friends Solanio and Salerio his inability to find
the source of his sadness. Notice how Antonio has a smack of Hamlet
in him:

> In sooth, I know not why I am so sad.
> It wearies me, you say it wearies you;
> But how I caught it, found it or came by it,
> What stuff 'tis made of, whereof it is born
> I am to learn.
> And such a want-wit sadness makes of me
> That I have much ado to know myself.

What *is* postmodernism? Where are its roots, its seeds? Attempting to define
postmodernism, to say when it came about, or even what it is or is not, may seem
as elusive as Antonio's sadness. The simplest definition—postmodern is what
follows the modern—tells us nothing. And many postmodern critics would bristle
at the attempt to historicize postmodernism. But that which is "post" must necessarily involve chronology. The movement, such as it is, must define itself against
time. So, we start with history.

Aspects of the postmodern appear in the version of existential philosophy
developed by Jean-Paul Sartre after World War II, especially in his atheism, in his

insistence upon the facticity of life, and in his belief that the self, to a significant degree, is shaped by cultural, political, and, most important, by economic forces external to it. Both postmodernism and Sartrean existentialism endorse the Marxist view of history as dialectic, but of course in different ways and in differing degrees. While Sartre never abandoned the idea of the self as authentic agent, postmodern thought, it seems to me, sees the self much more completely as constructed.

But the seeds of postmodernism were planted long before the existential movement. Sartre builds upon phenomenological theories of the German philosopher Martin Heidegger (1889–1976), and reaches back along a German philosophical fault line to Frederick Nietzsche (1844–1900). In *The Birth of Tragedy* (1872), Nietzsche, reacting against his view of the modern world as ruinously dominated by the pursuit of knowledge, looked back to the great tragedies of fifth-century BC Athens as the supreme moments in human history. Attic tragedy, according to Nietzsche, presented a near-perfect equipoise of the two contrary impulses that govern the human soul and thus all societies: first, the drive to differentiate, demarcate, and delimit life, to individualize and partition, which Nietzsche associated with the god Apollo; and second, the opposite drive to transgress law, exceed distinctions, obliterate boundaries; to drown the individual in excess. This was Dionysus. Nietzsche saw these two drives—the Appollonian represented by epic poetry and the Dionysian by choral song and dance—as contesting for the Greek soul in the tragedies performed in the amphitheaters of Athens.

This cultural high point was eclipsed by the advent of Socratic rationalism, which, according to recent editors of *The Birth of Tragedy*, "upsets the delicate balance on which tragedy depends, by encouraging people not to strive for wisdom in the face of the necessary unsatifactoriness of human life, but to attempt to use knowledge to get control of their fate. 'Modern culture' arises in direct continuity out of such Socratism."

Nietzsche ushers in the radical skepticism and doubt of twentieth-century thought. And he locates this skepticism specifically in the character of Hamlet. The ideal "Dionysiac man," Nietzsche writes,

> is similar to Hamlet: both have gazed into the true essence of things, they have *acquired knowledge* and they find action repulsive, for their actions can do nothing to change the eternal essence of things; they regard it as laughable or shameful that they should be expected to set to rights a world so out of joint. Knowledge kills action; action requires that one to be shrouded in a veil of illusion—this is

the lesson of Hamlet, not that cheap wisdom about Jack the Dreamer who does not get around to acting because he reflects too much, out of an excess of possibilities, as it were. No, it is not reflection, it is true knowledge, insight into the terrible truth, which outweighs every motive for action, both in the case of Hamlet and that of the Dionysiac man. Now no solace has any effect, there is a longing for a world beyond death, beyond the gods themselves; existence is denied, along with its treacherous reflection in the gods or in some immortal Beyond. Once truth has been seen, the consciousness of it prompts man to see only what is terrible or absurd in existence wherever he looks; now he understands the symbolism of Ophelia's fate, now he grasps the wisdom of the wood-god Silenus: he feels revulsion.

Nietzsche's Hamlet stares into the abyss of mortality, with no thought of the transcendence of his soul. In his dying hour Hamlet turns not to the heavens but to Horatio, his mortal friend, to tell his story, to perpetuate his memory. Hamlet places his faith not in God but in man. The perpetuation of life after death, which was so desperately important to Shakespeare's age, is dependent upon memory.

Nietzsche's Hamlet is a far cry from the Hamlet of Romantic tradition, the costly vase, as Goethe described him, into which is planted the unbearable burden of an oak tree. Neither is he the tidied up Prince of mainstream Anglo-American critics. Neither is he the psychological specimen modern critics made him out to be. Whether the Ghost is real or not would hardly seem to matter to Nietzsche. Hamlet is an emblem of death, or rather death in life. He has looked into the dark abyss of life and known it for what it is—a tale told by an idiot, full of sound and fury, signifying nothing. Hamlet hesitates to act because he knows that action is useless. When action becomes unavoidable, he commits himself to butchery with utter abandon, sacrificing his own life while killing Laertes, double-killing Claudius (with sword, followed by poison), while his mother dies in a grotesque exhibition of violence that, if imagined literally, would leave the stage awash in blood and vomit.

This is surely a Hamlet beyond good and evil, or rather one for whom good and evil are merely products of the mind, of thought that fashions reality. He is not an ideal young man crushed under a burden too heavy for anyone to bear, not a sensitive soul given to too much feeling, not an intellectual too mired in thought to know how and when to act. Rather, he is aware of the horrible emptiness of a world that merely reflects, in its own impenetrable darkness, his own bleak reality.

This darkest strain of criticism in the history of reception was taken up in 1930 by the Shakespearean scholar and critic G. Wilson Knight, who wrote that when we first meet him, Hamlet "has lost all sense of life's significance." Against the vibrant background of court life—ceremonies, the traffic of emissaries, carousing at the center of national power—Hamlet is strikingly out of step, a man who is bereft of purpose, who sees "no possibility of creative action," for whom "No act but suicide is rational." Romantic love, the antithetical impulse to death, exerts only a fleeting influence upon him, and he is drawn to the spectacle of death with a magnetic attraction. Knight writes, "[t]he horror of humanity doomed to death and decay has disintegrated Hamlet's mind." Whereas many eighteenth- and nineteenth-century productions had shortened or completely excised 5.1, Knight finds the magnificent "prose threnody of the Graveyard scene" compelling. In a summary comment he writes that Hamlet's "disease—or vision—is primarily one of negation, of death. Hamlet is a living death in the midst of life."

The Nietszchean Hamlet taken up by Knight anticipates postmodern thought, which dismisses the belief in a coherent, providentially driven history. There is no God, only gods; no History, only fragmented and localized histories. In philosophy, history, and literature of the postmodern era, the spiritual is rejected in favor of the material. How people actually lived becomes important in a way it had never been before. The record of "Early Modern England" (which replaces the value-weighted term "Renaissance") comprises all artifacts, the writings of and about monarchs, priests, poets, dramatists, philosophers, memoirists, physicians, explorers, tailors, physicians, anecdotalists—anyone who left a trace record. All this, everything, must be sorted through, investigated without any necessary regard to rank or status.

As defined by exponents such as Ihab Hassan and Jean-François Lyotard, postmodernism begins with the assumption of indeterminacy, a belief in relativism, that there are no transcendent truths, that all claims are temporal and contingent. Good and evil, right and wrong, are not given but constructed. It follows that there are no absolute distinctions between high and low culture. All media, all genres, are equally important or unimportant, and may be treated together without challenges to appropriateness or quality. Shakespeare's plays are a priori no more important or better than Marvel Comics. We can talk of Hamlet and Spiderman in the same breath, yoke Rosalind and Cher, pair the Wife of Bath and Madonna.

Following Sartre and other existentialist philosophers, postmodernism rejected what it saw as the modernist belief that the self is an inherent, natural entity, existing apart from the cultural, economic, and political forces that shape it. The self is the product of complex external forces that shape individual life, forces both microcosmic—the daily bombardment of media images, say—to the macrocosmic—the global economic forces that shape life from the slums of Colombia to TriBeCa lofts. Differences among individuals are the accidents of birth, circumstances over which we have little or no control. Given the absurd circumstance of life, postmodern man revels in transgressive acts—in "travesty, grotesquerie and parody." The love of play in its myriad senses is essential to postmodernism, theater being only one form that interests postmodernists. They are especially fond of word and image play. The fragmented and mirroring narratives of Thomas Pynchon are favored, as are films featuring such techniques, *Blade Runner*, *Natural Born Killers*, and *Pulp Fiction*. Given its interest in popular culture, you might expect postmodern criticism to be indifferent to politics, but exactly the opposite is the case. Postmodern critics are almost universally committed to effecting political change, especially in erasing class, racial, ethnic, and gender prejudices. Postmodernism is an amorphous, contradictory, and, at times, impenetrably dense set of propositions and procedures, but in practice, a devotion to a new view of history and a commitment to political change are its commonest goals.

Some of the important concerns of postmodernism, especially regarding the way history is read, coalesced in Stephen Greenblatt's seminal book, *Renaissance Self-Fashioning: From More to Shakespeare* in 1980. In *Renaissance Self-Fashioning*, Greenblatt inaugurated nothing less than a new way of thinking of literature as history, and history as literature. In Renaissance England he saw a culture where the anecdote was not incidental but central. Thus, in various nonliterary writings—medical accounts, legal tracts, and the like—Greenblatt saw the reciprocity of literature and the agents of social, political, and economic power. As Greenblatt explained in his introduction to *Renaissance Self-Fashioning*, the "texts"—no longer plays or poems but *texts*—are "viewed as the focal point for converging lines of force in sixteenth-century culture." Their importance is not that they reveal "underlying and prior historical principles." Instead, what's important is that "the interplay of their symbolic structures" is "perceivable in the careers of their authors and in the larger social world." The result of this interrelation of literature and history is a "single, complex process of self-fashioning" that brings us "closer to understanding how literary and social identities were formed in this culture."

The mission of the New Historicism, as opposed to old historicism, is to achieve, in the famous formulation of Louis Adrian Montrose, "the historicity of texts and the textuality of history." By *the historicity of texts*, Montrose meant "the cultural specificity, the social embedment, of all modes of writing—not only the texts that critics study but also the texts in which we study them." By *the textuality of history*, he wished to express two claims: first, that we can have no unmitigated, unmediated access to the past, the lived material existence; history can be approached only through textual artifacts, and not just or preeminently works of high literary culture, and secondly, that these texts corrupt the process of reading the past—they are "themselves subject to subsequent textual mediations"—when they are employed by historians to construct histories. New Historicism, therefore, doesn't privilege literature over other forms of "cultural performances." Thus, an account by Thomas Harriot of the English encounter with the Native Americans of the Roanoke Colony in 1587 can launch an analysis of power dynamics in *Henry V*; an Elizabethan diarist's erotic dream of a tryst with Queen Elizabeth can lead to a consideration of the diffuse display of royal power and allure in *A Midsummer Night's Dream*. In *Reinventing Shakespeare*, Gary Taylor, the highly influential editor (with Stanley Wells) of the 1986 Oxford edition of the *Complete Works*, somewhat dismissively sums up the New Historicist assumptions as follows: "Everything is related to everything else. So everything is relevant to Shakespeare, and Shakespeare is relevant to everything. Shakespeare, the apex of the inverted pyramid of interpretation, is also the tip of a funnel through which the whole world can be poured."

NEW DIRECTIONS IN SHAKESPEARE CRITICISM

I experienced the impact of radical reappraisals of Shakespeare studies firsthand in the summer of 1988 when I participated in a National Endowment for the Humanities Summer Institute at the Folger Shakespeare Library in Washington, D.C., titled "New Directions in Shakespeare Criticism." The fourteen of us (mostly young assistant professors) were from all over the country, from small colleges and large universities, from rich private schools and lean state schools. We were a Shakespearean gazpacho.

"New Directions" brought to the Folger critics who really were taking Shakespeare scholarship in new directions. Most seemed to have an "-ism" attached to them. Louis Montrose represented the New Historicism, which even in 1988 was beginning to deny that anything like New Historicism ever existed. Jonathan Dollimore presented Cultural Materialism, the British counterpart of New Historicism—much more politically committed and, to my way of thinking, more admirable because Cultural Materialists worked among small interdisciplinary groups in England, where salaries couldn't compare to America's. Joel Fineman presented his Lacanian psychoanalytic theory in a discussion of the Sonnets. Fineman's award-winning *Shakespeare's Perjured Eye: The Invention of Poetic Subjectivity in the Sonnets* was perhaps the hottest book of the year. Jean Howard stood for the powerful influence of Feminist and Gender Studies. The institute's director, Paul Werstine, pressed the new New Bibliography, which was in the process of radically destabilizing Shakespeare's texts, especially, as we have seen, *King Lear* and *Hamlet*.

I knew within a couple of sessions—we met Tuesday and Thursday afternoons in the basement of the Folger Library—that we were no longer in Kansas. Other people might be selling real estate or practicing medicine or passing laws or building cars, but we were charting new territories in this small but very influential area of study. After all, we would take these new directions in Shakespeare studies back to our classrooms. If we entered the institute as innocents, we left as some new fusion of Marxists, New Historicists, Cultural Materialists, Feminists, Lacanians—at least until the heady air of that summer faded from our heads, and our students brought us back to mundane reality with, "when Juliet says 'wherefore art thou, Romeo,' is it supposed to be really dark outside, so she can't see him?" But for that special time we were au courant.

That summer Shakespeare really mattered. I returned home to Chapel Hill newly energized. But I was also bemused. That fall I wrote what I meant to be a thoughtful and objective, though somewhat ironic, essay, "Commotion in the Wind," reporting our experience at the Folger in the summer of 1988. My thesis was uncontestable: a new generation was turning "the huge ship of Shakespeare criticism hard to port." From here Shakespeare's plays looked very different. Old notions of order were debunked; traditional readings stood on their heads. "The witches are the central figures of *Macbeth*," I wrote. "Shylock rather than Antonio or Portia is the focus of *The Merchant of Venice*. Calaban is the hero of *The Tempest*,

Prospero a usurping tyrant." "The swing to the left," I added, "is something like a grass-roots movement occurring within the now democratized American academy."

A yellow-dog Democrat, I've always been Left-leaning, in part as a reaction against an undergraduate upbringing in a regional university where my teachers were, with a few exceptions, stodgy conservatives who hardly ever contested traditional interpretations. For them, Shakespeare was the honey-tongued national poet, the sweet swan of Avon, the sentimental saint of beauty. They steered clear of any idea that might be controversial or that threatened their deeply ingrained values. I don't remember my teachers ever mentioning that Othello was a black man married to a white woman. Othello was a Moor—a Saharan of dark skin but chiseled European features. No thick lips here, no sooty bosom.

But my essay was not uncritical of the Left. I pointed out the irony that the radical critics of the "new New Left" featured in "New Directions in Shakespeare Criticism" were being funded by the very running dogs of capitalism they were attacking—at a library a block and a half from the United States Capitol. I noted furthermore that within the American university system if you wrote a book attacking capitalism, the dean awarded you tenure and/or a promotion, with a handsome raise. Your radical work had the effect of advancing you within the very system you purported to undo. Now, you could buy your suits from Georgetown tailors, and send your kids to private schools.

"With tenure, fame and a fat salary," I wrote, "life as a Leftist critic in the American academy is quite livable."

I also pointed to the fact that (then as now) the huge academic proletariat— "graduate students . . . short-termers and part-timers . . . lecturers and itinerant post-docs"—do the bulk of the work. "For marginalized faculty who bear the burden of production but yet take away only the scraps, Leftist theory offers an opportunity to attack the machine that feeds upon them." It troubled me, moreover, that if, in order to register a new inclusiveness, we were to rename English departments as departments of Cultural Studies, as was suggested, we might create the very conditions under which a new racist program might be fostered. Finally, I pointed out that English majors were steadily declining. In the new class of undergraduates, 30 percent would major in business.

My essay focused upon Jonathan Dollimore, whose *Radical Tragedy: Religion, Ideology and Power in the Drama of Shakespeare and his Contemporaries*, published four years earlier, had proved enormously influential. He was, to me, the most daring critic to address the institute that summer. His mission was to investigate the responses of power centers to transgressive sexuality, as that sexuality is played out on the carnivalesque Renaissance stage where boys played the female parts and then, as in *As You Like It, Twelfth Night,* and *The Merchant of Venice,* disguised themselves as boys, or men, who then become the love objects of other boys playing girls. Dollimore, then of the University of Sussex in England, came to academic life after stints in farming and factory work. He was also, beginning in the fall of 1988, a fellow at the National Humanities Center in the Research Triangle Park, only a few miles from Chapel Hill. Like me, he loved cars. Over the coming months, we became real acquaintances, if not real friends.

Here's how I introduced Dollimore:

> If you imagine a middle-aged man, paunchy and toothless in the usual guise of the English don, you're wrong. Dollimore slips into the room, a handsome, youthful, fashionably skinny man with jet hair and marble eyes like those of a small forest creature. He wears a blousy collarless white shirt, tight black jeans and hi-topped sneakers. A tiny earring glittering beneath a curling lock of hair, Dollimore looks as though he stepped out of a Pre-Raphaelite painting.

I meant this to be a flattering portrait. Looking back, it still seems that way to me.

When "Commotion in the Wind" appeared early that December in *The Spectator* magazine—a free alternative weekly tabloid—I had no reason to expect trouble.

A couple of days later I knew something unexpected was taking shape. Cards and phone calls started coming in from friends and strangers alike. Opinion was divided. Some applauded me for giving the boot to conservatives, others criticized me for attacking the Left. In my mind, both responses seemed wrong. Most of my essay was reportage, and my relative detachment from the issues (teaching at a small private college in North Carolina, I had nothing really at stake) seemed clear. Moreover, I had made an effort to be scrupulously balanced. I hadn't attacked or defended any position more than another. I was bewildered.

Just after dinner one night, the phone rang. It was Jonathan Dollimore. "I have just one question to ask you," he said. "Whose side are you on?" Stunned, I fumbled for a beat or two, and replied, "I'm on nobody's side."

"Well, you'd better make up your mind whether you're with us or them. And, for the record, I've never worn tight jeans in my life." He hung up. We've never spoken since.

Us or *them*. I had obviously failed to understand the depth of polarization that postmodern criticism had forged.

My little essay, published in a local free tabloid (I think I was paid fifty dollars for it), would not go away. I've never clearly understood how it happened, but "Commotion in the Wind" found its way to the highest levels of the National Endowment for the Humanities, the funding agency for "New Directions in Shakespeare Criticism." The Chairman of the NEH at the time was Lynne V. Cheney, the wife of Richard B. Cheney, later a two-term vice president. Without consulting me—much less asking my permission—someone at NEH used this essay, which was now seeming monstrous to me, as part of an institutional evaluation of "New Directions in Shakespeare Criticism," apparently with a negative spin, although I never saw a report of any kind. Some weeks later, however, I did receive a distressed and distressing call from the Folger asking me if I was aware of the potential damage my essay might have done. The fear seemed to be that funding agencies might decline to support controversial programs in the future.

Jump forward a couple of years. In a book titled *Shakespeare Left and Right*, Michael D. Bristol, one of the champions of the new wave of Shakespeare criticism, took me to task in an essay titled "Where Does Ideology Hang Out?" In what he called "surely one of the most bizarre examples of . . . journalistic 'contributions' to the cultural policy debate," he said that I had reported on "ideologically motivated critics plotting revolution in the basement of the Folger Library"—his remark, not mine. Bristol speculated that although I might be joking, my "estrangement from the activities of the Institute Seminar [was] evident." According to Bristol, I wanted "both to ridicule the radical scholars . . . for their hypocritical, self-serving vanity and to denounce them as a serious cultural threat." He mentioned "the neo-conservative readership of the *Spectator* magazine," a serious misappraisal of the *Spectator* audience, which was young and hip, consisting of readers seeking alternative sources of news.

How Bristol of McGill University in Montreal got his hands on "Commotion in the Wind," I can only guess.

I don't bring up this incident to settle an old score. The episode is minor at best and happened twenty years ago. Rather, it illustrates how much was (seen to be) at stake in the interpretation of Shakespearean theater during the 1980s. The "culture wars," pitting the Left against the Right, had already broken out of the narrow confines of university departments and into the pubic arena. On the Left, Stanley Fish, who was busily remaking the English Department at Duke University into a haven for what his detractors condemned as ideologues, was defending the new theorists and issuing challenges to conservative thought in the mainstream media. On the Right, Allan Bloom was passionately defending traditional values in education and attacking the relativism and revisionism of the Left. His *The Closing of the American Mind*, published the year before the Folger Institute gathering, had been a best-seller. Those heady days demanded that you take a side. Shakespeare had become a site, indeed the principal site, of a political contest between a conservative old guard and a new, politically committed Left. But this new New Left was anything but homogenous or united. It was amorphous and fluid, at times bitterly contesting within its ranks what it meant to be on the Left. Even as the principles and strategies of postmodernism were being formulated, leading figures of the Left, notably Frederic Jameson and Terry Eagleton, attacked postmodernism for its "depthlessness . . . its commitment to surfaces, to the signifier at the expense of the signified, and its consequent ahistoricity, its lack of a sense of a substantial past," according to Catherine Belsey.

The ambitions of postmodernism were grand, to say the least. Two symposia, in 1989 and 1990—and the two volumes of essays they yielded—illustrate these ambitions. Convened at the University of Essex in March 1989, the first of these three-day conferences brought together some of the leading figures in Renaissance studies to consider new possibilities for critical inquiry. For a broader sense of the possibilities postmodernism offered, the second volume is a better place to start, but since my concern is with Shakespeare, rather than the larger concerns of post-modern theories, I will restrict my discussion to the first volume of essays, *Uses of History: Marxism, postmodernism and the Renaissance*, edited by Francis Barker, Peter Hulme, and Margaret Iversen. In their introduction, the editors challenge old conceptions of history, from, "[b]roadly speaking . . . positions . . . situated on the political left." But, the editors ask, why investigate the past at all? One reason would be "the simply positivist (in Renaissance studies, often antiquarian) sense of knowledge being a good in itself and one relatively simply available."

The editors tell us that "[n]one of the contributors to this volume holds that position." The larger terms of the debate, they report, are "implicitly (and preferably explicitly) political."

Two essays contained in the first volume of the Essex symposium concern *Hamlet*. In "'No offence I' th' world: Hamlet and unlawful marriage," Lisa Jardine took up the much maligned character of Gertrude, in an attempt to address women's "agency"—the degree to which women in the period were able to establish and assert their own identities. She returned, as so many critics have, to T. S. Eliot's seminal essay in which he claims that "Hamlet (the man) is dominated by an emotion which is inexpressible, because it is in *excess* of the facts as they appear." Hamlet's "difficulty" is that the disgust occasioned by his mother "envelops and exceeds her."

Jardine countered this assertion by remarking that "what is striking in the play *Hamlet* is that Hamlet does not sleep with Gertrude; there is no incestuous event in the play, between mother and son, to match the excessive emotion on his side, and the excessive guilt on hers." It is rather the sexual relationship between Claudius and Gertrude that constitutes incest. Gertrude's crime is not that she has married Claudius but rather that by marrying Claudius she has robbed Hamlet of his right to the crown. Although this claim may not be entirely sound, given the crucial fact that Danish monarchy is elected, Jardine asserted that "in so far as Gertrude is supposed to have behaved monstrously and unnaturally towards her first husband *and* her son, her guilt—in direct contrast to Claudius's—is culturally constructed so as to represent her as responsible without allowing her agency." Women are not merely objects, she argued, but subjects as well, endowed with individual desires and aspirations. "To be always object and victim is not the material reality of woman's existence," she wrote, "nor is it her lived experience."

Francis Barker supplied the other *Hamlet* essay in this volume. His "Which dead? Hamlet and the ends of history" is densely written, at times almost uninterpretable. "Shakespearean tragedy," Barker cryptically claims, "dramatizes an end of history." Barker locates the play on the brink of modernity in its "critical disjunction between history and mourning." In *Hamlet* the "forms of memory, of the representation of memory—history and mourning are engaged in a pattern of displacement and substitution where historical memory is displaced on to and tendentially replaced by the personal version." But this displacement is further complicated by the fact that mourning "takes at least two forms. Within the displacement of history on to mourning, grief is the truly personal version, whereas commemoration is the 'public' form." Both are forms of "bad remembering" that "tend to fail." This, Barker claims, is "a mark of the cultural crisis, and an unwitting exposure of the limitations of the original displacement." He cites the maimed and missing burial rites—Ophelia's mangled funeral and the "secret rather than public" committals of

Polonius and Old Hamlet. What remains is "powerless personal grief . . . already hard to narrate and now redoubled in both its poignancy and its impotence." Displacement, furthermore, "covers its own traces by trailing a false option between grief and commemoration," offering "a faulty solution to the problem, tempting— even a radical—critique through the necessary criticism of desocialized 'private' grief on to the lure of collective memorialization as the answer to the problem of the access to, and practice of, history."

If Barker was nearly indecipherable in "Which dead," he had provided a more lucid analysis of *Hamlet* in his 1984 book *The Tremulous Private Body: Essays on Subjection*. In that work, Barker set about to dispel the widespread belief that Hamlet achieves a profound interiority. Barker places *Hamlet* at the cusp—but only at the cusp—of "an incipient modernity." Hamlet is not, that is to say, a product of post-Cartesian subjectivity. He has no authentic subjectivity at all. Rather, Hamlet's "self" is "a condition of dependent membership in which place and articulation are defined not by an interiorized self-recognition . . . but by incorporation in the body politic which is the king's body in social form." A "social plenum," Barker claimed, shapes the individual life and thus what in Hamlet we may think is a genuine individuality only *seems* so. In Shakespeare's time, authentic subjectivity is literally unthinkable. "The public and private as strong, mutually defining, mutually exclusive categories, each describing separate terrains with distinct contents, practices and discourses, are not yet extant."

Instead of generating an authentic autonomous interiority, then, *Hamlet* presents the reader/viewer with dazzling surfaces. "In *Hamlet*, social life is a succession of brightly lit tableaux set against black backgrounds whose darkness is not the symbol of mysterious alterity, but simply the meaninglessness of the void beyond the surface of signification itself." The "depth" the play achieves is not really depth at all but a *"doubling of the surface"* (Barker's emphasis). "The Mousetrap," which re-presents the narrative of murder and usurpation, is prime exampling of the superficial doubling, but so are, according to Barker, Fortinbras, Laertes, and Pyrrus, figures that replicate the Hamlet-surface. Hamlet's early assertion that he knows not "seems," that "forms, modes, shapes of grief" cannot denote his grief, for these are mere surface gestures, teasingly creates the appearance of substance, but this claim, like so much else in the Hamlet character, is an act. "[I]nteriority remains, in *Hamlet*, gestural" rather than authentic, because Hamlet arrives on the cusp of modernity, not within it. Thus, "from its point of vantage on the threshold of the modern but not yet within it, the text scandalously reveals the emptiness at the heart" of the self.

As a challenge to the tendency to read too much interiority into *Hamlet*, Barker's discussion is a helpful corrective, though his argument will not stand up to scrutiny. Not only do I disagree with his assertion that Hamlet's soliloquies create only the appearance of interiority to challenge the surface dimension of the play; Barker also ignores or suppresses important evidence to the contrary. For instance, in Barker's discussion of Hamlet, I don't find a single reference to the Ghost of Hamlet's father.

Yet no analysis of the issue of depth in *Hamlet* can fail to consider the Cellarage Scene in 1.5 when the Ghost issues his demands from *under* the stage. This situation emphatically—dramatically—underscores depth versus surface. Clearly, the Ghost comes from—and represents—some region other than the spectacular surface of *Hamlet*, which is no more invested in visual surfaces than any other play. All dramas are, after all, speaking pictures. I think, moreover, that Barker draws the line too sharply between pre- and post-Cartesian subjectivity. Descartes' pivotal assertion in his *Discourse on Method* (1637), "Cogito ergo sum"—"I think, therefore I am"—is quite clearly prefigured in Hamlet's remark to Rosencrantz and Guildenstern in F1 2.2 that "there is nothing good or bad but thinking makes it so." This evidence, which Barker doesn't bring up, counters his argument.

But Barker persists. Hamlet's many claims to an authentic self reveal "simply the meaninglessness of the void beyond the surface of signification itself," he writes. The words of Nietzsche reverberate in this comment: "Now no solace has any effect, there is a longing for a world beyond death, beyond the gods themselves; existence is denied, along with its treacherous reflection in the gods or in some immortal Beyond. Once truth has been seen, the consciousness of it prompts man to see only what is terrible and absurd in existence wherever he looks." But the impact of this line of thought—that Hamlet stares into empty meaninglessness of life—belies the argument that Hamlet is not an authentic self but rather a series of gestures. There must be a Hamlet who stares into nothingness.

Two years after *The Tremulous Private Body*, the Marxist critic Terry Eagleton extended this view of Hamlet in a brilliant little book deceptively titled *William Shakespeare*. Eagleton shunned the apparatus of academic writing, offering only 104 pages of text and fewer than twenty notes, producing what one critic called a "mock epic." In a chapter titled "Nothing," Eagleton acknowledged Hamlet as "an enigmatic being . . . legendary in world literature." Then he makes perhaps the most radical claim in the history of *Hamlet*'s reception. "Hamlet has no 'essence' of being whatsoever, no inner sanctum to be safeguarded: he is pure deferral and diffusion, a hollow void which offers nothing determinate to be known. His 'self' consists simply of a range of gestures with which he resists available definitions, not in a radical alternative beyond their reach." For Eagleton, Hamlet is "a superfluous man . . . sheer empty excess over the given, a being radically incommensurate with any other and so the ruin of all metaphor and exchange."

This is the most brilliant, perhaps the most perceptive and courageous reading of *Hamlet* ever offered over the course of five pages. But it stumbles on the problem that Hamlet is a character in a play, not a real man, not a prince but a construct of words and dramatic gestures. Postmodern critics of every ilk and turn seem, like the psychoanalytic critics they supersede, to forget that Hamlet is not a real person. No genuine selfhood can be extracted from a character in a play, which is, after all, an amalgam of words and actions.

TELMAH

Another important book of 1986, Terence Hawkes' *That Shakespeherian Rag: Essays on a Critical Process*, also effectively challenged inherited assumptions about *Hamlet* the play and, by implication, about Hamlet the character. Like Barker and Eagleton, Hawkes rejected the belief that the play "runs a satisfactorily linear, sequential course from a firmly established and well-defined beginning through a clearly placed and signaled middle to a causally related and logically determined end which, planted in the beginning, develops, or grows out of it." Instead, Hawkes cited evidence that the play is run "backwards." He expresses this notion in the title of his essay on *Hamlet*, "Telmah." Hawkes asked readers to see, especially in the action of "The Mousetrap," which replays the narrative of the murder, that *Hamlet* "reinforces its recursive mode, making it, as it were, move only unwillingly and haltingly forward, constantly, even as it does so, looking over its own shoulder." The effect of Shakespeare's method is to "buttonhole" readers into constantly revising our interpretation of the action.

But Hawkes' mission is larger than this point about the unfolding structure of the play. Explicitly—as opposed to implicit arguments in the works I've treated recently—Hawkes wants to expose the personal motives that underlie modern readings of *Hamlet*. To this end, he reconsiders John Dover Wilson's contribution to Shakespeare studies, beginning with Wilson's dedicatory letter to W. W. Greg in which Wilson recalls his train ride to Sunderland in November 1917. Dover Wilson's stated mission—the engine that drove so much of his career—was to prove "damnably wrong" Greg's claim that the Ghost is a hallucination. Dover Wilson focuses so much manic energy upon this matter, Hawkes argues, precisely because that interpretation disrupts the inherited belief that the play works according to a rational, linear design, implying, as Hamlet's remark that "[t]here is a special providence in the fall of a sparrow" suggests, a divine logic directing the affairs of men. Dover Wilson implicitly feared, Hawkes suggests, the threat of chaos that would be admitted into the most canonical work in English drama if Greg's claim were allowed to stand.

Hawkes notes also that in recalling the Sunderland trip of November 1917 Dover Wilson makes no mention of the Bolshevik coup that had taken place within a couple weeks, if not days, of the train trip. The omission is telling because Dover Wilson was a student of Russian society. He had written essays warning of the dangers to Europe if revolution broke out in Russia. Dover Wilson sided with the Tzarist faction, even endorsing its "commitment to terrorism," because Autocracy, Dover Wilson had written in 1914, "still has a long life before it and much work to perform in Russia. It is therefore wiser to face the facts and to recognize that Tsardom is after all Russia's form of democracy . . . [that] it is the kind of government the people understand and reverence."

As an emissary from the Ministry of Munitions, Dover Wilson had been dispatched to Sunderland, we should recall, to tend to "[s]ome trouble" that had arisen with local trade-union officials. Some of the local shop stewards at munitions factories were said to be "revolutionary socialists" who opposed the war. The implication is clear that Dover Wilson's mission was to attempt to defuse the Sunderland situation. That is to say, he operated as an instrument of conservative government, which feared and therefore opposed destabilizing social elements. By extension, according to Hawkes, Dover Wilson's interpretation of *Hamlet*—one that avoids unsettling aspects of the play—is motivated by anxiety, a fear of revolutionary aspects of the work, the sorts of things that Eastern European directors would emphasize during the Cold War. Dover Wilson's is a "brand of literary Tsarism."

When, in May 1919, Dover Wilson was appointed to a board charged with inquiring "into the position occupied by English (Language and Literature) in the educational system of England," he was provided the opportunity to institutionalize this literary Tsarism as part of the shaping principles and direction of the British educational system. The resulting Newbolt Report had two central concerns that were really, according to Hawkes, "related political ones: social cohesion in the face of potential disintegration and disaffection; and nationalism, the encouragement of pride in English national culture on a broader front." Addressing the matter of "Literature and the Nation," Dover Wilson conceived of "teaching literature to the working class [as] a kind of 'missionary work' aimed at stemming the tide of that class's by then evident disaffection." The risk to the nation if literature is not inculcated among the lower classes is not merely that they will not know "the 'comfort' and 'mirth' of literature," but that if the national literature, being the Arnoldian distillation "of the best thoughts of the best minds," is not disseminated among the unwashed masses, then that nation "must assuredly be heading to disaster."

Looking back on "Telmah" from twenty years' distance, Hawkes' attack seems rather harsh. After all, given the terrible nature of the war years, John Dover Wilson was certainly not alone in his aversion to chaos. Every thinking person must have been mindful of the threat of chaos, which loomed everywhere in 1917, from Moscow to the Somme to Sunderland. It was perhaps the darkest hour of a war that was killing thousands upon thousands. Danger was everywhere, so there's no surprise that Dover Wilson craved order. Order would have meant a cessation of the killing. Order might have saved the poet Wilfred Owen, and the remainder of a generation of young men who were dying like cattle led to slaughter.

Moreover, there is no reason for Hawkes—or any of us—to assume, as Dover Wilson clearly did, that literature would exert a calming, conformative influence upon the public. The opposite effect—that literature might wield a liberating force upon the disenfranchised, showing them the very necessity of resistance—is an obvious possibility. In *The Tempest*, Prospero taught the language to Caliban and Caliban, you'll recall, learned to curse, if not to effectively resist or free himself from slavery.

But at crucial times, certainly in America, learning to curse was the first step toward revolution. In the antebellum South, many a white mistress taught a slave to read the Bible, where he discovered that slavery was monstrous and that the only right course was to rise up against it. The most shocking—and revealing—consequence of the 1831 Nat Turner slave uprising were laws forbidding black people to be taught to read and write. Clearly, southern legislators learned that resistance is every bit as likely as compliance to be the consequence of reading great literature.

Historicists must be themselves historicized. Hawkes, writing two decades ago, adores American culture, especially jazz—the language of the African American deep South of fecund New Orleans, cooking up a new, improvisational music that would explode in one of America's most ancient (and postmodern) cities and spread throughout the world. To Terence Hawkes the music-lover, writing, I surmise, somewhere in Wales in 1985, New Orleans and, more broadly, the American South must have seemed like the Promised Land. Hawkes' analysis brilliantly illustrates how culture and history figure in what is finally cryptically and enigmatically personal: the interpretation of Hamlet/*Hamlet*. Hawkes' main title, *That Shakesepeherian Rag: Essays on a Cultural Process*, notable for its excrescent syllable, is taken from a refrain in the second movement of Eliot's "The Waste Land," a profound register of the impact of World War I on Western consciousness. But Eliot himself had borrowed the phrase from a popular ragtime song of the 1912 Ziegfield Follies. Like Eliot the poet, Hawkes the critic is inseparable from his involvement with American music, especially the improvisational dynamic rooted in jazz. Hawkes' work is a tribute to black American music, so transgressive and energetic and soulful, so much a part of life lived at the margins of poverty and desperation, where food and drink and music lessened the pain of life. At the end of "Telmah," Hawkes sees the name of the greatest black American trumpeter figured in the name "Fortinbras." Louis "Satchmo" Armstrong resides *in* Fortinbras, in an anagrammatized name that of course provides a path, through the mind of Hawkes and Eliot, worming back through time to popular music, into the play's deep structure.

THE SMELL OF DEATH

While one strain of postmodern critics was denying Hamlet the interiority that I've been arguing for in this book, another strain was not only according Hamlet an authentic selfhood, but subjecting that self to psychoanalysis. In this tradition, the most important post-Freudian is the Frenchman Jacques Lacan (d. 1981). For literary critics the special appeal of Lacan's very difficult, sometimes indecipherable writings—made all the more difficult by appearing in translation—lies in the fact that he figures the unconscious as structured like language itself. I will not attempt to explain Lacan's complex and elusive theories here—I'm quite sure I'm not up to the task—but rather direct the interested reader to the records of Lacan's own writings, most of which are transcripts of lectures. Instead, I will move directly to a consideration of Lacan's contribution to the *Hamlet* history in his lengthy essay, compiled from series of seminar lectures given the late 1950s and published in *Yale French Studies* in 1977 as "Desire and the Interpretation of Desire in *Hamlet*." Even so, Lacan's analysis, while very important in the critical tradition, is very difficult to understand, and I beg the reader's indulgence while I attempt to summarize his argument.

Lacan begins with an assertion that the play is driven by Hamlet's desire for Ophelia; but this desire is not physical but rather psychic. Lacan sees in Ophelia the principle of "the Mother as Other," that is, the unattainable object of desire, which Lacan elsewhere terms *object petit a* ("the object little-a"). Since Ophelia is a desire Hamlet can never fulfill, he is deprived of something, and this something, according to Lacan, is the phallus. Lacan shares Freud's obsession with the penis—now almost a quaint notion—which he argues is symbolically transferred to Ophelia, whose name suggests that meaning in "O phallus." "The phallus," Lacan writes, "is our term for the signifier of [Hamlet's] alienation in signification. When the subject is deprived of this signifier, a particular object becomes for him an object of desire."

Because he can't possess Ophelia, Hamlet is trapped always "in the time of the Other." However cryptically, this explains his delay. "[F]or Hamlet, the appointment is always too early, and he postpones it. Procrastination is thus one of the essential dimensions of the tragedy." Lacan focuses upon the hour of Ophelia, in which Hamlet's apparent estrangement from her, as she reports it in the second act, registers the "decomposition" of Hamlet's fantasy crossing "the limits originally assigned to it." Hamlet's abuse of Ophelia soon after is evidence of this decomposition of the fantasy. "Ophelia is at this point the phallus, exteriorized and rejected by the subject as a symbol signifying life."

We should note, though Lacan doesn't, that this decomposition of the fantasy becomes corporeal, fated to rot; it becomes olfactory. Hamlet's vicious association of conception with putrefaction—"if the sun breed maggots in a dead dog, / Being good kissing carrion" he says to Polonius in 2.2, "—have you a daughter?"—links fecundity with the smell of ripe road kill. Hamlet condemns Ophelia to a "nun-nery," which, in Shakespeare's time, could mean a brothel. According to Lacan, "the reintegration of the [petit] object a" takes place in 5.2, when Hamlet leaps into Ophelia's grave, the place where her body will accomplish its putrefaction under-ground, out of smell as well as sight.

Mourning her loss in the graveyard scene, Hamlet is confronted with the frus-trated sense, which Lacan later links to castration, of impossible fulfillment. "[O]nly insofar as the object of Hamlet's desire has become an impossible object can it become once more the object of his desire." For her part, Ophelia, the object of desire, "becomes the signifier of this impossibility." When he leaps into her grave, Hamlet is animated by an "object whose loss is the cause of his desire, an object that has attained an existence that is all the more absolute because it no longer cor-responds to anything in reality." For Hamlet, the loss of the object of desire, now "essentially the veiled phallus," creates a gap or a hole that is now filled by "swarms of images" that "assume the place of the phallus." Nothing can fill the hole, indeed, "except the totality of the signifier."

The "totality of the signifier" is, in turn, captured in ritual, in the maimed rites that are famously hidden or deformed in *Hamlet*. Old Hamlet is interred with his sins "Unhouseled, disappointed, unaneled." Polonius is buried in secret. And the suicidal Ophelia is given a Christian burial over the objections of the presiding priest, who would have her body lodged in "ground unsanctified," and "for charita-ble prayers / Flints and pebbles should be thrown on her."

Hamlet's habitual punning, his use of metaphors, conceits, and other verbal tricks links him, in Lacan's judgment, to Shakespearean fools, a point I developed in greater detail earlier in this book. "It is in this playfulness, which is not merely a play of disguises but the play of signifiers . . . that the very spirit of the play resides." In Hamlet's remark to Laertes, "I'll be your foil," Lacan sees a significant pun on "foil" as spoiler and "foil" as weapon. "In this pun there lies ultimately an identifica-tion with the mortal phallus."

The fight with Laertes is the culmination of game-playing in *Hamlet*. Here in the register of the imaginary Hamlet confronts his double, his mirror image. This is an image that he must kill. But he enters this contest—this game—with a blunted sword, "without, shall we say, his phallus." A castrated Hamlet enters the duel with his mirror. The exchange of swords provides Hamlet with a weapon of destruction, "an instrument of death" that he can receive "only from the other," with Lacan figuring that the exchange of weapons, the trading of a blunted tip for a sharpened and poisoned one, takes place offstage. "In the realm beyond, there is the phallus."

"The position of the phallus," Lacan remarks near the end of his lecture, "is always veiled."

Hamlet is mourning the loss of that thing, his penis (his *objet petit a?*), which he has sacrificed to others, most painfully to the usurping Claudius, who has stepped between Hamlet and the crown, and who nightly plows his mother with a penis Hamlet doesn't have. And so, it is always the hour of the Other, the hour of Claudius, that prevents Hamlet from killing the King earlier in the prayer scene: "Claudius, as he knelt there before him, wasn't quite what Hamlet was after—he wasn't the right one." Hamlet cannot strike Claudius until he sheds all narcissistic attachments—all attachments to life itself—at the moment of complete sacrifice.

Lacan concludes his lectures on *Hamlet* by drawing attention to Hamlet's words to Rosencrantz and Guildenstern, who, after the killing of Polonius, order Hamlet to accompany him to the King. "The body is with the King," Hamlet says, "but the King is / Not with the body" (4.2.25–6). Lacan asks us to substitute the word "phallus" for "King," and we shall see how "the body is bound up in this matter of the phallus . . . but the phallus, on the contrary, is bound to nothing"—

HAMLET: The king is a thing.
GUILDENSTERN: A thing, my lord?
HAMLET: Of nothing.

M. D. Faber's 1993 essay "Hamlet and the Inner World of Objects" provides a helpful complement to Lacan's analysis, though Faber makes no mention of Lacan's work. "Western tragedy," Faber asserts, "invariably presents us with characters who undergo a traumatic reactivation of infantile feelings." This claim rests upon Freudian—that is, misogynistic—assumptions involving what Faber sees as "the splitting of the maternal image"—a tantalizing echo of Lacan's hole or gap—that results from "the mother's confusional behavior, rejecting at times, accepting at others." Though this splitting is never explicitly defined, he presumably knows that the mother exists in two separate visions, that of the idealized mother who "cherishes and seduces" her son, and the debased mother who attempts "to abuse and destroy" him. "[R]aised at the hands of an ambivalent Western mother," the male child—who at the imaginative level appears as the tragic hero—experiences Freudian "anxiety over loss, mutilation, abandonment, betrayal . . . and a deep, regressive predilection that is ultimately oral in nature but that can receive expression at the genital level" as incestuous impulses. Faber assumes that "Western tragic heroes will be vulnerable to female influences or the power of women who are able to reawaken through their behavior the anxiety of the early period." The hero's task is to "resolve the mystery of maternal ambivalence." He is ultimately "destroyed by patriarchal forces," however, and through his sacrifice reestablishes the patriarchal hierarchy. Remarkably, there are no female characters alive at the end of the play.

Hamlet's "disintegration," consequent upon the splitting of the mother into "good" and "bad," stems from his unwillingness or inability "to re-examine his origins, to rethink the idealized version of his parents, to admit their imperfection." The Ghost initiates this splitting during his first encounter with his son. Here Hamlet Sr. functions as a "powerful super-ego figure," idealizing his marriage (imposing upon his son the role of "the good boy") on the one hand, while, on the other, presenting Hamlet "with a picture of the lustful bad object, the adulterous mate of the satyr preying upon 'garbage.' " The Ghost forces Hamlet to imaginatively "witness the primal scene"—the sex act in both its licit and illicit contexts—which reactivates the son's infantile impulses. The Ghost splits the mother into two incompatible versions: one won to lust by Claudius, the other linked to "a radiant angel." The result is a "seeming-virtuous Queen."

We should note here what Faber doesn't: that in his 1.2 soliloquy, Hamlet had anticipated this splitting in the desire he witnessed his mother express for his father and the forbidden desire that drove her to incest. The Ghost, clearly echoing the disgust that his son had voiced, is a version of the witches in *Macbeth*, infiltrating the mind of his victim with thoughts instantly ingrained in the victim's consciousness. Hamlet's abuse of Ophelia is a consequence of this implantation.

With his unconscious fears of separation "reawakened" by the ambivalent mother, Hamlet desires to incorporate his mother within himself, literally to consume her. Simultaneously, Faber thinks, these anxieties cause him to "desire to be taken in by the object, to be devoured by the object" so as to achieve a "symbolic union." Again, we should note what Faber doesn't: that this reawakening sets in motion in Hamlet's psyche an alimentary cycle, the process of ingestion, digestion, and elimination—a process necessarily involving decay and corruption and stench—that becomes an integral part of the play's imaginative structure. This surfaces most forcefully in 4.3 after the murder of Polonius,

when Hamlet imagines Polonius at dinner: "Not where he eats but where he
is eaten."

A

certain convocation of politic worms are e'en at him.
Your worm is your only emperor for diet. We fat all
creatures else to fat us, and we fat ourselves for
maggots. Your fat king and your lean beggar is but
variable service, two dishes to one table. That's the end.

The remains of a king fed upon by worms that are, in turn, fed upon by fish then
eaten by a cadger show "how a king may go a progress through the guts of a beggar." "Those who are alive must *eat*," Faber writes, "or strive to; those who are dead
are eaten and, as Hamlet feels it, *fed to*" (emphasis in original). If in the king-beggar
analogy, Claudius is the fat one and Hamlet lean, then Hamlet is entering a fantasy
in which he eats the king. This is a stark transference of his desire to eat and be
eaten by the mother as object, a substitution of husband for wife, man for woman,
King for Queen. Hamlet himself evokes this transference in a turn of bitter
sophistry. "Farewell, dear mother," he says to Claudius:

KING: Thy loving father, Hamlet
HAMLET: My mother. Father and mother is man and wife.
Man and wife is one flesh. So—my mother.
(4.3. 47–50)

In an interesting twist on Lacan's reading of this scene, and the placement of
Claudius' phallus inside Gertrude, Faber writes that "Hamlet would have Claudius
inside him because, as Hamlet sees it, Claudius possesses Gertrude." Eating is a distorted analogy for sexual intercourse: Hamlet will possess Claudius just as Claudius
possesses Gertrude. Consuming Claudius amounts to consuming Gertrude, since
father and mother are one. Certainly, this feint has about it religious overtones that
deepen the resonance of the moment. Stephen Greenblatt, in *Hamlet and Purgatory*,
calls it "a grotesquely materialist reimagining of the Eucharist."

The talk about dining implies the digestive process that ends in defecation—
"the whole business of Polonius and worms has excretory overtones and is anally
aggressive," Faber writes. Hamlet wishes to ingest Claudius to shit him, the ultimate degrading victory over his rival. The putrefaction that encompasses all of

Denmark—both his mother and her husband—has, according to Faber, in effect found its way into Hamlet's bowels.

Similarly deployed to show the debasement of the great in death, the gustatory cycle reappears in Hamlet's 5.1 meditation on the fate of Alexander, delivered while he holds the stinking skull of Yorick. "Why may not imagination trace the noble dust of Alexander till 'a find it stopping a bung hole." Alexander died, rotted, was transformed to loam to stop up a barrel. As I mentioned earlier, "bung hole" is a slang term for the anus. Taken together with the king's progress through the guts of a beggar, Hamlet's remarks about Alexander conjure for us the image of a great conqueror's remains constipating a mendicant.

In the context of this alimentary cycle, culminating in 5.1, primal odors over-whelm us. "Everywhere," Faber writes, "we are confronted with strong smells, with decaying corpses, worms meat, gnawed carcasses, the very bones of the dead. Death as devourer, death as ingester, death as a kind of dumb feeder with an unstoppable mouth." "Pah," Hamlet exclaims, sniffing Yorick's death's head. The total effect is one of utter, naked debasement, stripping the play of its philosophical, and I would argue even its psychological frameworks, as remains are infinitely recycled amid the conjured stench of rotting flesh and fecal matter—all of this linked retrospectively to Ophelia and a rotting dog breeding maggots, kissing carrion and conception, and back further still to lust of Claudius and "the bad mother" Gertrude preying on "garbage." And behind Shakespeare's play we find similar imagery of decay in the Danish saga. There Amleth/Hamblet had refused to eat swine that had fed on the corpses of men. This strongly suggests that something like Hamlet's talk of Polonius being fed upon by worms, and his tracing the body of a king through the guts of a beggar were present in Shakespeare's source, the missing *Hamlet* of the 1580s. If not the Ur-*Hamlet*, then Shakespeare might have reworked material he took directly from Belleforest, if not Saxo.

In *Hamlet in Purgatory*, Stephen Greenblatt calls attention to the stench of rotting bodies that was commonplace for people of Shakespeare's day, especially in the most holy and sacred of places, the church itself in whose yard bodies rotted in shallow graves. Walking to church, you would have encountered the foulest, most sickening odors imaginable, more intensely the closer one got to the sanctuary itself, and especially inside the building, where the bodies of the wealthy were buried under the floors and in the walls. "Even the liberal use of incense, flowers and sprigs of rosemary," Greenblatt writes, "could not altogether have masked the smell of decay that medieval and early modern burial practices almost inevitably introduced into the still air of churches." Shakespeare himself was buried in such a place of smelly honor, the floor of the Holy Trinity Church in Stratford, where, from the grave, he curses anyone who would raid his tomb. This extreme olfactory unpleasantness is everywhere present, literally or suggestively, in *Hamlet*, though we should be quick to remind ourselves that both the alimentary cycle and the foul odors that accompany it are present both in Saxo and Belleforest, and so must have been present in some fashion in the Ur-*Hamlet*. This, needless to say, in no way detracts the smell of death in 5.1 of *Hamlet*.

Finding Hamlet's problem in an attraction to and revulsion from the mother, displaced onto the daughter Ophelia—who, interestingly, has no trace of a mother in the play—Freudian tradition seems perversely obsessed with the degradation of women. In *Hamlet* Gertrude and Ophelia are victims of this degradation. Misogynistic impulses, needless to say, are deeply ingrained in Western consciousness. I needn't rehearse the Book of Genesis for you. But is Hamlet necessarily misogynistic? Might there be alternative views that show Gertrude and Ophelia in a more favorable light?

Feminist critics of the 1980s and '90s attempted to wrest Gertrude and Ophelia from the grip of the Oedipal curse, to lay claim to the women of the play, so often maligned by male critics. In 1985, Elaine Showalter asked the fundamental question: "How should feminist criticism represent Ophelia in its own discourse? What is our responsibility towards her as character and woman?" Showalter identified three strategies that feminism has employed to answer these questions. One is for critics to act as advocates for Ophelia, as lawyers for a client. Two related problems hinder this strategy, however. First, Showalter raises the problem of deciding which story is Ophelia's. Is it "the story of her life? The story of her betrayal at the hands of her father, brother, lover, court, society." Or is it the extratextual "story of her rejection and marginalization by male critics of Shakespeare?" Deciding which story to tell is complicated by the fact that she is so sketchily drawn. She appears in only five scenes. As a result, we know little or nothing of her past; her relationship with Hamlet "is known only by a few ambiguous flashbacks." Here, Showalter confronts an essential interpretive problem: that we conceive of Hamlet without Ophelia, but Ophelia has no existence apart from Hamlet.

A second strategy, emerging in the French feminist tradition, by definition accords Ophelia virtually no being whatsoever. In this tradition, the feminine is that "which escapes representation in patriarchal language and symbolism." In the Renaissance, women were said to be "nothing"—that is, women have no "thing," no penis. They are figures of absence, defined against the male presence underscored by the possession of the phallus. "Deprived of thought, sexuality, language," Showalter writes, "Ophelia's story becomes the Story of O—the zero, the empty circle or mystery of feminine difference, the cipher of female sexuality to be deciphered by feminist interpretation." A third strategy is "to read Ophelia's story as the female subtext of the tragedy, the repressed story of Hamlet." She comes to represent the powerful emotions, often irrational and only incompletely realized, that seethe in the unconscious of the play. But this approach can only return us, sooner or later, to Freudian readings.

Where, then, can we look for an Ophelia of substance and some degree of autonomy? For Showalter, the answer is not to be found in language or plot, but rather in representations of the stage, and in paintings and photography. Because Ophelia ultimately commits suicide, she becomes the representation of female madness. If not dead in the stream, as in the famous Pre-Raphaelite painting by John Everett Millais, she is often depicted as raving mad. And not only in paintings. Showalter reports, shockingly, that with the invention of photography in the mid-nineteenth century, mad women in English asylums were sometimes posed in attitudes that consciously recalled Ophelia.

But Showalter sees progress in the depictions of Ophelia. The great Victorian actress Ellen Terry notably rehabilitated Ophelia "in feminist terms" by representing her as victimized by the men in her life. She is a "study in sexual intimidation, a girl terrified of her father, of her lover, of life itself." Terry broke with tradition by abandoning the white costume, which suggests "transparency, an absence that took on the colors of Hamlet's mood," appearing in black dress in the mad scene.

To be sure, in some representations, Ophelia appears in postures that suggest sexual repression, which only reassert Freudian ownership of the character. But Showalter sees a positive development especially since the 1970s when Ophelia's madness came to stand for "protest and rebellion." "For many feminist theorists," Showalter concludes, "the madwoman is a heroine, a powerful figure who rebels against the family and the social order; and the hysteric who refuses to speak the language of the patriarchal order, who speaks otherwise, is a sister."

Seven years later, Janet Adelman advanced a psychoanalytical interpretation of the Queen in *Suffocating Mothers*, a reading that calls upon Freudian treatments of her but nevertheless significantly alters the tradition and, in doing so, sheds light on aspects of the play that otherwise remain obscure. Like Ophelia, Gertrude is a shadow presence: "Given her centrality in the play," Adelman writes, "it is striking how little we know about Gertrude; even the extent of her involvement in the murder of her husband."

However guilty she may or may not be, Gertrude occasions extraordinary effects in her son. Her sexuality is criminally "uncontrolled" by "a [moral] revulsion as intense as anything directed toward the murderer Claudius." Given the shadowy nature of her character, Hamlet's response amounts to an overreaction, thus returning Adelman to Eliot's remark that Hamlet's reaction "is in *excess* of the facts as they appear." But for Adelman, the source of this disproportionate reaction lies not in an orthodox Oedipal explanation but rather, *for Shakespeare as well as Hamlet*, in deep "fantasies of maternal malevolence, of maternal spoiling, that are compelling exactly as they are out of proportion to the character we know . . ." (my emphasis). These fantasies are rooted, Adelman claims, in Hamlet's refiguration of Old Hamlet and Gertrude as Adam and Eve. In this "highly compacted and psychologized version of the fall," Gertrude is the poison that renders the primal garden a place of "rank corruption," which no husbandry can weed. Her sexuality is, in effect, the poison that kills her husband while he sleeps in a garden that the sexualized mother has spoiled. Hamlet's image of an unweeded garden, of course, presupposes the time of his living father when that garden was weeded.

The result is, as we saw in Lacan and Faber, a splitting, not of the mother but rather of the father, which is registered in Hamlet's division of the father into the lofty, asexual Hyperion and the base, sexualized satyr: "So excellent a king, that was to this / Hyperion to a satyr." But Adelman argues that this splitting cannot be maintained. Hamlet's father and Claudius collapse back into one another: "For if Gertrude's appetite for the two men is the same, then Old Hamlet is as fully implicated in her sexuality as Claudius. This Hamlet seems to recognize in the Prayer Scene, when he resolves to kill the usurper in the same condition as the usurper killed his father"—that is, "as Old Hamlet says of his own murder, 'Cut off even in the blossoms of my sin.'" In Hamlet's bitter association of conception and corruption— "For if the sun breed maggots in a dead dog," he tells Polonius, "being a good kissing carrion—have you a daughter?"—Hamlet sees his own origin "spoiled . . . in the rank flesh of the maternal body." This amounts to the "subjugation of the male to the female": "Beneath the story of fratricidal rivalry is the story of the woman who conduces to death, of the father fallen not through his brother's treachery but through his subjection to the woman."

As this fantasy evolves, Gertrude becomes ever darker, more malevolent. She becomes "the horrific female body," "the night-witch" against whom Marcellus in 1.1, when the cock announces the coming of dawn and the Ghost fades, invokes the protection of the virgin-born Savior. Gertrude becomes "the aspect of this night-body, herself becoming the embodiment of hell and death: the fires in which Hamlet's father is confined, the fires that burn and purge the foul crimes done in his days of nature." Thus, the only way for Hamlet to escape this horrific fantasy of the sexualized maternal body is to neutralize sexuality in his mother, to in effect separate her from her body, "to remake her in the image of the Virgin Mother." This Hamlet partly succeeds in accomplishing during the Closet Scene. After his initial comparison of Old Hamlet with Claudius, Hamlet's effort is not so much to make her avoid allowing Claudius to make love to her, but to neutralize sexual desire in her.

Whether this effort to reclaim Gertrude as a pure mother is successful we can never certainly know. This is because we never see Gertrude in her own light but only reflected in the light of others, her husband and her son. Nevertheless, the evidence suggests to Adelman that after 3.4 Hamlet "seems securely possessed of [Gertrude] as an internal good mother; and this possession gives him a new calm about his place in the world." This purification comes at a considerable cost: the sacrifice of maternal sexuality.

The final essay I want to consider avoids these dark views of women by rejecting an Oedipal approach altogether. Louise Schleiner in 1990 challenged the largely untested assumptions that underlie Freudian readings of Hamlet. Hamlet, she insists, "is at no risk of marrying or having sex with his mother. He is at considerable risk of killing her." Following the lead of Nicholas Rowe in the eighteenth century, Hegel in the nineteenth, and Gilbert Murray in the early part of the twentieth, Schleiner claims that Hamlet "is much more a version—even a purposeful revision—of Orestes than of Oedipus."

Schleiner traces a route by which Shakespeare might have come into contact with Aeschylus' *Oresteia* and Euripides' *Orsetes*, in either the Latin translation of Aeschylus by Jean de Saint-Ravy (1555), possibly in the library of Ben Jonson, the preeminent classicist-playwright of his day, or another member of the circle of contemporary dramatists, John Marston or George Chapman, perhaps; or through witnessing two plays produced (but never published) by the Admiral's Men in 1599 as *Agamemnon* and *Orestes' Furies*.

According to Schleiner, "[t]he general parallel between Orestes and Hamlet as legendary heroes is that they are initiates of death, moral judges and punishers of their mothers, and avengers of their fathers." She sees more concrete connections between the Oresteian narrative and Hamlet in the 5.1 Graveyard Scene, and in the remarkable similarity between the roles of Horatio and Pylades, the loyal friend of Orestes in Aeschylus and Euripides. *The Libation Bearers*, the second part of the Oresteian trilogy, opens with Orestes and Pylades mourning over the grave of Agamemnon. As his sister Electra and a train of women mourners approach, Orestes and Pylades move offstage. The moment closely parallels 5.1, when Hamlet and Horatio hide at the approach of the funeral party bearing the body of Ophelia. As Electra grieves at her father's grave and wonders where her brother might be, Orestes, with Pylades, reenters the stage to the amazement of the mourners, a move paralleled by Hamlet, who, with Horatio, steps forward to interrupt the interment of Ophelia. Schleiner asks us, the next time we watch or read the graveyard scene of *Hamlet*, "to test the air . . . and see if it doesn't bring distinctly to mind a procession of approaching 'libation bearers.'"

The Pylades-Horatio connection at its core depends upon the mutual friendship of these seconds with their principals, Orestes and Hamlet. "Horatio [is] a modern Pylades," Schleiner writes. But an important difference emerges. Whereas later in *The Libation Bearers* Pylades presents no opposition to Orestes' killing of his mother, in *Hamlet* both Hamlet's vow to speak daggers to his mother but use none, and the Ghost's injunction to leave Gertrude to heaven, constitute a resistance to matricide that Pylades doesn't provide. If Horatio the loyal friend plays no direct part in preventing Hamlet from killing Gertrude, the play itself takes on that role in diffuse ways. The voice of conscience that, coming from the loyal friend, should prevent Hamlet from killing is dispersed among Hamlet and the Ghost, thus accounting for the most striking difference between *Hamlet* and *The Libation Bearers*: that Orestes butchers his mother as well as his usurping cousin, her paramour, whereas Hamlet exacts revenge only upon his murdering uncle. The play thus successfully resists the deep-seated urge supplied by its Oresteian origins to kill the mother. Finding the central dynamic of *Hamlet* in the Oresteian rather than the Oedipal tradition, Schleiner takes us down a different avenue of interpretation, one free of the need for a suffocating and corrupting female sexuality that poisons the mind of the son.

All three of these "feminist" readings of *Hamlet* provide fruitful new ways of understanding Ophelia and Gertrude. All of them place less emphasis—and in Schleiner's case, none at all—upon traditional Oedipal readings, which are based in an acute psychopathology that construes women as monsters creating monstrous effects in their sons. In the final analysis, however, these readings clearly don't succeed in cleansing the play of its deeply rooted misogyny. Yes, as Showalter points out, women are associated with the beneficial symbolic values of water, water that might wash away madness and the stench of corruption, if there were enough water. But there isn't, and water, consequent upon her madness, becomes the cause of Ophelia's death. For Adelman, Gertrude is a source of corruption originating in the act of procreation itself. The recuperation of this sullied mother, this poisoned garden, is achieved only at the conclusion of the play, and then only by desexualizing Gertrude. And as for Schleiner, whose approach is entirely detached from Freudian moorings, she presents us in Clytemnestra with a mother who kills her husband and marries his enemy, reminding us, if her reading is to be credited, how deeply embedded is the impulse to avenge the killing of the father by killing the mother. The fulfillment of the Oresteian destiny is only narrowly averted in *Hamlet* by the diffuse agency of a surrogate Pylades.

We are left to wonder why, despite these admirable efforts, can't we eradicate misogyny from *Hamlet*? Well, because we can't rewrite the play, of course. But this doesn't mean that Shakespeare, though he certainly must have shared the general patriarchal disposition of his age—and the denigration of women that disposition entailed—was himself a misogynist. At least, we can't use *Hamlet* to make that case. We must keep in mind that the fierce misogyny of *Hamlet* was there before Shakespeare, in the material he inherited and reworked. Thus it is untenable to claim, as Adelman does, that Hamlet's neuroses are Shakespeare's. We need to be always mindful of what Robertson stressed in *The Problem of Hamlet*, discussed earlier, that Hamlet is "a play of adaptation and adjustment." We can't allow ourselves to forget that *Hamlet* is a palimpsest, a work in which many hands are, however indistinctly, present. The misogyny of Hamlet must be understood as the collective misogyny of the traditions Shakespeare inherited. Likewise, the astonishing psychological depth and complexity of Hamlet is the product of a collective subconscious of which Shakespeare was perhaps the greatest but certainly not the only part.

POST-POSTMODERN *HAMLET?*

I think of Greenblatt's *Hamlet in Purgatory*, which I've mentioned several times, as a development out of and beyond postmodernism. Though the book covers an enormous amount of material, most of it, in the New Historicist manner, is only ancillary to the play itself. Still, this very accomplished book seems to me a rather conventional history, except perhaps in the extent to which Greenblatt's own experience is imbedded in it. It may be, I concede, that critics have become so accustomed to Greenblatt's acuity that it only *seems* conventional now. Given his role in radically revising our approaches to history and literature, Greenblatt's reasons for undertaking this study seem if not quaint then remarkably old fashioned. "My only goal," he says,

> was to immerse myself in the tragedy's magical intensity. It seems a bit absurd to bear witness to the intensity of *Hamlet;* but my profession has become so oddly diffident and even phobic about literary power, so suspicious and tense, that it risks losing sight of—or at least failing to articulate—the whole reason anyone bothers with the enterprise in the first place.

Asserting the primacy of esthetic values in literary criticism, a regard for power of beauty and meaning in their everyday senses, seems distinctly uncharacteristic of Greenblatt's own history. Some may see him as selling out his revolutionary past; others may think he's simply taking the turn of an opportunistic critic who, sensing the shift in the winds, a weariness with theory-based analysis, signals a new era in his own development and, perhaps, in literary studies in general—a post-postmodernism.

I do not know what is true of Greenblatt personally. I do know that he has been working above the fray for decades. This is not to say that he hasn't been the target of whips and scorns. But he has demonstrated a singular ability to remain, at least seemingly, unfazed by his critics. Indeed, Greenblatt has emerged in the twenty-first century as a very successful popular author. His eminently readable 2004 biography of Shakespeare, *Will in the World: How Shakespeare Became Shakespeare*, was a bestselling finalist for every major literary prize and award offered for non-fiction trade books.

If Greenblatt's methods are conventional in *Hamlet in Purgatory*, his subject is anything but. Greenblatt surveys a remarkable range of material—British and Continental liturgical literature, ghost lore, legends, homilies, knights' tales, visual depictions—to show how purgatory, this middle state where souls in terrible flames were purged of their sins, found expression in the imagination and memory of medieval and Renaissance society. It was both a horrible and blessed experience, this prison-house of flames. As opposed to the eternal suffering of the damned, for purgatorial souls the long fiery perdition—thousands of years—was finite; they would eventually be released and soar out of the flames, accompanied by angels, to heaven.

What route did these souls take to the underworld? One widespread story held that the entrance to purgatory was through a cave in Ireland, the entrance to Saint Patrick's purgatory. Purgatory was thus both "real" and imaginary, a place of terrible flames and torments, which haunted dreams and spawned ghosts. Hamlet Sr. draws his breath in dread to tell of this prison-house. The "lightest word" of this scorching torment, we recall,

> Would harrow up thy soul, freeze thy young blood,
> Make thy two eyes like stars start from their spheres,
> Thy knotted and combined locks to part
> And each particular hair to stand on end
> Like quills upon the fearful porpentine.

The frightful vision of a realm of torment was useful to the Catholic Church in material ways: in effect, to extort money from believers, who were taught that donations—indulgences—would remit sins of their dead relatives. You paid money to the Church to lessen the time your ancestors spent in this terror, speeding along the moment when they would be set free, ascending through that hole, that gap, through which souls were loosed into heaven.

The evolving Protestant movement of late medieval and early modern Europe despised the doctrine of purgatory as a commercial scam. Protestants derided purgatory as a metaphor, or as poetry, which may attest more than anything else to its social essence. Purgatory was ridiculed as a convenient and lucrative fable responsible, according to one defender of the doctrine, for founding all bishoprics, churches, oratories, colleges, schools, and charities. Similarly, Protestants noted, if people can eat the body of Christ, then maggots and carrion birds might also be able to eat of the Savior's body.

When Greenblatt brings this conflict between Catholic and Protestant belief to the role of the Ghost in *Hamlet*, we are on familiar ground tilled by many earlier critics, including Greg, Wilson, and Prosser. Greenblatt illuminates the function of memory and its failure in the latter stages of the play, but when it comes to deciding whether the Ghost is "a spirit of health or goblin damned," and whether, in the larger context, it implies in Shakespeare a Catholic or Protestant disposition, Greenblatt is cagily noncommittal. He points to "the bewildering array of hints that the play generates," but refuses to become mired in the quagmire of conflicting and inconsistent evidence of whether the Ghost comes from purgatory or hell, whether it is an aid to Hamlet or the instrument of his ruin and damnation. This is not to say that Shakespeare is guilty of being simply inconsistent or haphazard. "There is, rather, a pervasive pattern, a deliberate forcing together of radically incompatible accounts of almost everything that matters in *Hamlet*." Thus, we can't possibly determine when or whether Hamlet is actually mad or feigning madness, or whether Hamlet really delays or "only berates himself for delaying," or whether Gertrude is or isn't complicit in her first husband's death. The many generations of readers who have debated these issues have presented powerful but starkly dissonant answers to these questions. But "what is at stake is more than a multiplicity of answers," Greenblatt writes, "[t]he opposing positions challenge each other, clashing and sending shock waves through the play." Concerning Hamlet and the nature of the Ghost, all that can be finally said is that "a young man from Wittenberg, with a distinctly Protestant temperament, is haunted by a distinctly Catholic ghost."

Given the complexity of the issues under consideration here, Greenblatt's remark might seem frustratingly insufficient; or, given the interpretive stakes, it may seem a convenient version of Keats's "negative capability," an ability to resist the urge to reach for certainties in the midst of uncertainties. But this isn't really the case. In fact, in his next book, *Will in the World*, Greenblatt makes this yoking of ideas in conflict the crux of his interpretation of *Hamlet*. In *Hamlet*, Greenblatt argues, Shakespeare made a crucial imaginative breakthrough that distinguishes this work from all that had come before it, and shapes the work that followed. He attenuated causality and "psychological rationale" in favor of what Greenblatt terms "strategic opacity." "With Hamlet," he writes, "Shakespeare found that if he refused to provide himself or his audience with a familiar, comforting rationale that seems to make it all make sense, he could get to something immeasurably deeper." It isn't that Shakespeare wished to create mere indecipherable riddles which, after all, could yield only nonsense. "Rather, Shakespeare came increasingly to rely on the inward logic, the poetic coherence that his genius and his immensely hard work had long enabled him to confer on his plays." At once both conceptual and technical, this breakthrough involved the "tearing away of superficial meanings" to fashion "an inner structure through the resonant echoing of key terms, the subtle development of images, the brilliant orchestration of scenes, the complex unfolding of ideas, the intertwining of parallel plots, the uncovering of psychological obsessions." This opacity was the product of "Shakespeare's experience of the world and of his own inner life: his skepticism, his pain, his sense of broken rituals, his refusal of easy consolations." It is not Greenblatt who finds sanctuary in "negative capability," but Shakespeare himself.

I think Greenblatt is certainly correct to return us to the fundamental indeterminacy of *Hamlet*. Indeed, it is precisely indeterminacy that has been the engine that has driven centuries of investigation. The enigma of *Hamlet* is never likely to be satisfactorily unraveled, to be sure, but that enigma may not be the product of a deliberate strategy on Shakespeare's part, as Greenblatt believes. Shakespeare was a very busy man in the period of *Hamlet* and most probably, it seems to me, he left these problems and conflicts—the nature of the Ghost, the issue of Hamlet's madness, the causes of delay—unexplained because he had other things to do than to resolve them. I assume that Shakespeare had no reason to think that future generations of readers and commentators would pore over *Hamlet* in such detail and with such concentration. Had he been able to foresee the problematics in the reception of *Hamlet*, he might have taken greater care to tidy things up. But that would be beyond the powers even of Shakespeare.

TEN

LOOKING FOR HAMLET

$\mathcal{N}$ear the end of the very long and involved 3.2, Polonius intrudes on Hamlet's space, which the editors of the 2006 Arden edition of Q2 gloss as "an indoor Court setting large enough to accommodate the performance of the interlude, *The Murder of Gonzago*." For the last twenty minutes Hamlet has been abusing everyone involved. As "The Mousetrap" opened, he had thrust himself between Ophelia's legs, playing upon the meanings of "lie"—to have sex with but also to speak falsely. In conversation with Ophelia, he had taunted his mother with the darkest accusations, asking how long it's been since her husband died—two years, two months, two days?—then in effect had condemned her remarriage in the play scene. (Here, Q1 insists on Gertrude's complicity in her husband's murder with "none weds the second but *she* kills the first.") Claudius, realizing perhaps for the first time what Hamlet is up to, stops the action where the murdering brother pours poison in the King's ear, crying, "Lights! Lights! Lights!"

The stage is then cleared of all but Hamlet and Horatio. Hamlet asks whether Horatio noted the King's guilty reaction. Horatio confirms Claudius' guilt and the veracity of the Ghost with "I did very well note him." Immediately Rosencrantz and Guildenstern enter the scene and tell Hamlet that the King has retired "marvelous distempered" and that Hamlet's behavior has plunged the Queen "into amazement and admiration." She desires a conference with her son, Rosencrantz reports. Hamlet, seizing a recorder, a kind of flute, then confronts them directly with the charge of being spies for the King. They would play upon him like a "recorder," assuming to know his stops. They would "pluck out the heart of my mystery." But they will fail. "Call me what instrument you will," he says, "though you fret me you cannot play upon me."

After this intense sequence of revelatory events, Polonius enters the scene with, "God bless you, sir."

Physically and psychically exhausted, Hamlet replies with a curious, wearied redirection. He points the soon-to-be "grave" councilor's attention to a cloud. This means, among much else, that the Arden mention of an "indoor" court is at this moment, strictly speaking, wrong. The scene has shifted; Hamlet is looking skyward.

"Do you see yonder cloud that's almost in shape of a camel?" Hamlet asks.

Polonius agrees: "By th' mass and 'tis like a camel indeed."

Hamlet turns agreement against Polonius: "Methinks it is a weasel."

"It is backed like a weasel," Polonius toadishly replies.

"Or like a whale," Hamlet challenges.

"Very like a whale," Polonius agrees.

This series of feints suggests how deeply *Hamlet* is, as Harry Levin noted, a kind of Rorschach test, a changing cloud formation that appears as something different depending upon our culture, history, and personal experience. When anthropologist Laura Bohannon told the story of Hamlet to elders of the Tiv tribe of northern Nigeria, to call upon a famous example of cultural difference, they denied that the Ghost of Hamlet's father was in any sense "real." The Tiv don't believe in the survival of the individual spirit beyond death. Their interpretation of Hamlet's Ghost, emerging from discussions around a pot of beer, held that the apparition was "an omen sent by a witch." Perplexed by this reaction, Bohannon brought up the initial confrontation between Hamlet and the Ghost in which Hamlet Sr. speaks. In a tantalizing reminder of Renaissance spiritualism, which held that Ghosts did not speak unless and until spoken to, the elders denied this emphatically: "Omens can't talk!"

No, Bohannon insisted, this wasn't an omen but rather the spirit of the dead king. It was visible and could talk. Why then, the elders said, it must have been a zombie, a dead body animated by a witch, which appeared to Hamlet. "One can touch zombies," they insisted. Bohannon ventured to explain that no one touches the Ghost of Hamlet's father, nor did anyone make him walk. "He did it himself," she insisted. The elders protested that "dead men can't walk."

Casting about for a way of explaining what's happening, Bohannon described Hamlet's father as a "dead man's shadow."

"Dead men cast no shadow," they replied.

"They do in my country," Bohannon said.

When Bohannon revealed that Hamlet appears mad to Polonius, their interest was heightened. To the Tiv, there are two causes of madness: witchcraft and something like heightened perception, the ability to see "the beings that lurk in the forest." Since only male relatives could bewitch a person, they explain, Claudius must be responsible for Hamlet's madness. Bohannon introduced the Players whom Hamlet uses to test Claudius's guilt. A "famous storyteller," she explained, tells the Great Chief the story of the murder. But why was this necessary? they asked. Because, Bohannon explained, Hamlet wasn't certain whether the Ghost was telling the truth. But why, they wondered, would a father lie to his son? Well, Hamlet wasn't sure if the Ghost really was his father. Then, as they had already explained to this interloper, it was an omen. Hamlet was a fool not to seek the council of a man "skilled in reading omens and divining truth. Hamlet could have called the elders to settle the matter." Revenge against Hamlet's father's brother is unacceptable, they assert. Vengeance belongs to the "age-mates."

The Tiv have a keen sense of irony, however. Had Claudius bewitched Hamlet with madness and then in this madness Hamlet had attempted to kill Claudius— now that would be "a good story."

Bohannon moved to the Closet Scene, in which Hamlet chastises his mother. No circumstances, however urgent or important, could justify such mistreatment of the mother, the elders said. For their part, the Tiv women saw nothing wrong with Gertrude's hasty remarriage. "Who will hoe your farms for you," they asked, "if you have no husband?"

And what of Ophelia? Who drove her mad? Laertes, the elders concluded, must have "killed his sister by witchcraft, drowning her so as to sell her body to the witches." But Ophelia's body was recovered and buried. Indeed, Laertes leapt into her grave, followed by Hamlet. This only confirmed for the Tiv that Laertes was "up to no good" with his sister's body. Hamlet blocked him because as the dead chief's son, Hamlet didn't wish to see Laertes "grow rich and powerful" by employ-ing witchcraft. He would thus have killed his sister without gaining any benefit for himself, and for this reason he would want to kill Hamlet. "Is this not what hap-pened?" they asked Bohannon. More or less, she conceded.

Bohannon explained Claudius' treachery in arranging the swordfight, and the consequent slaughter, with Hamlet managing to kill his father's brother before dying himself. The Tiv approve of the story but explain one detail of 5.2 that Bohannon, in their opinion, seemed to have missed. The poisoned cup was meant for Laertes in case he won the fight, for the usurping king couldn't allow the only person who knew of Claudius' scheme to live. Then Claudius wouldn't have to fear Laertes' powerful witchcraft.

Obviously, the Tiv cultural perspective produces a reading quite different from that of the West. The Ghost could not have been in any sense "real," so they offer the only available interpretation of the apparition. It is a zombie. Among the Tiv, fathers don't lie to their sons, so the story of a questionable father seems improba-ble to them. Hamlet's madness, like Ophelia's, has a ready cause that we in the West don't allow. It is a curse or hex cast by an enemy. Whereas four centuries of Western interpreters have agreed with Hamlet that Gertrude's second marriage is incestuous, Tiv women exonerate her, insisting upon the necessity of a quick remarriage after the death of a husband, and appropriately enough to her dead husband's brother. Most important, perhaps, the Tiv have a level of arbitration, a council of elders—"age-mates"—that would have determined the nature of the case and meted out justice, thus releasing Hamlet from the necessity of exacting revenge. Had there been a level of arbitration such as the Tiv elders in *Hamlet*, of course, much slaughter would have been averted.

What we find in *Hamlet* is also a product of one's historical circumstance. Consider the experience of the Warwickshire historian Charlotte Carmichael Stopes, who, you'll recall, proposed that the Ghost was a hallucination. Searching the coroners' inquests among the "Ancient Indictments" housed at the Record Office, she found, in the roll of 1580–81, an account of the drowning of one Katherine Hamlet in the Avon River near Stratford-upon-Avon, when Shakespeare was a teenager. Was this an accident, as the record seems to indicate, or had Katherine Hamlet drowned herself? She asks, "Had this little incident floated through Shakespeare's brain from his youth, till it was recalled by the name of 'Hamlet'?"

Stopes (1841–1929) was a remarkable woman. Informally educated at Edinburgh University in a time before women were allowed to take university degrees, in 1879 she married Henry Stopes, an architect with an interest in paleontology, with whom she explored the Nile River. Back in London, she became an early champion of women's rights, and took up scholarly pursuits during her husband's frequent absences. She attended meetings of the New Shakespeare Society, which provided her with access to the most important Shakespeare scholars of the time. "With all her feminist ardor," writes S. Schoenbaum in *Shakespeare's Lives*, "she determined to excel in a field overwhelmingly dominated by men." Her passionate devotion to Shakespearean scholarship never waned, even when her husband's death left her in penury, with the burden of raising two children. During her career as an amateur Shakespearean, she published dozens of articles, which she collected into several books, including *Shakespeare's Warwickshire Contemporaries* (1897, revised and enlarged 1907), *Shakespeare's Family* (1901), and *Shakespeare's Environment* (1914).

As these titles suggest, Stopes' interest was in Warwickshire genealogy and history rather than literary criticism proper. As a researcher, she was formidable yet flawed. "Tough-minded and critical," in Schoenbaum's judgment, she was an early opponent of the anti-Stratfordian Movement—the effort to disprove that William Shakespeare was the author of the plays—and a supporter of the now widely held belief that the Earl of Southampton rather than the Earl of Pembroke is the Fair Young Man of Shakespeare's sonnets. She brought a helpfully corrective, objective approach to her researches, one that eschewed the sentimental Bardolatry that reigned in her time. Yet her work is marked by "slovenliness" and "appalling carelessness" and "gross blunders"—again, the words of Schoenbaum. Not only did she misreport facts and misquote the most familiar lines from *Hamlet*, her overweening ambition led her to claim other people's discoveries as her own and to sabotage the work of competing researchers.

Although in the late 1920s Edgar I. Fripp reported the drowning of Katherine Hamlet, I don't know of anyone who disputes that this was Stopes' discovery, one made all the more noteworthy precisely because Stopes was an amateur and a woman struggling to make a name for herself as an outsider in a male-dominated profession. But the historical context in which she was working is of even greater interest. She announced her finding in the *Transactions of the Royal Society of Literature* in late February 1915—six months into the slaughter of the Great War, which had already seen the ghastly debacle along the Marne, and in three months would see another, even greater catastrophe in the Dardanelles, where Rupert Brooke, the loveliest flower of Edwardian innocence, who had written "If I should die, think only this of me: / That there's some corner of a foreign field / That is forever England"—would fulfill that ironic prophesy, succumbing to blood poisoning aboard a troop ship en route to the Battle of Gallipoli on St. Georges Day, 1915—April 23, Shakespeare's birthday and death day. Amid such horrors, we are left with a larger contextual question: May not the war itself, in some way too personal for us ever to recover, have led Stopes to the coroners' roll at the Record Office?

The best searches for Hamlet are motivated by intense and idiosyncratic experiences. The postmodern political fervor of the late 1980s and early '90s is similarly the product of historical circumstance, thriving in the decade of Reagan-Thatcherism against which the participants in the Essex symposia were reacting. What is true of Stopes and Dover Wilson and Barker is true, I think, of everyone who becomes deeply involved with *Hamlet*, this camel, this weasel, this whale. Our own place in time figures deeply in what we find when we look for Hamlet.

The cultural and historical converge at the much more enigmatic and, if I may use the word, neurotic level of the individual mind and personality. The individual psyche is perhaps the most important of all shaping influences. This is especially clear among Romantic critics—Hamlet as a precious vase shivered by a monstrous oak, for example, is inseparable from Goethe's own mind and experience—but even among moderns and postmoderns, interpretation is deeply shaped by personal experience and disposition. This is certainly true of psychological readings. Indeed, Freud, perhaps indirectly the single most influential figure in the search for Hamlet, is the most self-involved of all thinkers. By the same token, the political ends to which postmodern critics wish to enlist *Hamlet* are also personal ends. In all cases, the search for Hamlet is finally personal, a search, as I suggested at the outset, for some idealized version of the self. Hamlet is the Western world's collective dead son, a missing person made conspicuous by his absence. Centuries of interpretation have directed us inward to an exploration of what we have lost, or are losing, in the search for Hamlet.

But Hamlet is obviously more than an inert image—a mirror in which we see ourselves reflected, an empty chair at the table; he is rather a shaping force, a literary character of supreme importance in the fashioning of Western thought and personality. Harold Bloom's hyperbolic claims for Shakespeare and Hamlet—that Shakespeare, largely through his greatest creation, "has become a mortal god," that "Shakespeare invented us"—have annoyed many. But the history of *Hamlet*'s reception amply demonstrates that this character has played a preeminent role in making us what we are. If we find untenable Bloom's extreme claims for Shakespeare the writer, and Hamlet his supreme creation, we certainly must acknowledge as absolutely true Greenblatt's more circumspect conviction that "we are in part the unintended consequences of *Hamlet*."

FRIGHTED WITH FIRE

If every engagement with Hamlet is at once cultural, historical, and personal, if we all of us have a version of the train to Sunderland, let me explain how my own knit of identity brought me to this book. I'm a fan of Duke University football. That's not a misstatement. Duke football, not basketball. For the record, I was a graduate student at The University of North Carolina at Chapel Hill during the James Worthy/Michael Jordan era, and my allegiance to UNC basketball is unshakable. But my earliest sports affinity was to Duke. My father, then a divinity student there, took me to my first Blue Devil football game in 1960 or '61. Just a boy, I'd spent my years in rural communities in southern Virginia where my father served small parishes. I remember the visceral shock of walking into Wallace Wade Stadium that crisp fall afternoon and seeing the huge colorful crowd arrayed around the horseshoe-shaped stadium. Duke was playing Notre Dame or Navy that day, I don't remember which, but I do remember a sea of gold and green on the visitor side of the stadium and an even greater mass of blue and white on our side. I had never seen a spectacle like this, so many people, so many colors; had never heard so much music and noise. I remember the band, the fans cheering, the players in their beautiful uniforms crashing into one another, the roars and groans, the kickoffs, punts, and passes that sent the ball soaring through the air. My father was a hotheaded fan, unseemly for a man of the cloth. In the middle of the game, he stood up and challenged a heckling Notre Dame or Navy fan sitting behind us to a fight.

The rich memory of that day came flooding back through me years later when, having finished graduate school and moved back to Durham, with two children in middle school, I took my son to a Duke game, hoping John would feel the same thrill I had felt so many years ago. He didn't, of course. Just barely a teenager, he'd seen more of the world by the time he was ten than I had well into my adult years. He was already beyond such an experience. A football game left him cold.

But not me. The old thrill came back that day, the unfolding drama of the game blending with a powerful nostalgia. This was my past, this stadium, these aging fans. The next season, I corralled a couple of friends from my college years and we became regulars on Saturday afternoons at Duke games. It didn't matter that Duke teams were perennial cellar-dwellers. Indeed, the fact that the Blue Devils lost so many games, and so regularly, had very real benefits: cheap season tickets and easy parking.

We developed a tradition of locking on one incoming freshman player and following him through his Duke career. In the fall of 2001, I selected Micah Harris, a 6' 3," 235-pound freshman defensive end from a suburb of Youngstown, Ohio. Micah was talented enough to see considerable playing time his freshman year, though offenses regularly ran over him. The next year Micah was bigger and stronger, and didn't get pushed around as much. He had a few great moments that season, breaking into the backfield to disrupt a play, or holding his position at the line to stop a running back in his tracks. In his junior year Micah emerged as a defensive stalwart in a long season of losing causes, punctuated by a mid-season coaching change that produced the next week a spectacular victory over Georgia Tech. Duke students tore down the goal posts, the only time I've seen that happen at Wallace Wade.

Our seats that season were adjacent to the parents' section, and I frequently saw Micah's mother and father, who came from Ohio for home games. Polonius-like, I watched them watching Micah, though I never approached them or their son. Resting on the sideline, Micah would take off his helmet to reveal a shock of black hair tied back with a red headband. I imagined this was the work of his girlfriend.

In the final game of his junior year, against archrival UNC, Micah was a monster, swatting down passes, dragging runners to the turf, fighting through or around offensive players, wrecking havoc in Carolina's backfield. Duke won the game hands down, giving us long-suffering Duke fans something to really cheer about, finally, and setting up great expectations for the 2004 season.

It was not to be. On the morning of June 11, 2004, Micah left Durham in his Volvo, headed north on I-85 for Richmond, Virginia. Just over the state line he fell asleep at the wheel. With the cruise control apparently engaged, his car drifted into the median, plowed through brush, smashed into a tree and exploded in flames. Micah Harris, *aetat* twenty-one, was immolated.

By the oddest of coincidences, my aged parents were traveling the same stretch of interstate that day and passed just minutes after the accident. At a rest stop a few miles up the road, they overheard some EMS workers talking about the crash. My mother called me from the road to say that a Duke football player had been killed, but she didn't know who he was. That afternoon I learned of Micah's death from news reports. Just the barest of accounts: who, what, when, where. The resulting silence, the empty chair, I have attempted to fill with words.

The dream that opens the final chapter of Freud's *Interpretation of Dreams* is premonitory and profoundly evocative. In it, an exhausted father is sleeping after having spent days tending to his dying son. In another room, the boy's body lies in a coffin surrounded by candles. The corpse is guarded by an old man muttering prayers. Suddenly in the father's dream, the son appears in flames at his side, tugging at his arm and whispering, *"Father, don't you see I'm burning?"* These words are uttered, *reproachfully*, Freud says. At this point in the dream, the father wakes up to see a bright light coming from the other room and rushes in to find the old man asleep. The boy's body is in flames, the implication being that the nodding old man has knocked a candle over into the coffin. Freud sees this "moving" dream as simple enough to interpret. Perhaps the father "had felt some concern when he went to sleep as to whether the old man might . . . be incompetent to carry out his task." For Freud, the point is that the father's dream of the child coming to him in flames momentarily extends his life, if horribly. The dream shows the father his child alive again. If he had awakened before the flaming boy rose from his coffin, the father would have been spared a terrible experience, but he "would have shortened the child's life by that moment of time."

As a means of bringing *Looking for Hamlet* to an end, let me venture a brief interpretation of this dream. The flaming child is Hamlet, of course. The old man who spills the fire onto the corpse is the Ghost dousing his son in the flames of purgatory, his sleep representing the fading memory of the father enacted in *Hamlet*. The old man sacrifices the son, covering young Hamlet's "smooth body," as Claudius had the father's, "with vile and loathsome crust." We—everyone who has read and seen the play through the history of its reception—are the father asleep in the other room, exhausted from the ravages of time. We receive, over and over again, the most horrible but most compelling of visitations.

One particular aspect of this episode, which for me links it through the death of Micah Harris to Hamlet, is crucial: the dream of the burning child is *reported*; its "source" Freud says, "is still unknown to me." It was told to him by a woman who heard it described at a lecture on dreams. It was so powerful that she internalized it; she "re-dreamed" it, repeating elements of it in her own dream work, only to propagate the dream when she reported it to Freud, who then conveyed it to untold thousands who have read, and will read, *The Interpretation of Dreams*. Like *Hamlet*, it circulates through audiences who must grapple with its haunting images and enigmatic meanings, in effect copy-dreaming it, internalizing the dream of the reproachful child in flames who implores his father with, "Don't you see I'm burning?"

Finally, let me note that the dream of the burning child appears in a chapter of *The Interpretation of Dreams* concerned with forgetting *in* dreams, *while* dreaming. But Freud actually discusses how dreams fade, or are repressed, during our waking hours. There is anecdotal evidence to suggest that history might be forgetting *Hamlet* just as Hamlet had forgotten his father. Writing in 1989, Gary Taylor remarked that "Shakespeare's words are disappearing before our eyes; their sound is lost already, tentatively reimagined in specialized monographs written and disputed by phonologists and linguists, but spoken by no one . . . the code that communicated his meanings [is] becoming unintelligibly obsolete. . . ." If, as we regularly hear, we are now in a postliterate age, there is no reason to assume that *Hamlet* will survive this sea change. Curricular changes in American colleges and universities, moreover, may be speeding Hamlet on his way to oblivion. In my department, as in many others around the country, neither undergraduate nor graduate majors—to say nothing of nonmajors—are any longer required to take a course in Shakespeare. In many institutions of higher learning, it is entirely possible for students to graduate with degrees in English and never read this great play. *Hamlet*, which has done so much to shape the psyche of the Western world, may be a dream we are forgetting.

BIBLIOGRAPHIC ESSAY

INTRODUCTION

In 1993, R. A. Foakes claimed that *King Lear*, a vision of apocalyptic ruin brought about by the mistakes of old men, had supplanted *Hamlet* in importance. But the editors of the recent Arden, Third Series *Hamlet*s, Ann Thompson and Neil Taylor, dispute this claim. They count 400 items on Hamlet/*Hamlet* appearing in the 2001 *Shakespeare Quarterly Annual Bibliography*. *Lear* appears about half that often. I quote *Hamlet* from the Arden *Shakespeare*, Third Series, edited by Thompson and Taylor (London: Thomson, 2006). Thompson and Taylor publish three separate versions of the play, in two volumes. Unless otherwise indicated, mine are taken from the Second Quarto (Q2). At other times, as indicated, I quote the First Quarto (Q1) and First Folio (F1). T. S. Eliot's 1919 essay "Hamlet and his Problems" has been widely reprinted. Here and elsewhere, I quote from the essay as it appears in his *Selected Essays: New Edition* (New York: Harcourt, 1950). De Grazia's *Hamlet without Hamlet* (Cambridge: Cambridge UP, 2007) arrived just as *Looking for Hamlet* was entering production—too late, I'm sorry to say, to give her very fine book the consideration it deserves.

For the number of stage and film productions of *Hamlet*, see David Crystal and Ben Crystal, *The Shakespeare Miscellany* (Woodstock, NY: Overlook, 2005). See also Thompson and Taylor, "*Hamlet* on Stage and Screen" in their "Introduction" to the Arden *Hamlet* Q2. The Richard III—William the Conqueror anecdote was recorded by John Manningham, a law student, in his diary entry for March 13, 1601. See S. Schoenbaum, *Shakespeare's Lives* (Oxford: Oxford UP, 1970). For an extensive account of the performance of *Hamlet* aboard the *Red Dragon*, and of English attitudes toward Africa and Africans in Shakespeare's age, see Gary Taylor, "*Hamlet* in Africa 1607" in *Travel Knowledge: European "Discoveries" in the Early Modern Period*. Ed. Ivo Kanps and Jyotsna G. Singh (New York: Palgrave, 2001), 223–48. Jesús Tronch-Pérez offers a concise listing of *Hamlet* in quarto and folio versions in *A Synoptic Hamlet: A Critical and Synoptic Edition of the Second Quarto and First Folio Texts of Hamlet* (Sederi: Universitat de Valencia, 2002). On the Davenant/Betterton *Hamlet*, see John A. Mills, *Hamlet on Stage: The Great Tradition* (Westport, CT: Greenwood, 1985) and

Russ McDonald, *The Bedford Companion to Shakespeare: An Introduction with Documents*, Second Edition (New York: Bedford/St. Martin's, 2001); the Cornmarket Press issued a facsimile of the 1703 text of Davenant's *Hamlet* in 1969. Levin's comments on the impossibility of being comprehensive in treating Hamlet/*Hamlet* commentary appear in *The Question of Hamlet* (New York: Oxford UP, 1959).

ONE   THE PREHISTORY OF HAMLET

My quotations from Saxo and François de Belleforest's subsequent rendering of the Hamlet legend are taken from the translations of the *Historica Danica* and the *Histories Tragiques* by Sir Israel Gollancz (London: Cass, 1926; rpt. New York: Octagon, 1967). I have silently updated his spelling. Selections from the Danish sources can also be found in Horace Howard Furness, ed., *A New Variorum Edition of Shakespeare: Hamlet*. Vol. II (New York: Lippincott, 1877; rpt. New York: Dover, 1963), and Geoffrey Bullough, ed., *Narrative and Dramatic Sources of Shakespeare*. Vol. VII (London: Routledge, 1973). On the derivation of the name Amleth, see Gollancz, Kemp Malone, *The Literary History of Hamlet* (New York: Haskell, 1964) and Marion A. Taylor, *A New Look at the Old Sources of Hamlet* (Hague: Mouton, 1968). On the changes Shakespeare made to the old sagas, see Furness, Thompson and Taylor, as well as William F. Hansen, *Saxo Grammaticus and the Life of Hamlet: A Translation, History and Commentary* (Lincoln and London: U of Nebraska Press, 1983).

The devastating effects of the Ghost's appearing to Hamlet and not to Gertrude in 3.4 becomes an issue of much debate in the late nineteenth and twentieth centuries, especially for W. W. Greg, John Dover Wilson, and Eleanor Prosser, among others. I discuss these works in detail in chapter eight, "Hamlet Among the Moderns."

The Ur-*Hamlet* title for the old play about Hamlet has been favored since 1919, when W. W. Greg used it. Bullough, in the "Introduction" to *Narrative and Dramatic Sources*, Vol. VII, offers a helpful overview of the possible relationship of *The Spanish Tragedy* to the Ur-*Hamlet*, though Bullough concedes that the relationship "is impossible to define." The remarks of Nashe, Meres, and Lodge in relation to *Hamlet* are conveniently available in Furness' *Variorum Shakespeare*, Vol. II and in Tronch-Pérez's *Synoptic Hamlet*. *Fratricide Punished* is included in both Furness and Bullough. In his groundbreaking study of the sub-genre of revenge tragedy in Elizabethan-Jacobean theater, Fredson Bowers concludes that Kyd wrote the Ur-*Hamlet* in 1587, based on his reading of Belleforest; and that he reworked this material the following year as *The Spanish Tragedy*. This raises, but does not answer, the question why Shakespeare chose the Ur-*Hamlet* rather than the more sophisticated *The Spanish Tragedy* as the source for his play. I suggest contextual reasons that might explain this choice. See Bowers, *Elizabethan Revenge Tragedy, 1587–1642* (Princeton: Princeton UP, 1940). On Shakespeare's relations with his contemporary playwrights, see Stanley

Wells, *Shakespeare and Co.: Christopher Marlowe, Thomas Dekker, Ben Jonson, Thomas Middleton, John Fletcher and other Players in his Story* (New York: Pantheon, 2007). On the dating of *Hamlet*, see E. A. J. Honigmann's important essay "The Date of *Hamlet*," *Shakespeare Survey* 9 (1956): 24–34. Honigmann dates the play before the War of the Theatres (1601), since the second published version of *Hamlet* (Q2, 1604/5), which he and many others think was written before the first edition of the play (Q1, 1603), doesn't have this digression, but this supposition is far from incontestable. It is just as likely that the 1603 edition of *Hamlet*, which contains the allusion to the War of the Theatres, was written first. On the dispute as it was waged in plays by Jonson on the one side, and Dekker and Marston on the other, see E. K. Chambers, *The Elizabethan Stage*. Vol. III (Oxford: Clarendon, 1923; rpt with corrections, 1974).

I have taken my account of the Essex uprising from J. E. Neale, *Queen Elizabeth I: A Biography* (London: Cape, 1934; rpt. New York: Doubleday, 1957); see also relevant sections of Paul Johnson's *Elizabeth I, A Biography* (New York: Holt, Rinehart, 1974), and Christopher Haigh's *Elizabeth I* (New York: Longman, 1988). McDonald, *Bedford Companion*, reproduces William Lambarde's account of Elizabeth's reaction to the 1601 resurrection of *Richard II*.

TWO   THE THREE *HAMLETS*

Anyone interested in pursuing the relationships among the three versions of *Hamlet* with claims to authority—the First Quarto (Q1, 1603), the Second Quarto (Q2, 1604/05), and the First Folio (F1, 1623)—relationships as fascinating as they are perplexing and inconclusive, should begin with the texts themselves. These are available in several different formats. Tronch-Pérez (*A Synoptic Hamlet*) presents Q2 and F1 collapsed upon one another, with Q2 readings presented as superscript and F1 readings as subscript. This allows for an immediate grasp of the differences between Q2 and F1. *The Three-Text Hamlet: Parallel Texts of the First and Second Quartos and First Folio*, Second Edition, edited by Paul Bertram and Bernice W. Kliman (New York: AMS, 2003) allows one to study variants among all three versions across the page. Less conveniently useful for comparative purposes is the 2006 Arden *Hamlet*, edited by Thompson and Taylor, which prints Q2 in one volume and Q1 and F1 together in another.

From the texts themselves, the next step is to study the commentaries accompanying these volumes, especially those of Tronch-Pérez and Thompson and Taylor (introduction and appendices), who offer extensive histories of investigations of the texts of *Hamlet*, as do Stanley Wells and Gary Taylor, with John Howett and William Montgomery, in *William Shakespeare: A Textual Companion* (Oxford: Oxford UP, 1987). Hamletworks.org is also a helpful resource. Lukas Erne offers a helpful history of twentieth-century evolution of the understanding of the three *Hamlet* texts in *Shakespeare as Literary Dramatist*

(Cambridge: Cambridge UP, 2003). My consideration of the three *Hamlet*s is based on the order in which they were published, a strategy by which I largely avoid complex issues that are, after all, mainly irrelevant to my line of inquiry. As I suggested above, however, it is by no means clear that the sequence in which these three *Hamlet*s appeared in print—Q1>Q2>F1—reflects the order in which they were composed. While Q1 may in fact be Shakespeare's first draft of *Hamlet*, written perhaps in consultation with the missing Ur-*Hamlet*, which Shakespeare then revised as Q2, which was, in turn, republished with alterations as F1, many scholars believe that, owing to pronounced affinities between Q1 and F1, Q2 must represent Shakespeare's original version of *Hamlet*, which was abridged as a theatrical version of the play, Q1, which was consulted in the production of F1 in 1623. Thus the sequence of composition might in fact be Q2>Q1>F1. But as Tronch-Pérez, after an extensive survey of the evidence, concludes: "narratives of the textual history of *Hamlet*, which account for the textual differences in terms of authentic readings and corruptions, have only resulted in tentative and sometimes contradictory explanations that always contain some problematic point in their argument and ultimately depend on assumptions concerning, and reflect subjective views on, literary production and transmission." Thompson and Taylor reach a similar conclusion. "The textual history of *Hamlet*," they write, "is full of questions and largely empty of answers."

The term "bad quarto" was coined by A. W. Pollard in *Shakespeare's Folios and Quartos: A Study in the Bibliography of Shakespeare's Plays 1594–1685* (1909). On the "striking" similarity between the roles of Marcellus, Lucianus, and Voltemar (Voltemand in F1) in Q1 and F1, see Kathleen O. Irace, *The First Quarto of Hamlet* (Cambridge: Cambridge UP, 1998). On the possibilities of "doubling," where one actor may have played multiple roles in the same production, see Thompson and Taylor; also " 'Your Sum of Parts': Doubling in *Hamlet*," in Lukas Erne and Margaret Jane Kidnie, eds., *Textual Performances: The Modern Reproduction of Shakespeare's Drama* (Cambridge: Cambridge UP, 2004). My discussion of the outbreaks of plague in London is drawn from Chambers, *Elizabethan Stage*, Vol. IV.

In her "Introduction" to the First Quarto, Irace provides a valuable discussion of the evidence of Q1 as a memorial reconstruction, as a theatrical adaptation, and as a memorially reconstructed theatrical adaptation, as well as differences in plot and characterization between Q1 and later versions. My discussion of the ensemble theory is based upon Erne in *Shakespeare as Literary Dramatist*, who provides a detailed discussion of the ways this scene consolidates material and thus supports the belief that a deliberated theatrical adaptation stands behind Q1. Irace, and Thompson and Taylor, reproduce this unique exchange between Horatio and the Queen as scene 14 of Q1 *Hamlet*. On the psychological function of forgetting and remembering in *Hamlet*, see James Schiffer's "Mnemonic Cues to Passion in Hamlet" in George Walton Williams and Barbara J. Baines, eds., *Renaissance Papers* 1995 (Southeastern Renaissance Conference, 1996): 65–79.

The figure of 4,056 lines for Q2 is Tronch-Pérez's total. Thompson and Taylor count of 3,902 "separate lines of printed text." Harold Jenkins, editor of the Arden Second Series

Hamlet (London: Metheun, 1982), counts 3,723 lines, excluding stage directions. The claim that Q2 *Hamlet* is a work conceived to be read as literature, as opposed to being seen as dramatic performance, is the argument advanced by Erne in *Shakespeare as Literary Dramatist*. Similarly, Giorgio Melchiori claimed that "behind Q2, there is a play for the closet, not for the stage" in "Hamlet: The Acting Version and the Wiser Sort," in Thomas Clayton, ed., *The Hamlet First Published (Q1, 1603): Origins, Form, Intertextualities* (Newark: U of Delaware Press, 1992).

The exception to the use of Q2 as copy text is the Oxford *Complete Works of William Shakespeare*, edited by Stanley Wells and Gary Taylor (Oxford: Oxford UP, 1986). Wells and Taylor base their edition of *Hamlet* upon F1, relegating Hamlet's 4.4 soliloquy beginning "How all occasions do inform against me," which does not appear in F1, to "Additional Passages" at the end of the play.

On Shakespeare's rise to prominence on the Elizabethan stage, see Schoenbaum and Honan; Wells, *Shakespeare and Co.*; as well as Stephen Greenblatt, *Will in the World: How Shakespeare Became Shakespeare* (New York: Norton, 2004). Regarding the Pyrrhus interlude, see Harry Levin's essay "An Explication of the Player's Speech" near the end of his *The Question of Hamlet*. Mark Taylor provides a helpful reading of the Player's Speech in ironic relation to Hamlet's subsequent soliloquy on his inaction, in *Shakespeare's Imitations* (Newark: U of Delaware P, 2002). Robert Weimann, ("Mimesis in *Hamlet*," in Patricia Parker and Geoffrey Hartman, eds., *Shakespeare and the Question of Theory* [New York: Methuen, 1985]: 275–291), stresses the extraordinary levels of mimesis, or imitation, in this scene (including his advice to the players on acting), which presents Hamlet as theoretician, theater critic, dramatist, director, chorus, and actor.

In contributing "some dozen lines, or sixteen lines" to *The Murder of Gonzago*, Hamlet becomes, as it were, a coauthor of *Hamlet*.

On the child acting companies and the "War of the Theatres," see Chambers, Vol. III. On the number and dispersion of theaters in London, see Chambers, Vol. II, and Steven Mullaney, *The Place of the Stage: License, Play and Power in Renaissance England* (Chicago: U of Chicago P, 1988). I quote Milton's *Paradise Lost* here and elsewhere from Merritt Y. Hughes, ed., *John Milton: Complete Poems and Major Prose* (New York: Odyssey, 1957). On the de Bène heresy, and the support Amaurians received from the Capetian monarchy, see Robert E. Lerner, "The Uses of Heterodoxy: The French Monarchy and Unbelief in the Thirteenth Century," *French Historical Studies* 4.2 (Autumn 1965): 189–202.

THREE YORICK'S SKULL

Shapiro (*A Year in the Life*) assumes that Armin played the gravedigger in the original productions of *Hamlet*. On the exchange of titles and identities between fools and their betters in Shakespeare, compare the encounter between the fool /clown Feste and the Lady Olivia in 1.5 of *Twelfth Night*. Olivia is mourning the death of her brother:

FESTE   Good Madonna, why mourn's thou?

OLIVIA   Good fool, for my brother's death.

FESTE   I think his soul is in hell, Madonna

OLIVIA   I know his soul is in heaven, fool.

FESTE   The more fool, Madonna, to mourn for your brother's soul, being in
          heaven. Take away the fool, gentlemen.

See the similar imposition of the title of fool upon Lear by his fool in 1.5 of *King Lear*. Acknowledging David Aers, "A Whisper in the Ear of Early Modernists; or, Reflections on Literary Critics writing in the 'History of the Subject,'" in Aers, ed., *Culture and History 1350–1600: Essays on English Communities, Identities, and Writing* (Detroit, 1992): 177–201, Thompson and Taylor concede that "the kind of interiority or subjectivity identified by scholars working on the Renaissance can be found much earlier in the poetry of William Langland and Geoffrey Chaucer," but they affirm that the play invites speculation about precisely what it means to claim, as Hamlet does, that "I have that within which passes show." On the matter of inwardness in *Hamlet*, see, among many others, Michael Schoenfeldt, *Bodies and Selves in Early Modern England: Physiology and Inwardness in Spenser, Shakespeare, Herbert and Milton* (New York: Cambridge UP, 1999), Katherine Eisaman Maus, *Inwardness and Theater in the English Renaissance* (Chicago: U of Chicago P, 1995), and Anne Ferry, *The "Inward" Language: Sonnets of Wyatt, Sidney, Shakespeare, Donne* (Chicago: U of Chicago Press, 1983). On boundaries in *Hamlet*, see Marjorie Garber's chapter on the play in *Shakespeare After All* (New York: Pantheon, 2004), and Janet Adelman's discussion of *Hamlet* in her *Suffocating Mothers: Fantasies of Maternal Origin in Shakespeare's Plays, Hamlet to The Tempest* (New York: Routledge, 1992). Wright's essay "Hendiadys and Hamlet" appeared in *PMLA* 96.2 (1981): 168–93. See also Shapiro's discussion of this rhetorical device in his *Year in the Life*.

I am indebted to Mark Taylor for pointing out that Montaigne anticipates this distinction between signifier and signified in the beginning of his essay, "Of Glory." "There are names and there are things," Montaigne writes. "A name is the spoken sound which designates a thing and acts as a sign for it. The name is not part of that thing nor part of its substance: it is a foreign body attached to that thing; it is quite outside it." For an application of Saussurian logic to another important Renaissance work, see my "Charactonymic Structures in Sidney's *Arcadias*," *Studies in English Literature: 1500–1900* 33.1 (1993): 1–20. On the connection between madness and prisons in Early Modern Europe, see Michel Foucault's *Madness and Civilization: A History of Insanity in the Age of Reason* (New York: Random House, 1965). We should note that the confinement of folly is enacted in *Twelfth Night*, with Malvolio's descent into "madness" eventuating in his confinement, is in contrast to the freedom of the "fool" Feste who enjoys unfettered privilege to move between the courts of his lady Olivia and Duke Orsino. See Mullaney, "Mourning and Misogyny," for a fuller consideration of the reaction to the death of Queen Elizabeth enacted in *Hamlet* and *The Revenger's Tragedy*.

FOUR   DEAD SON HAMLET

There is certainly no explicit presence of Old Hamlet after the Ghost's final appearance in 3.4. However, Shakespeare's own father, who worked in the leather trade, may be cryptically remembered in the gravedigger's 5.1 remark that a tanner's body "will last you nine years"— that is, the corpse of a tanner will not rot for nine years. See Shapiro's discussion of Hamnet's death and Shakespeare's travels between London and Stratford-upon-Avon in *A Year in the Life*. See also Stephen Greenblatt, "The Death of Hamnet and the Making of Hamlet." *New York Review of Books* (51.16), October 21, 2004. There is a record of the drowning in the River Avon of one Katharine Hamlet in the coroner's inquests in 1580–81, which may have contributed to Shakespeare's dispatching of Ophelia by drowning. Katharine Duncan-Jones notes the increase in children named Hamlet in the early seventeenth century in *Ungentle Shakespeare: Scenes from his Life* (London: Arden, 2001). Lawrence Stone, in *The Family, Sex and Marriage in England, 1500–1800* (New York: Harper, 1977), argues that, with the exception of the eldest son who stood to inherit "title, positions and property," "fathers . . . tended to take. . . . [a] cold-blooded attitude towards their children" (pp. 112–13). Individual responses, I am arguing, differ widely from this generalization. Quotations from Montaigne's essays are taken from M. A. Screech, ed. and trans., *The Complete Essays* (London: Penguin, 1987; rpt. 2003). Quotations from Joyce's *Ulysses* are taken from the Vintage International edition (New York, 1990), a reprint of the 1934 Modern Library edition of the novel. Everett's comments appear in *Young Hamlet: Essays on Shakespeare's Tragedies* (Oxford: Clarendon, 1989). Derrida's discussion of the sacrifice of Isaac appears in *The Gift of Death*, trans. David Willis (Chicago: U of Chicago P, 1995), originally published by Metailie-Transition, Paris, 1992.

FIVE   CONTRARIANS AT THE GATE

The history of the Royal Society is found at www.royalsoc.ac.uk. Crystal and Crystal list eighteenth-century editions of Shakespeare in *The Shakespeare Miscellany*. Lengthy discussions of these editions can be found in a variety of sources already mentioned. Quotations from Dryden, Rowe, Dennis, the anonymous 1752 Observations on the Tragedy of Hamlet, Johnson, Steevens, Voltaire, and Stubbes are taken from *Critical Responses to Hamlet*, Volume I (1600–1790), ed. David Farley-Hills (New York: AMS, 1997).

Quotations from the *London Chronicle*, Goldsmith's *Works*, and William Richardson's *Essays on Some of Shakespeare's Dramatic Characters* are taken from Claude C. H. Williamson, ed., *Readings on the Character of Hamlet 1661–1947* (New York: Allen and Unwin, 1950; rpt. 1972). In the case of some widely dispersed or otherwise difficult to access material, for the sake of convenience I direct readers to the compilations by Farley Hills and Williamson, having, whenever possible, checked excerpts against originals and, where necessary, made silent corrections.

Like Hamlet, Johnson struggled with depression for much of his life. See John Wain, *Samuel Johnson* (New York: Viking, 1974). Critical reactions to *Hamlet* are by no means restricted to the eighteenth century, nor are they restricted to this play. Tolstoy called Shakespeare "a man quite devoid of the sense of proportion and taste," a writer who is manifestly an "insignificant, inartistic, and not only non-moral but plainly immoral writer." His plays "have absolutely nothing in common with art or poetry," but rather are "works which are beneath criticism, insignificant, empty and immoral." Tolstoy determines that Hamlet is no true character at all. And yet "the learned critics," a mystified Tolstoy writes, "write volumes upon volumes, until the laudations and explanations of the grandeur and importance of depicting the character of a man without a character. . . ." See G. Wilson Knight, *Shakespeare and Tolstoy*, The English Association, Pamphlet 88 (1934; rpt. London: Folcroft Library Editions, 1976). And, of course, detractors haven't all been Continental. As earlier noted, T. S. Eliot, who called Hamlet the "Mona Lisa of literature," pronounced the play an artistic failure. If Eliot's pronouncement seems essentially provocative rather than genuinely censorious—Eliot deeply appreciated Shakespeare's achievement—the same can't be said of D. H. Lawrence, who in *Twilight in Italy* (1916) called Hamlet "a creeping, unclean thing. . . . His nasty poking and sniffing at his mother, his setting traps for the King, his conceited perversion with Ophelia make him always intolerable. The character is repulsive in its conception, based on self-dislike and a spirit of disintegration." Lawrence, soaking up sunlit Italy with his new wife Frieda von Richthofen, pronounced the ghost of Hamlet's father "one of the play's failures . . . trivial and unspiritual and vulgar." See *D. H. Lawrence and Italy*, introduction by Anthony Burgess (New York: Viking, 1972).

Discussions of the Davenant/Betterton and the Garrick *Hamlet*s are based on the accounts of these productions by Mills in *Hamlet on Stage*. My quotations from Pope's *An Essay on Man* are from *The Poems of Alexander Pope*, ed. John Butt (New Haven: Yale UP, 1965).

SIX   HAMLET AMONG THE ROMANTICS

My quotations from *Wilhelm Meister's Apprenticeship and Travels* are taken from Thomas Carlyle's 1824 translation (rpt. New York: Scribner's, 1899). Vol. I. The essential passages can also be found in Farley-Hills, Vol. II. I quote Georg Gottfried Gervanius on Hamlet as expressing the soul of Germany from his 1849 *Commentary* on *Hamlet* in Farley-Hills, Vol. III. I quote Schlegel's *Lectures* as translated by John Black (London: Harrison, 1811). For Coleridge's lectures and commentaries on them, see R. A. Foakes, ed., *Lectures 1808–1819 on Literature*. Vol. V of *The Collected Works of Samuel Taylor Coleridge*, eds. Kathleen Coburn and Bart Winer, Bollingen Series LXXV (Princeton: Princeton UP, 1987). On the Hamlet-like aspects of Coleridge's character, see Martin Greenberg's *The Hamlet Vocation of Coleridge and Wordsworth* (Iowa City: U of Iowa Press, 1986). Kurt Fusso calls Hamlet "the soliloquist of mortality" in *Buried Communities: Wordsworth and the Bonds of Mourning* (Albany: State U of New York P, 2004). Hazlitt's remarks are quoted from R. S. White, ed., *Hazlitt's Criticism of Shakespeare: A Selection*, Studies in British Literature Vol. 18 (Lewiston, NY: Mellen, 1996). My quotations from Dostoevsky are taken from Williamson, ed., *Readings*. Quotations from Berlioz are gleaned from Farley-Hills, Vol. III, and Williamson, *Readings*. For a more recent translation of Berlioz's comments, see David Cairns, trans. and ed., *The Memoirs of Hector Berlioz* (New York: Knopf, 2002).

SEVEN   "THIS DISTRACTED GLOBE"

My account of Ferrers is based upon the e-text of *The Complete Newgate Calendar*. Vol. III, Tarlton Law Library, The University of Texas Law in Popular Culture Collection: http://tarlton.law.utexas.edu. Horace Walpole mentions that "Hamlet was read to the prisoner at his own request" in a letter to Sir Horace Mann of May 24, 1760. See W. S. Lewis, Warren Hunting Smith, and George L. Lam, eds., *Horace Walpole's Correspondence with Sir Horace Mann*, V. 21.5 (New Haven: Yale UP, 1960). On the notion of wise folly in the Humanist tradition, see Desiderius Erasmus, *The Praise of Folly*, trans. with Introduction and Commentary by Clarence H. Miller (New Haven: Yale UP, 1979). Sir Thomas More, *Sir Thomas More, Utopia: A New Translation, Backgrounds, Criticism*, trans. Robert M. Adams (New York: Norton, 1975). While I place Hamlet in the tradition of the wise fool, Robert Weimann associates Hamlet's "madness" "with the element of clowning, punning, and 'impertinency,' the tradition of topsy-turvydom, and the 'mad' nonsensical Vice" of medieval theater. See his "Mimesis in *Hamlet*" in *Shakespeare and the Question of Theory*. The classic study of melancholy in Renaissance England is Lawrence Babb's *The Elizabethan Malady: A Study of Melancholia in English Literature from 1580 to 1642*, Studies in Language and Literature (East Lansing: Michigan State, 1951). For the theory of humors, see Babb, and Richard L. Gregory and O. L. Zangwill *The Oxford Companion to the Mind* (Oxford: Oxford UP, 1987). I quote Robert Burton from Floyd B. Dell and Paul Jordan-Smith, eds., *The Anatomy of Melancholy* (New York: Tudor, 1927). Victor Hugo, *William Shakespeare*, trans. Melville B. Anderson (Chicago: McClurg, 1887).

EIGHT   HAMLET AMONG THE MODERNS

In the final chapter of *Shakespeare Among the Moderns* (Ithaca: Cornell UP, 1997), Richard Halpern provides a complex but enlightening discussion of the modernist construction of Hamlet on the Continent. Strachey's lengthy comment is found in Farley-Hills. Vol. III. My summary dismissal of mainstream Victorian contributions to our understanding of *Hamlet*/Hamlet is not likely to sit well with the contributors to the two-volume *Victorian Shakespeare*, ed. Gail Marshall and Adrian Poole (London: Palgrave, 2003). But as Richard W. Schoch's essay "Shakespeare Mad," in volume one of that work, suggests, more entertaining, and perhaps more interesting, nineteenth-century reactions to *Hamlet* may be found in the many published and unpublished burlesques of the play, ranging from John Poole's *Hamlet Travestie* in 1810 (which was reprinted at least seven times in England and twice in America) through A. C. Hilton's *Hamlet, or Not Such a Fool as He Looks* in 1882. Some of these burlesques, which increase in number during the Victorian period, are rather unimaginative simplifications of the plot. Others, such as *Hamlet! The Ravin' Prince of Denmark!! or, The Baltic Swell!!! and the Diving Belle!!!!* (anon., 1866) are crude but funny. Still others, such as W. S. Gilbert's *Rosencrantz and Guildenstern* (1874), have some claim to literary merit. Three *Hamlet* travesties appeared on the American stage after mid-century. Typically, Hamlet's serious speeches, as well as the great soliloquies, are set to contemporary tunes. Charles Beckington's 1847 *Hamlet the Dane: A Burlesque Burletta*, for example, parodies Hamlet's " 'Seems,' madam—nay it is" speech to the tune of "Love's Retornello": "Oh, it is not my cloak, though so inky, mamma, / Not, not the crape on my hat for papa," etc. Hamlet's "To be, or not to be" soliloquy, is a jig set to the tune of "Jim Crow." It begins "To be or not to be's the rub: / Then tell me, if you know, / Which is best, to die, or live / And jump James Crow. / To turn about and wheel about, / And do just so; / I think 'tis better still to live, / And jump James Crow." In his five-volume anthology, *Shakespeare Burlesques* (Wilmington, DE: Michael Glazier, 1978), Stanley Wells includes ten *Hamlet* travesties. See also James Ellis, "The Counterfeit Presentment: Nineteenth-Century Burlesques of *Hamlet*," *Nineteenth Century Theatre Research* 11 (1983): 29–50. Burlesque adaptations of the play persist in our own time, as in, for example, Rob Krakovski's and Geoff Lower's rap *The Trage-D of Prince Hammy-T*, which was produced at the NADA Theatre and House of Candles Theatre in the Fall of 1993. See Michael E. Mooney, ed., *Hamlet: An Annotated Bibliography of Shakespeare Studies 1604–1998* (Asheville, NC: Pegasus Press, 1999), number 188. The Tiny Ninja Theater's entertaining *Hamlet*, featured in the 2007 Shakespeare in Washington Festival, might fit into the category of burlesque as well.

My summary of "subjectivist" and "objectivist" positions in German criticism is based upon J. M. Robertson's discussion of German criticism in *The Problem of "Hamlet"* (London: Allen and Unwin, 1919; rpt. Folcroft, 1970). My précis of the development of psychology is drawn from *The Oxford Companion to the Mind*. For an in-depth and enlightening consideration of Shakespeare's plays, particular *Hamlet*, in the psychoanalytic tradition, one that takes the reader well beyond my sketch of the tradition, see Philip Armstrong, *Shakespeare in Psychoanalysis*, Accents on Shakespeare Series (London: Routledge, 2001). Onimus' *La Psychologie de Shakespeare*, Kellog's *Shakespeare's Delineations of Insanity, Imbecility and Suicide*, and Chambers' *Hamlet* are excerpted in *Readings*.

Bradley greatly admired Hegel, whose comments on *Hamlet*/Hamlet are collected in Anne and Henry Paolucci, eds., *Hegel on Tragedy: Selections from The Phenomenology of Mind, Lectures on the Philosophy of Religion, The Philosophy of Fine Art, Lectures on the History of Philosophy*, Second Edition (Smyrna, DE: Griffon House, 2001).

Freud's "Mourning and Melancholia" is found in James Strachey, trans. and ed., et al., *The Standard Edition of the Complete Psychological Works of Sigmund Freud*. Vol. XIV (London: Hogarth, 1953). Freud proposed *Hamlet* as a reworking of the Oedipus story— stating that Shakespeare's play "has its roots in the same soil as *Oedipus Rex*"—first as a footnote in the 1900 edition of *The Interpretation of Dreams*, which he moved into the body of the text in the 1914 edition of that work. Given the importance of Freud to subsequent readings of *Hamlet*, it is surprising that his most influential comments on the play first appeared as a footnote. Avi Erlich significantly amplifies and adjusts Harold Goddard's reading of *Hamlet* in *Hamlet's Absent Father* (Princeton: Princeton UP, 1977).

The possibility that Shakespeare was of a Catholic disposition has long been suspected. Tradition has it that Shakespeare in his youth lived for two years with the Hoghton family at Lea and Hoghton Tower in Lancashire. Lancashire was "backward and feudal"— that is to say, fiercely Catholic—according to Honan. One William Shakeshafte is listed as living in the Hoghton household as a "servant." Interestingly, this Shakeshafte (along with another member of the household, one Fulke Gillom) is associated with "all maner of playe clothes"—that is, actors' clothes—in Hoghton's will of August 3, 1581. Hoghton bequeaths his instruments and costumes to his half-brother Thamas, and asks that if Thomas will not keep an acting troupe, then Hoghton's friend, Sir Thomas Hesketh, should "be ffrendlye vunto ffoke Gyllome and william Shakeshafte & eyther to thake theym vunto his Servyce or els to helpe theym to some good master as my tryste is he wyll." We cannot know whether this Shakeshafte is Shakespeare, of course, but the association of this servant with the accoutrement of actors is tantalizing. No less interesting is the possibility that the family Shakespeare was residing with was Catholic. See Honan and Greenblatt for discussions of this episode.

Stopes is quoted from *Transactions of the Royal Society of Literature*, Second Series, v. 23 (1915); Greg is quoted from Sir Israel Gollancz, ed., *A Book of Homage to Shakespeare* (Oxford: OUP, 1916). Greenblatt (*Hamlet in Purgatory*) lists other important studies of the Ghost, ranging from Roy Battenhouse's "The Ghost in Hamlet: A Catholic 'Linchpin'?" *Studies in Philology* 68 (1951) to Roland Mushat Frye's *The Renaissance "Hamlet": Issues and Responses in 1600* (Princeton: Princeton UP, 1984), and concludes that these "intricate arguments . . . are not completely evacuated by the fact that they are almost certainly doomed to inconclusiveness."

I quote Fussell from *The Great War and Modern Memory* (Oxford: Oxford UP, 1975). I quote Eliot's "The Waste Land" from *The Complete Poems and Plays, 1909–1950* (New York: Harcourt, 1971). The comments of Brecht and Kott appear in Kott's *Shakespeare Our Contemporary*, trans. Boleslaw Taborski (Garden City, NY: Doubleday, 1964). I quote Shurbanov from his "Politicized with a Vengeance: East European Uses of Shakespeare's Great Tragedies," in Jonathan Bate, Jill L. Levenson, and Dieter Mehl, eds., *Shakespeare and the Twentieth Century: The Selected Proceedings of the International Shakespeare Association World Congress, Los Angeles, 1996* (Newark: U of Delaware P, 1998). See also Eleanor Rowe, *Hamlet: A Window on Russia*, New York University Studies in Comparative Literature, VII (New York: New York UP, 1976).

NINE   POSTMODERN HAMLET

Concise definitions of postmodernism are available in various handbooks. See, for example, William Harmon, ed., *A Handbook to Literature*. Ninth Edition (Upper Saddle River, NJ: Prentice Hall, 2003) and Edwin J. Barton and Glenda A. Hudson, eds., *A Contemporary Guide to Literary Terms with Strategies for Writing Essays about Literature*. *Second Edition* (Boston: Houghton Mifflin, 2004). Jean-François Lyotard's *The postmodern Condition: A Report on Knowledge*, trans. Geoff Bennington and Brian Massumi (Manchester: Manchester UP, 1979), is the original manifesto of the movement in philosophy. My summary of existentialism is based upon the *Stanford Encyclopedia of Philosophy*, http://plato.stanford.edu/entries/existentialism. I quote Nietzsche from *The Birth of Tragedy and Other Writings*, ed. Raymond Geuss and Ronald Speirs, trans. Ronald Speirs, Cambridge Texts in the History of Philosophy (Cambridge: Cambridge UP, 1999). Knight's comments are quoted from his *The Wheel of Fire: Interpretations of Shakespearean Tragedy, With Three New Essays*. Fifth Edition (New York: Meridian, 1957). I quote Montrose from his *The Purpose of Playing: Shakespeare and the Cultural Politics of the Elizabethan Theatre* (Chicago: U of Chicago P, 1996). Greenblatt links Thomas Harriot's record of the Roanoke Colony with Second Henriad in "Invisible Bullets: Renaissance Authority and its Subversion, *Henry IV* and *Henry V*," in Johanthan Dollimore and Alan Sinfield, eds., *Political Shakespeare: New Essays in Cultural Materialism* (Ithaca: Cornell UP, 1985); Montrose links the dream of Simon Foreman with *A Midsummer Night's Dream* in "'Shaping Fantasies': Figurations of Gender and Power in Elizabethan Culture," in Stephen Greenblatt, ed., *Representing the English Renaissance* (Berkeley: U of California P, 1988).

I own what is perhaps the only extant copy of "Commotion in the Wind," which appeared in the *Spectator Magazine*, December 8–14, 1988, and that's not an original but a photocopy. So many fish to wrap, so little time. Bristol's essay "Where Does Ideology Hang Out?" appears in Ivo Kemps, ed., *Shakespeare Left and Right* (New York: Routledge, 1991).

That *Hamlet* is not especially congenial to politically minded postmodern critics is suggested by the fact that the first edition of Dollimore's *Radical Tragedy: Religion, Ideology and Power in the Drama of Shakespeare and His Contemporaries* (Chicago: U of Chicago P, 1984) makes no mention of the play.

Catherine Belsey's summary of the critique of postmodernism appears in her essay "Masking Histories Then and Now," in Barker, Hulme and Iverson, eds., *Uses of history*. Quotations from Barker, Eagleton, and Hawkes are taken from, respectively, *The Tremulous Private Body: Essays on Subjection* (London: Methuen, 1984); *William Shakespeare* (New York: Blackwell, 1986); and *That Shakespeherian Rag: Essays on a Critical Process* (New York: Methuen, 1986). Hawkes quotes from Dover Wilson's essays on Russia, and the Newbolt Report in "Telmah," in *That Shakespeherian Rag*. Hawkes advances his reading of *Hamlet* in a chapter titled "The Old Bill," in his *Shakespeare in the Present*, Accents on Shakespeare Series (London: Routledge, 2002).

I quote Lacan's essay from *Yale French Studies*. It is reprinted in Shoshana Felman, ed., *Literature and Psychoanalysis* (Baltimore: Johns Hopkins, 1982): 11–52. Faber's "Hamlet and the Inner World of Objects" appears in B. J. Sokol, ed., *The Undiscover'd Country: New Essays on Psychoanalysis and Shakespeare* (London: Free Association, 1993).

Showalter's essay, "Representing Ophelia: Women, Madness, and the Responsibilities of Feminist Criticism," appears in Parker and Hartman, eds., *Shakespeare and the Question of Theory*; Adelman's "Man and Wife is One Flesh: Hamlet and the Confrontation with the Maternal Body" is chapter two of her *Suffocating Mothers: Fantasies of Maternal Origin in Shakespeare's Plays, Hamlet to The Tempest* (New York: Routledge, 1992); Schleiner's essay, "Latinized Greek Drama in Shakespeare's Writing of *Hamlet*," appeared in *Shakespeare Quarterly* 41.1 (Spring 1990): 29–48. For an insightful fictional (and exonerating) portrayal of the Gertrude character prior to the action of the play, see John Updike's *Gertrude and Claudius* (New York: Knopf, 2000).

If Greenblatt says no more, in the end, than that Hamlet is a Protestant prince confronting a Catholic ghost, John E. Curran, in *Hamlet, Protestantism, and the Mourning of Contingency: Not to Be* (Aldershot: Ashgate, 2006), explores the tensions between Protestant and Catholic mindsets in *Hamlet* in great detail, arguing that Hamlet, in the final act, is forced to shed the Catholic assumption of contingency, of man having options, perhaps infinite possibilities, for a Calvanistic vision in which, finally, "the search for possibility" succumbs to the operation of Providence, and Hamlet's fate seems predestined.

TEN   LOOKING FOR HAMLET

Laura Bohannan's "Shakespeare in the Bush" appeared in *Natural History* 75 (1966): 28–33. Stopes is quoted in *Transactions*. Schoenbaum's comments on Stopes appear in

Shakespeare's Lives. Fussell's remarks appear in his *The Great War and Modern Memory* (London: Oxford UP, 1975). Harold Bloom's remarks appear in *Shakespeare: The Invention of the Human* (New York: Riverhead, 1998). I quote Freud's account of the flaming child dream from *The Interpretation of Dreams*, in *The Standard Edition*, Vol. V.

THE GALLERIES

I have relied heavily on Mills' *Hamlet on Stage: The Great Tradition* for much of the commentary in the galleries. See also, Bernice W. Kliman, *Hamlet: Film, Television, and Audio Performance* (Rutherford, NJ: Fairleigh Dickinson UP, 1988). On the early images of Amblett/Amblet, see William F. Hansen, *Saxo Grammaticus and the Life of Hamlet: A Translation, History and Commentary* (Lincoln and London: U of Nebraska P, 1983). On Bernhardt, see Gerda Taranow, *The Bernhardt Hamlet, Culture and Context* (New York: Peter Lang, 1996). The 1849 Astor Place riots are the subject of Nigel Cliff's *The Shakespeare Riots: Revenge, Drama, and Death in Nineteenth-Century America* (New York: Random House, 2007). On the feminization of Hamlet, see Catherine Belsey, "'Was Hamlet a Man or a Woman?': The Prince in the Graveyard, 1800–1920," in Arthur F. Kinney, ed., *Hamlet: New Critical Essays* (London: Routledge, 2002), 135–158.

INDEX